W9-DBT-612

MUSIC IN LONDON
1890–94

CRITICISMS CONTRIBUTED WEEK BY WEEK
TO THE WORLD

IN THREE VOLUMES

VOLUME II

©

SHAW THE MUSIC CRITIC

STUDIO PORTRAIT BY FREDERICK H. EVANS

BERNARD SHAW

MUSIC IN LONDON

1890–94

CRITICISMS CONTRIBUTED WEEK BY WEEK TO THE WORLD

IN THREE VOLUMES

VOLUME II

NEW YORK
VIENNA HOUSE
1973

This 1973 VIENNA HOUSE edition is reprinted
by arrangement with The Society of Authors, London.
International Standard Book Number: 0-8443-0060-8
Library of Congress Catalogue Number: 70-183508
This volume is the second in a set of three (ISBN 0-8443-0062-4)
comprising Shaw's Music in London 1890-94.
The three volumes are also published in a set (ISBN 0-8443-0063-2)
with Shaw's London Music in 1888-89 As Heard By
Corno Di Bassetto Later Known As Bernard Shaw.
Manufactured in the United States of America

MUSIC IN LONDON 1890–94

6 January 1892

NEED I say anything more in justification of The Mountebanks, a Gilbert opera with Cellier as composer *vice* Sullivan, retired, than that it made me laugh heartily several times. The brigands whose motto is "Heroism without Risk"; the alchemist who pays his bills with halfpence, accompanied by a written undertaking to transmute them into gold as soon as he discovers the philosopher's stone; the girl who thinks herself plain and her lover handsome, but has to confess to him that she finds herself in a hopeless minority on both subjects; the unsuccessful Hamlet who so dreads to be ever again laughed at by the public that he has turned clown; the mountebank who, pretending that he has swallowed poison and is in the agonies of stomach-ache, is forced to swallow an elixir which has the magic property of turning all pretences into realities; the transformation by this same elixir of the brigands into monks, the clown and columbine into automatic clockwork figures, the village belle into an old hag, the heroine into a lunatic, and the rustic hero into a duke:—if all these went for no more than one laugh apiece, the opera would come out ahead of many of its rivals in point of fun. With them, however, the merit of the piece stops: every line that goes a step further is a line to the bad.

Mr Gilbert has gone wrong in his old way: he has mixed his *genres*. In this Shakespear-ridden land one cannot be a stickler for the unities of time and place; but I defy any dramatist to set the fantastic and the conventional, the philosophic and the sentimental, jostling one another for stage-room without spoiling his play. Now The Mountebanks begins in an outrageous Sicily, where the stage-struck people want to play Shakespear, and where impossible brigands, prosecuting farcical vendettas, agree to hold a revel for twenty-four days on wine, ordered from the chemist's, and not to cheer during all that time above a whisper, because of a bedridden alchemist upstairs, shattered by the repeated explosions which have attended his researches into the transmutation of metals. As aforesaid, brigands, mountebanks, and everyone else become enchanted by drinking a magic potion, and are restored to their natural, or rather normal, condition by the burning of the label of the bottle which contains the philtre.

Clearly there is no room here for the realism of Ibsen or the idealism of Drury Lane. That a man so clever as Mr Gilbert could have supposed that the atmosphere of such a Sicily could be breathed by a figure from the conventional drama is a startling example of the illusions of authorship. He undoubtedly did suppose it, however; for one of the characters, a girl who loves the hero and is cordially detested by him, might have been turned out by Tom Taylor himself. When Alfredo impersonates the duke, and is caught in that assumption by the action of the elixir, she impersonates the duchess and shares his fate, thereby becoming his adored wife. Incidentally she delays the action, bores the audience, and, being quite unfancifully conceived, repeatedly knocks the piece off its proper plane. In the second act, she goes to the incredible length of a sentimental *dénouement*. She "relents" at the entreaty of the heroine, not in the fashion of the Pirates of Penzance on learning that his prisoner is an orphan—the only variety of ruth conceivable in Gilbertland—but actually in the orthodox manner of Hubert in King John.

I am afraid that Miss Lucille Saunders will think me grossly inconsiderate when I say, as I must, that if her part were completely cut out, the opera would be vastly improved; but that is certainly my opinion. Alfredo could quite Gilbertianly be represented as devoted to an absent duchess whom he had never seen; and the incident of Pietro losing the charm might easily be managed otherwise, if not wholly omitted. Under these circumstances, it is little to be thankful for that Ultrice, though she is ugly, is at least not old. The old woman of the play is happily not a new Lady

Jane or Katisha, but a young maiden who takes the elixir when simulating octogenarianism, and pays the penalty like the rest.

Another weakness in the scheme is that there is no dramatic action in the second act—nothing but a simple exhibition of the characters in the plight to which the elixir reduced them at the end of the first. They walk on in twos; sing comic duets recounting the anomalies of their condition in Gilbertian verse; and go off again, all except the incorrigibly malapropos Ultrice, who sings a tragic *scena* which nobody wants to hear. And nothing else happens except an incident planned in the first act and deprived of its *raison d'être* by the charm, and the sentimental *dénouement*, which is dragged in by the ears (if I may so mix my metaphors) when the fun begins to wear out. The result is that the opera is virtually over ten minutes before the curtain falls; and this means that the curtain falls rather flatly, especially as the composer signally failed to come to the rescue at this particular point.

Cellier's strength never lay in the working up of finales; but this one flickers and goes out so suddenly that one can almost hear ghostly muffled drums in the orchestra. The rest of the score is what might have been expected from the composer—that is, better than the occasion required it to be; and in this very superfluity of musical conscience one recognizes his want of the tact which has saved Sir Arthur Sullivan from ever wasting musical sentiment on Mr Gilbert. Musicians will not think the worse of Cellier for this. There are many points, such as the graceful formalism of the little overture, with its orthodox "working out," and the many tender elaborations in the accompaniments, all done from sheer love of music, which will shield Cellier more effectually than his new dignity of *de mortuis* from that reproach of musical unscrupulousness which qualifies every musician's appreciation of the Sullivanesque *savoir-faire*.

But from the more comprehensive standpoint which is necessary in judging an opera, it must be confessed that, since Sullivan is spontaneously vivacious where Cellier was only energetic—and that, too, with an effort which, though successful, was obvious—and since Sullivan is out of all comparison more various in his moods, besides being a better song-writer, Mr Gilbert cannot, on the whole, be said to have changed for the better when he left the Savoy for the Lyric. Only, Cellier's master, Sterndale Bennett, would not have thought the worse of him on that account; nor do I set it down here as any disparagement to him.

In speaking of Cellier as generally less vivacious than Sullivan, I do not of course imply that he is behindhand in those musical facetiousnesses which tickled the public so hugely at the Savoy. The duet for the automata with the quaint squeaking accompaniment, the clockwork music, and the showman's song with big drum obbligato by Mr Monkhouse, are quite up to the Savoy standard—if, indeed, that does not prove too modest an appreciation of the popularity of Put a penny in the slot. The old and easy expedient of making the men sing a solemn chorus and the women a merry one successively (or vice versa, as in Patience), and then repeat them simultaneously, is achieved in the second act to the entire satisfaction of those who regard it as one of the miracles of counterpoint.

One of the operatic jokes is the best in the whole Gilbertian series. The monkized brigands receive the Duke with a mock ecclesiastical chorus on the syllable La. He expresses his acknowledgments by an elaborate recitative in the same eloquent terms, and, having to finish on the dominant, and finding himself at a loss to hit that note, explains that he is "in want of a word," whereupon they offer him La on the tonic. He shakes his head, and a monk gives him La on the dominant, which he immediately accepts with an air of relief, and so finishes triumphantly. Not to damp my readers too much, I may add that anybody with an ear can appreciate the joke when they hear it without in the least knowing what "the dominant" means.

Mr Gilbert has not much to complain of in the way his

work is given to the public. Miss Aida Jenoure makes a hit as the dancing girl who becomes an automaton. She is clever, funny, pretty, a sufficient singer and dancer, with the only woman's part in the opera worth having. Poor Miss Lucille Saunders does her work earnestly, in spite of the fact that the better she does it the more heartily the audience (through no fault of her own) wish her at the Adelphi. Miss Geraldine Ulmar can do little except clothe herself in the dignity of leading lady, and get through her part as prettily as possible. She rather declines to be mad in the second act, mistrusting, as I surmise, the effect of vociferous lunacy on the voice. Miss Eva Moore, as one of a subsidiary pair of lovers, brings in a second tenor, Mr Cecil Burt, who, though condemned to impersonate a particularly fatuous brigand, and to answer to the name of Risotto—all of which he does without apparent reluctance—looks like an early portrait of Daniel O'Connell by Sir Thomas Lawrence. Mr Robertson, the leading tenor, retains all his freshness, even to the extent of an occasional rawness of voice which suggests that it has not yet attained full maturity, and an air of unfamiliarity with the stage which often clings for long to men who are not mummers by natural temperament. The comedians are as funny as could be desired. Mr Monkhouse's Bartolo is a genuine creation: he shews a thoroughly artistic perception of the fact that as the pseudo-Ibsenite clown with drum and pipes he has to make his part funny, whereas in the automaton scenes his part makes him funny, and he has only to be careful not to spoil it by trying to help it too much. Mr Brough gets everything that is to be got out of the business of the chief mountebank; and Mr Wyatt is in the highest spirits, dancing less than usual, but executing every step with all his old air of receiving the most exquisite anguish from the exercise. Furneaux Cook, as the innkeeper, describes the alchemist with an unembarrassed conviction which sends the fun well across the footlights. And the band, under Mr Caryll, is excellent. I am bound to mention, though, that I am writing all this before the first public performance, on the strength of a dress rehearsal. But I do not think I shall have occasion to change any of my judgments, however the cat may jump.

The death of Cellier has diverted public attention from that of Weist Hill, who was chiefly remarkable, as far as my knowledge of him went, for what he did as a conductor. The set of concerts he conducted for Madame Viard Louis, when orchestral music in London was at its lowest ebb, can hardly yet be forgotten by the survivors of that famine. Had he been lucky enough to find a capitalist of sufficient staying powers, he would undoubtedly have anticipated Mr Henschel's London Symphony enterprise. He knew that the London orchestral forces of his day were capable of extraordinary feats of combined speed and precision; and he saw, what everybody has since learned from Richter, the need for enlarging the orchestra and insisting on the importance of broad handling and sustained tone. It is not altogether to the credit of English musical enterprise that it should have been possible for him to give such signal proofs of capacity as he did with Madame Viard Louis without succeeding in finding another backer when that lady's resources were exhausted.

13 *January* 1892

PROFESSOR RISELEY, conferring with an assembly of professional musicians at Newcastle, complains of the absence of orchestras in England. I have often complained of this myself, without receiving any encouragement to believe that my grievance received the smallest attention. Mr Riseley, I see, appeals to Church and State for aid; and it is just possible that persistent hammering away in this direction might get something done in the course of half a century or so. At present every parish in England has a parish church in which instrumental and vocal music is performed at least once a week, and in which the congregation, however impatient of serious and elevated art on weekdays, resigns itself on Sunday to countenance the highest pretensions that music can make. Unfortunately, most of these churches are provided with nothing better in the way of instrumental music than a huge machine called an organ, which, though capable of great things in the hands of a first-rate player dealing with solo music specially written for it, is in many ways highly objectionable for accompanying choral music, and a quite atrocious substitute for orchestral accompaniments. The manipulator of this mechanical monster is generally selected by a sort of open competition, one applicant after another playing before a few gentlemen who bring a trained judgment of horses, crops, groceries, or dry goods to the assistance of the clergyman, who may perhaps know the difference between the Greek β and B flat, or perhaps may not. Every organist will tell you stories of the games he has had with these tribunals, and of the ingenious dodges, wholly irrelevant to his musical fitness, with which he has borne off appointments from less adroit competitors. Once accepted, an organist is underpaid; his authority in directing the services is jealously limited by the clergyman; and he is relegated to a social status intermediate between that of a gentleman and an organ-blower or gravedigger. Clearly, then, a church which has only an organ in the hands of an organist of no more than ordinary force of character will do little or nothing for music, and will presumably do less for The Church (as distinguished from the church) than it might if its services were musically decent. For my part, I have hardly ever heard a service at a country church without wondering at the extraordinary irreverence of the musical arrangements—the gabbling and bawling of the boys in the psalms, the half-hearted droning of the congregation in the hymns, and the trumpery string of modulations and tunes played by the organist, with perhaps a flight into comparative classicism with a number from Mozart's Twelfth Mass, the Cujus Animam from Rossini's Stabat, or the march from Le Prophète, to play the people out. When there is anything better than that, you always find, either that the incumbent (not the organist) is a musical enthusiast, or else that there are several churches in the neighborhood which compete hotly with the parish church for worshippers. Deplorable as this state of things is, and deeply corrupted as the ears of most English people become by their being trained from youth up to listen patiently to bad music once a week, it is not easy to see where the remedy is to come from so long as no musical qualification is expected from those who have the supreme control of a service that is half music. This is hardly to be wondered at in view of the fact that many bishops will ordain men who, though they can satisfy the chaplain of their ability, under stress of preparation, to blunder through the Gospels in Greek, cannot read a chapter of the Bible aloud in English intelligibly. And indeed I do not pretend that The Church could fill its pulpits if its ministry were to be made musical as well as spiritual. The artistic part of the service should be placed under the separate control of a capable artist, just as the heating arrangements are placed in the hands of a capable plumber. But since only those few clergymen who are themselves artists can recognize or even understand this, present circumstances offer no chance of the emancipation of the organist from the despotism of the rector. The organist is, and will always be, a slave. But if there were an orchestra in the church the organist would have to be a conductor, capable of inspiring some degree of confidence in a whole band; and the most inveterately obtuse incumbent could no longer make him feel that he might be replaced by any person who knew enough about the organ to strum through a service, pending whose appointment one of the young ladies from the rectory could keep things going for a week or two. Besides, the artistic conscience of a band is a stronger resisting force than that of an individual organist. It is always easier to say "We object" than "I object." The parish church bands would give the orchestral nuclei which Professor Riseley wants. As a first step in reconciling public opinion to them, let everyone of musical pretensions do his or her best to discredit the notion that the organ is a specially sacred kind of music machine. It is, as a matter of fact, quite the reverse; for I doubt if there is any instrument which so frequently and irresistibly provokes the player to profanity. Indeed, organists are far from being the majestic and self-contained men their office might lead outsiders to expect.

As to Mr Riseley's other suggestion, of bands maintained by the municipalities, or at least subventioned by them, I have urged that also, being quite unable to see why a County Council or Town Corporation should refrain from providing bands in parks when they provide flower-gardens. However, we must first educate the rate-paying classes on the subject, as they seem at present to have no idea of the plain fact that people who are bred in towns where there is no good theatre, no good picture-gallery, and no good orchestra, are ill-bred people, and that this is the reason why provincial society consists so largely of men who, though they are positively wallowing in money, are, with the best intentions, the dreariest boors imaginable. The twenty thousand bandsmen of Lancashire (I do not guarantee the figure, which I quote from an old number of the British Bandsman) are all men who work for weekly wages.

There was a time, as any instrument manufacturer will inform you, when gentlemen also broke into spontaneous musical activity of this kind, and amateurs of the key bugle, cornetto, serpent, and other musical weapons were not uncommon. My own father, armed with a trombone, and in company with some two dozen others of ascertained gentility, used to assemble on summer evenings on a riverside promenade on the outskirts of my native town, and entertain their fellow-citizens with public spirited minstrelsy. In fact, my father not only played his trombone part, but actually composed it as he went along, being an indifferent reader-at-sight, but an expert at what used to be known as "vamping." What my father's son might have said had he been compelled to criticize these performances in his present capacity is a point upon which I shall pursue no unfilial speculation: suffice it that such music must have been infinitely better and more hopeful than no music at all. At any rate, it did not encourage that sort of materialism which makes England a desert wherein music has to resort to the most degrading shifts for a living. We are all very angry when anyone calls us an unmusical nation; but let the holder of that opinion come from the general to the particular by proposing a rate of half a farthing in the pound for musical purposes; and he will soon have plenty of documents to support his contention.

Meanwhile, we have, outside London, just one first-class orchestra, the result of Hallé's life work at Manchester. And all the music in London last week was its two performances of Berlioz' Faust. One of the advantages of being a critic in London is that at all seasons of rejoicing and holiday making, Music vanishes from the critical sphere and takes to the streets, where she is very vociferous between eleven and two at night. The drunken bachelor sings, four or five strong, beneath my window; and the drunken husband passes doggedly on his way home, with his hardly sober wife one pace behind, nag, nag, nagging, except at such crises of screaming as are produced by the exasperated husband proving himself unworthy the name of a British sailor. This is a leading feature of our English Christmas, with its round of slaughtering, gorging, and drinking, into the midst of which this time comes Hallé with his orchestra, and finds his stalls anything but well filled, though the gallery is faithful even to "standing room only," and not too much of that.

When he first introduced The Damnation of Faust here, there were no rival performances to compare with that of the Manchester band. Now the work is a stock piece at the Albert Hall and the Richter concerts; and it has been heard at the Crystal Palace. The result is that London is utterly eclipsed and brought to naught. In vain does Mr Barnby guarantee metronomic regularity of *tempo* and accurate execution of every note in the score: the work is usually received at the Albert Hall as an unaffectedly pious composition in the oratorio style. Richter, by dint of incessant vigilance and urgency, only gets here and there a stroke of fancy, power, or delicacy out of his orchestra in its own despite. Mr Manns conducts Faust conscientiously, but without opposing any really sympathetic knowledge to the blank ignorance of the orchestra. Hallé simply indicates the quietest, amblingest *tempos* at his ease; and the score comes to life in the hands of players who understand every bar of it, and individualize every phrase.

The Hungarian March, taken at about half the speed at which Lamoureux vainly tries to make it "go," is encored with yells—literally with yells—in St James's Hall. Nobody mistakes the Amen parody for a highly becoming interlude of sacred music, nor misses the diabolic *élan* of the serenade, the subtler imaginative qualities of the supernatural choruses and dances, or the originality and pathos of the music of Faust and Margaret. Here is the experimental verification of my contention that no precision in execution or ability in conducting can, in performing Berlioz' music, supply the want of knowledge on the part of the band of the intention of every orchestral touch. Victories over Berlioz are soldiers' victories, not generals'. The long and short of the matter is that our London men do not know the works of Berlioz and the Manchester men do; hence the enormous superiority of the latter on such occasions as the one in question.

The principal parts were taken by the Henschels, Herr Georg of that ilk singing on this occasion better, if less prettily, than his wife. The gentleman who sang Brander's music only needs to raise his standard of accuracy of intonation to gain my unqualified approval. During the recent fog, when Messrs Besson were cheering me up one afternoon by the pipings of their new contrabass clarionet, they also submitted a new compensating piston, by which they have improved certain false notes in the scale of the cornet. If this compensating piston can be applied successfully to English bass singers, I do not hesitate to pronounce it the greatest invention of modern times.

Mr Barton McGuckin had to take Mr Lloyd's place, at the disadvantage of a very superficial acquaintance with a difficult part. His words were quite unintelligible; and in the invocation, at the very climax of the tremendous burst into C sharp major, he altered the cadence in a way that robbed me of breath. I see no reason why Mr McGuckin should not some day make an excellent Faust—quite as good as Mr Lloyd, who is not at his best in the part—as soon as he learns it. Pending which event, I reserve further criticism.

27 *January* 1892

I HAVE seldom been more astonished than I was last week, when the manager of the Haymarket Theatre offered me an opportunity of hearing the music which Mr Henschel has just composed for Hamlet. Not only had I never heard of a tragedian regarding incidental music as having any interest separable in the remotest degree from his own performance, or as being a less mechanical part of that than the last touch of paint or limelight, but I had been brought up to believe that Hamlet in its natural state consisted musically of the march from Judas Maccabæus for the entry of the Court, and the Dead March in Saul for Hamlet's death, the *entr' actes* being selected from no longer popular overtures such as La Sirène, etc. My opinion of Mr Tree consequently rose to such a pitch as to all but defeat the object of my visit to the last rehearsal; for instead of listening to Mr Henschel's interludes, I spent the intervals in explaining to Mr Tree exactly how his part ought to be played, he listening with the patience and attention which might be expected from so accomplished an actor. However, I heard enough with one ear to serve my purpose.

What Mr Henschel has done with his opportunity cannot be described off-hand to those who have never thought over the position of the composer in the theatre. For him there are two extremes. One is to assume the full dignity of the creative musician, and compose an independent overture which, however sympathetic it may be with the impending drama, nevertheless takes the forms proper to pure music, and is balanced and finished as a beautiful and symmetrical fabric of sounds, performable as plain Opus 1000 apart from the drama, as satisfactorily as the drama is performable apart from it. Example: Egmont, in which Beethoven and Goethe associate as peers in their diverse arts, Beethoven not merely illustrating Goethe's masterpiece, but adding a masterpiece of his own on the same subject. The other extreme is to supply bare *mélodrame*, familiar samples of which may be found in the ethereal strains from muted violins which accompany the unfolding of transformation scenes in pantomimes, the animated measures which enliven the rallies in the harlequinade, or the weird throbbings of the ghost melody in The Corsican Brothers.

The production of these is not musical composition: it is mere musical tailoring, in the course of which the *mélodrame* is cut and made to the measure of the stage business, and altered by snipping or patching when it comes to be tried on at rehearsal. The old-fashioned actor got his practical musical education in this way; and he will tell you that certain speeches are easy to speak "through music" and frightfully hard without it; or, as Richard III, he will work himself up to the requisite pitch of truculence in the "Who intercepts me in my expedition?" scene, partly by listening to the trumpets, and partly by swearing at them for not playing louder.

Beyond this he is so untutored that he will unhesitatingly call upon the *chef d'orchestra* to "stop that music" in the very middle of a suspension, or with a promising first inversion of the common chord, or on a dominant seventh or the like, quite unconscious of the risk of some musician rising in the theatre on the first night and saying, "I beg your pardon for interrupting you, sir; but will you kindly ask the band to resolve that four-to-three before you proceed with your soliloquy?" The idea that music is written in sentences with full stops at the end of them, just as much as dramatic poetry is, does not occur to him: all he knows is that he cannot make the audience shudder or feel sentimental without music, exactly as the comedian knows that he cannot make the audience laugh unless the lights are full on. And the music man at the theatre seldom counts for more than a useful colleague of the gas man.

This state of things at last gives way to evolutionary forces like other states of things. The rage for culture opens a career for cultivated men (not merely cultivated players) as theatrical managers and actors; and the old-fashioned actors and managers find themselves compelled by stress of competition to pose as connoisseurs in all the arts, and to set up Medicean retinues of literary advisers, poets, composers, artists, archæologists, and even critics. And whenever a masterpiece of dramatic literature is revived, the whole retinue is paraded. Now the very publicity of the parade makes it impossible for the retinue to be too servile: indeed, to the full extent to which it reflects lustre on the manager can it also insist on having a voice in the artistic conduct of his enterprises.

Take the composer, for instance. No actor-manager could tell Sir Arthur Sullivan to "stop that music," or refuse to allow Mr Henschel to resolve his discords. On the other hand, no manager will engage an orchestra of from eighty to a hundred performers for an overture and *entr' actes*; and no actor will sacrifice any of the effectiveness of his business in order to fit it to the music; whilst at the same time the actor-manager expects all the most modern improvements in the way of "leading motives," which make excellent material for press-cuttings. The situation being thus limited, the composer submits to become a musical tailor as far as the *mélodrame* is concerned, but throws over the manager completely in the overture and *entr' actes* by composing them with a view to performance as "an orchestral suite" at the Crystal Palace or London Symphony concerts, laying himself out frankly for a numerous orchestra and a silent audience, instead of for a theatre band contending feebly with the chatter of the dramatic critics. Clearly he might venture upon a great overture like Egmont or Coriolan but for the modern improvements—the leading motives—which are an implied part of his contract. The tragedian must have his motive; and the leading lady, even when she is not the most influential person in the theatre, is allowed to have one also as a foil to the tragedian's. Macduff, Richmond, and Laertes will soon advance their claims, which are obviously no more valid than those of high reaching Buckingham, Duncan, Polonius, and Claudius.

Mark my words: as actors come to understand these things better, we shall have such scenes at rehearsal as have never before been witnessed in a theatre—Rosencrantz threatening to throw up his part because his motive is half a bar shorter than Guildenstern's; the Ghost claiming, on Mozart's authority, an absolute monopoly of the trombones; Hamlet asking the composer, with magnificent politeness, whether he would mind doubling the basses with a *contrafagotto* in order to bring out the Inky Cloak theme a little better; Othello insisting on being in the bass and Olivia on being in the treble when their themes are worked simultaneously with those of Iago and Viola, and the wretched composer finally writing them all in double counterpoint in order that each may come uppermost or undermost by turns.

Pending these developments our composers lean towards compromise between the leading motive system and the old symphonic form. At first sight a double deal seems easy enough. Use your bold Richard motive or your tragic Hamlet motive as the first subject in your overture, with the feminine Ophelia theme as the second subject ("happily contrasted," as the analytic programist is sure to say if he is a friend of yours), and then proceed in orthodox form. Unfortunately, when this formula comes to the proof, you find that a leading motive is one thing and a symphonic subject another, and that they can no more replace one another than drawings of human figures in dramatic action can replace arabesques. It is true that human figures can be expressed by curved lines, as arabesques are; and there are arabesques composed of human figures, just as there are pictures in which the figures are decorations. In the hands of the greatest masters the success of the combination of decorative and dramatic seems complete, because every departure from perfect grace and symmetry produces a dramatic interest so absorbing that the spectator feels a heightened satisfaction instead of a deficiency.

But take a picture in which the epic and dramatic elements have been wrought to the highest pitch—say Ford Madox Brown's Lear and Cordelia—and contrast it with a shutter decorated by Giovanni da Udine. Imagine Giovanni trying to tell the story of Lear in his own way as convincingly as Madox Brown has told it, or Madox Brown attempting to give his picture the symmetry of Giovanni's shutter. The contrast at once reveals the hollowness of the stock professorial precept about uniting the highest qualities of both schools, which is seen to mean no more than that a man may reasonably prefer Tintoretto's Annunciation in the Scuola di San Rocco because the flight of angels shooting in through the window is more graceful than Giovanni's designs, whilst the story of the Virgin is as well told as that of Cordelia. But in subjects where flights of angels are unworkable, Tintoretto had, like Brown, to fall back on qualities of beauty not in the least arabesque.

Bring up a critic exclusively on such qualities, and he will find Giovanni vapidly elegant, empty, and artificial; whereas if you nurse him exclusively on arabesque he will recoil from Madox Brown as being absolutely ugly and uncouth. In fact, though Madox Brown is no less obviously the greatest living English epic painter than Mr Burne-Jones is the greatest decorative painter, his friends are at present collecting a thousand pounds to get him out of pecuniary difficulties which are no fault of his own, but a consequence of the nation being still too exclusively addicted to arabesques and pretty sentimentalities. Just as pictorial story-telling, having a different purpose from arabesque, has necessarily a different constructive logic, and consequently must seek a different beauty; so the dramatic composer must proceed differently from the composer of absolute music. If he tries to walk with one foot in each way, he may be as fine a musician as Sterndale Bennett was, and yet not be safe from producing futilities like Paradise and the Peri.

Take, for example, the overture to Richard III, which Mr Edward German, a musician of considerable talent, composed for Mr Mansfield. In this work the first subject begins as a genuine Richard motive; but in order to adapt it to sonata treatment it is furnished with an arabesque tail, like a crookbacked mermaid, with the result that the piece is too clumsy to be a good overture, and yet too trivially shapely to be a fitting tone symbol of Richard III. It is far surpassed by Grieg's Peer Gynt music, which consists of two or three catchpenny phrases served up with plenty of orchestral sugar, at a cost in technical workmanship much smaller than that lavished on Mr German's overture. But the catchpenny phrases are sufficiently to the point of the scenes they introduce, and develop—if Grieg's repetitions can be called development—according to the logic of those scenes and not according to that of Haydn's symphonies. In fact, Grieg proceeded as Wagner proceeded in his great preludes, except that, being only a musical grasshopper in comparison with the musical giant of Bayreuth, he could only catch a few superficial points in the play instead of getting to the very heart and brain of it.

Mr Henschel has wisely taken the same course, avoiding arabesques, and sticking to the play and nothing but the play throughout, except in one passage where he casts the oboe for the part of "the cock that is the trumpet [not the oboe] to the morn." This bird is usually *persona muta*; and Mr Henschel had better have left him so. Save in this one bar, the *mélodrame* is the simplest and most effective I can remember. Then there are preludes—Hamlet tragic but irresolute for Act I, Ophelia a trifle gushing for Act II, Hamlet ferocious and deaf to Ophelia's blandishments for Act III, Dirge for the Drowning for Act IV, and Pastorale (with real birds) for Act V. Of all which I shall have more to say when I hear them in full orchestral panoply at the postponed London Symphony concert. For the present, suffice it to say that they go deeper than Grieg, besides confining themselves, as aforesaid, strictly to their own business, without any digressions into arabesque.

3 *February* 1892

WHEN I received an invitation to a Grand Scotch Festival at the Albert Hall on the Burns anniversary, I was a little staggered; but I felt that a man should have the courage of his profession, and went. The population of the Albert Hall was scanty and scattered, probably through crofter emigration. I had no sooner entered when bang went two saxpences for a program! Now I am not a Scotchman—quite the reverse: my nature is an exceptionally open and bounteous one; and a shilling more or less will neither make me nor break me. All the meaner is the conduct of those who take advantage of my lavishness. And at the Albert Hall they always do take advantage of it. I look at this matter as a political economist. The charge made for a program is exactly a hundred per cent on the charge for admission at the margin of cultivation—I mean in the gallery. This program is not, like the sixpenny program at the Crystal Palace or the Popular Concerts, full of elaborate analyses, quotations in music type, latest historical discoveries concerning the compositions performed, and so forth. It is a bare list of the names of the pieces played, with the words of the songs more or less accurately copied, and spread out as widely as possible over sixteen quarto pages. Now in a huge building like the Albert Hall, where a couple of thousand copies could be easily sold if the price were reasonable, it would be possible, without any help from advertisers, to sell a sixteen-page program, quite sufficient for the purposes of the evening, at a penny, and make a profit on the transaction. At twopence the profit per cent would be huge. I am a sufficiently old hand at pamphleteering to know this off-hand, without the trouble of making inquiries. Fancy my feelings, then, on being compelled to disburse a whole shilling for the sixteen quarto pages aforesaid, made to that size for the more effective setting forth, on a dozen other pages, of the excellencies of Quinine and Iron Tonics, Dental Institutes, Scientific Dentrifices (with seductive illustration), Voice Production Studios based on the purest Italian methods, Parisian diamonds, Steinway pianos, and Yorkshire Relish. Of course, not one Scotchman in twenty will buy a program on such terms. This means that the price is too high to extract the largest obtainable booty from the audience. It is obviously more profitable to receive from ten people a penny apiece than to receive eightpence from one person, when both operations fit equally into the night's work. And this is why I, as a critic, meddle in the matter.

I cannot say that the concert was particularly Scotch in anything but the name. The part-songs given by Mr Carter's choir were so primly British in their gentility as to suggest that the native heath of the singers must be Clapham Common at the very wildest. Perhaps the highest pitch of emotional excitement was reached in that well-known Caledonian *morceau*, the Miserere from Il Trovatore, with military accompaniments from the band of the Scots Guards, in which Madame Giulia Valda expressed the distraction of the heroine by singing convulsively out of time. The effect of the entry of the organ and side drum *ad lib.* on the concluding chord was sublime; and the idea of having Manrico imprisoned in the cellar instead of in the tower was not unhappy in its effect; but, on the whole, I should not like to answer for Verdi's unqualified approval of the performance.

Most of the songs were in the last degree unlike themselves. I presume Mr Dalgety Henderson is a Scotchman; for only a Scotchman could have been so bent on making the vengeful Macgregors' Gathering into a sentimental English ballad. From Sims Reeves it was memorable—almost terrible; but when Mr Henderson sang Give their roofs to the flame and their flesh to the eagles, with his most lackadaisically pathetic *nuance* on "eagles," I felt that the whole Macgregor clan might be invited to tea with every confidence in the perfect propriety of their behavior. Miss Rose Williams's nationality is unknown to me. She is a contralto of the school of Madame Antoinette Sterling, singing very slowly and with a steady suffusion of feeling (physically a steady pressure of chest voice), which only admits of the most mournful expression. Her song was A man's a man for a' that; and she sang it exactly as if it were The Three Fishers. It was pretty; but it would have damped a whole revolution had there been one on at the moment.

Even Miss Macintyre was not in the least racy of the soil in her cosmopolitan rendering of Mary Morison. In short, the only singer who hit the mark in the first part of the concert (I did not wait for the second) was Mr Norman Salmond, who, having nothing Scotch about him, sang—and sang to perfection—what a cockney printer next morning described as Green grow the rashers O. The only other item in which any sense of the beauty and romantic dignity of Scotch folk-music was shewn by the artist was a movement from Max Bruch's Scottish Violin Fantasia, finely played by Mr Seiffert (a Dutchman), under the heavy disadvantage of a pianoforte accompaniment and a silly misdescription in the program, which led the audience to believe that he was to play a simple transcription of a Scotch melody. On the whole, I would not ask to hear a less Scotch concert.

The London Symphony Concert on the 26th was none the worse for its postponement as far as the band was concerned, though it unluckily found Mrs Henschel on the sick-list. The Lohengrin prelude and Schubert's unfinished symphony in H moll were played *con amore*, and went splendidly, in spite of a rough detail or two. Mr Gorski gave a respectable performance of Max Bruch's first violin concerto. The Hamlet music, eked out a little by some illogical repeats, was naturally much more effective in its stormier phrases than it is when played at the Haymarket by a band of forty thrust under the stage. In dramatic force and consistency it is undoubtedly better than anything which our great theatrical revivals have yet produced. The impetuous interlude (No. 3), in which occur the remarkably graphic passages for the piccolo which laugh away the Ophelia motive, is, on the whole, the best number. The pastorale, the march, and the dirge would probably have been better done by Sir Arthur Sullivan or any of our "absolute musicians."

The Hamlet music reminds me of the Haymarket conductor, Mr Carl Armbruster, and of a lecture on Wagner which I heard him deliver the other evening at the London Institution. It is my special merit that I have always seen plainly that in this Philistine country a musical critic, if he is to do any good, must put off the learned commentator, and become a propagandist, versed in all the arts that attract a crowd, and wholly regardless of his personal dignity. I have propagated my ideas on other subjects at street corners to the music of the big drum; and I should not hesitate to propagate Wagnerism there with a harmonium if I were sufficiently a master of that instrument, or if the subject were one which lent itself to such treatment. Failing that, Mr Armbruster's lectures, under the auspices of educational bodies, with magic lantern and vocal illustrations, are clearly the next best thing. Of course the modern Arcedeckne, being unable to say, "You should have a piano, Thack," will say, "You should have an orchestra, Armby"; but in view of the impossible expense, the conclusive reply is, "Dont you wish you may get it?" Once or twice I thought Mr Armbruster was more ornate than candid in his descriptions. It is all very well to represent Bayreuth as a quiet spot where Nature invites the contemplative peace in which Wagner's message comes to you with the full force of its deepest meaning (or words to that effect); but in solemn truth the place is such a dull country town that the most unmusical holiday-maker is driven into the theatre to avoid being bored out of his senses.

The proper way to enjoy Parsifal is to step into the temple straight out of the squalid rush and strain and vulgar bustle of London, with every faculty in keen activity, instead of loafing up a country road to it in a slack, unstrung, vagabondizing, overfed and underworked holiday humor, when a stroll through the pines seems better than any theatre. I once, on a Parsifal night, when there was a wonderful sky outside, spent the last act on the hills pretending to terrify myself by venturing into pitchy darkness in the depths of the woods. You do not suppose, probably, that I would have wandered about Drury Lane under the same circumstances.

However, it is no use complaining of the absurd things people will say about Bayreuth. It is a European centre for high art mendacity; and Mr Armbruster, who is always professionally busy inside the theatre, and so carries his London activity thither with him, has never realized what the genuine tourist-suited Bayreuth pilgrim experiences at the shrine of the Meister. The lecture, however, unmistakeably roused considerable interest and curiosity; and although I doubt if the London Institution audience quite knew how well Miss Pauline Cramer sang Isolde's death-song, they were left well on the way to a state of greater grace.

Mr D'Oyly Carte has withdrawn The Nautch Girl at the Savoy, and put on The Vicar of Bray. Mr Rutland Barrington is very funny as the Vicar; but in the work as a whole there is no life. It is, at best, a tolerable stop-gap.

10 February 1892

THE musical season is still very dull. Miss Macintyre's charity concert was quite an event last week, though it was of the miscellaneous order, with A fors e lui on top of O luce di quest' anima, and Un di si ben to finish up. Such concerts always give me an uneasy sensation of being still a boy of twelve, just wakened from a mad dream of maturity. And my impulse most decidedly is to add, Ah, do not wake me: let me dream again! to the program. There is, perhaps, a faint critical interest in hearing how Miss Fanny Moody makes the provincial dilettanti think that she is a great prima donna, and in watching the result of Miss Macintyre's original and very modern views as to how Verdi's music should be treated. Mind, I do not imply any sort of disparagement, or the opposite; no miscellaneous concert can stimulate me to face the risk and effort of forming a critical judgment, much less expressing it. I greatly enjoyed the performance of the Meister Glee Singers, and admired the success with which Miss Macintyre brought off her enterprise; but I mention the subject chiefly as an excuse for saying a word or two on the subject of charity concerts generally, concerning which I have often to act with apparent callousness to the claims of the poor and ailing. Every lady who has any turn for getting up such entertainments is keenly aware that a few lines in this column, costing me no more than a turn of the wrist, may help to feed many hungry persons, clothe many shivering children, and provide an extra bed or so at the hospital for some suffering and indigent fellow-creature. An announcement beforehand will sell tickets for any concert which is to provide funds for these purposes; whilst a word of notice afterwards will gratify the artists, and make it easier to get them to sing or play again for nothing next year. Under these circumstances, it cannot but appear the height of wanton hardheartedness in me to withhold my help and receive all appeals for it in stony silence. But the very ease with which I might help if I chose is so obvious, that the idea of asking for it occurs to someone or other at least twice a day during the crises of charity-concert organization which occur from time to time. If I were to comply, my compliance would soon defeat its own object; for what I wrote would cease to be read, nothing being less interesting than strings of puffs preliminary, however pious their objects may be; whilst as to criticizing the performances subsequently, I always think it as well not to look gift-horses in the mouth, particularly when the verdict might be anything but gratifying to the donors. In short, it is impossible for me to notice on charitable grounds concerts which I should not mention if they were ordinary commercial speculations; and I appeal to the charitable not to make me feel like a monster by writing me touching and artful appeals, which I must, nevertheless, disregard. All I can say is, that if a concert is musically important, I shall not be deterred from noticing it by the fact that the aims of its promoters are philanthropic.

The closing of the New English Opera House has elicited a chorus of indignant despair from us all as to the possibility of doing anything for a public which will not support The Basoche. It does not appear to be certain that The Basoche is stark dead—I see it stated that it is only speechless for the moment; but, assuming that it has had its utmost run, let me point out that it is not true that it has received no support. There are many degrees of failure. If I compose an opera, and get Mr Carte to produce it at his theatre, with the result that not a single person is found willing to pay to hear it, that will undoubtedly be a failure.

Suppose, however, that Mr Carte, bent on surpassing all previous examples of managerial enterprise and munificence, spends £1,000,000 sterling in mounting my opera, and that it is played for a thousand nights to a thousand people every night with the free list entirely suspended, that will be a failure too. Failure means simply failure to replace the capital expended with a fair profit to boot in a single run; and this may be brought about by the manager spending more than the first run is worth, as well as by the public paying less. The fact is, there is no grand opera in the world which will run long enough in one capital to pay for a complete and splendid *mise-en-scène*. On the other hand, such a *mise-en-scène* will last for years as part of the stock of the house.

What Mr Carte wants is a repertory, and a position in the social economy of London like that occupied in Germany by such opera-houses as those of Frankfort or Munich, where works like The Trumpeter of Sakkingen or The Barber of Bagdad may have a prodigious vogue without the manager dreaming for a moment of running them exclusively and leaving the town for months bereft of all opportunity of hearing Der Freischütz, or Fidelio, or Die Walküre, or Le Nozze di Figaro. And here Mr Carte will recoil, and ask me whether I seriously propose that he should attempt to recover his outlay on Ivanhoe and The Basoche by mounting half-a-dozen grand operas to sandwich them. Certainly not, if the mounting is to be as sumptuous as that of these two operas. But why should it be? Of course, it is impossible to insult gentlemen like Messager and Sir Arthur Sullivan with less than the best of everything; but there is no need to be particular with Mozart, Beethoven, Weber, and Wagner. They are all dead; and when they were alive they had to put up with what they could get. Signor Lago has shewn that the way to make money out of the classic masterpieces of lyric drama is to practise the severest asceticism, not to say downright mortification, in respect of scenery, dresses, and everything in which Mr Carte is habitually extravagant.

Not that I would have Mr Carte too slavishly copy Signor Lago, who, perhaps, overdoes his Lenten severities a trifle; but there is no avoiding the conclusion that if the expensive ventures of the Royal English Opera are to be spread over the full period needed to produce a reasonable return on them, their runs must be broken by performances of attractive operas mounted neatly but not gaudily, and perhaps performed on "popular nights" with lower prices than when the stage is *en grande tenue* for Ivanhoe, etc. I see nothing else for it, unless Mr Carte by chance discovers some individual performer whose magnetism may do for The Basoche what Mr Irving's does for the Lyceum plays. The smallness of the cultivated section of our population is the disabling factor in all these costly schemes for performing musical works of the best class. London, artistically speaking, is still a mere village.

Meanwhile, Sir Augustus Harris is said to be about to modernize the Covent Garden repertory to the extraordinary extent of introducing world-famous operas which were composed as recently as 1860 or thereabouts, and which have not been familiar to the German public for more than fifteen years. This is not bad for an impresario whose musical education consisted in watching the spectacle of post-Rossinian Italian tragic opera slowly dying of Madame Titiens at one house, without any serious attempt at rescue by Madame Patti at the other. I do not say these things by way of a fleer at Sir Augustus Harris; for I also am an old subject of the Titiens dynasty.

Imagine being inured from one's cradle to the belief that the sublime in music meant Titiens singing the Inflammatus from Rossini's Stabat Mater; that the tragic in operatic singing, far overtopping anything that Mrs Siddons could ever have done, was Titiens as Lucrezia Borgia; that majesty in music-drama reached its climax in Titiens tumbling over the roulades in Semiramide; that Valentine in Les Huguenots, the Countess in Le Nozze, Pamina in Die Zauberflöte, all weighed eighteen stone, and could not be impersonated without a gross violation of operatic propriety by anyone an ounce lighter. I was brought up in these articles of faith; and I believe Sir Augustus Harris was brought up in them too. Nothing will persuade me that he was not moved by some desperate yearning to recall the ideals of his boyhood when he allowed Mlle Richard, who is more like Titiens than any living artist, to play La Favorita at Covent Garden a couple of seasons ago.

What I am not so sure of is whether Sir Augustus Harris ever found Titiens out—whether he ever realized that in spite of her imposing carriage, her big voice, her general intelligence, and, above all, a certain goodhearted grace which she never lost, even physically, the intelligence was not artistic intelligence; the voice, after the first few years, was a stale voice; there was not a ray of creative genius in her; and the absurdity of her age, her pleasant ugliness, and her huge size (which must have been to at least some extent her own fault), the public got into a baneful habit of considering that the end of opera-going was not to see Lucrezia, Leonora, Valentine, or Pamina, but simply Titiens in these parts, which was tantamount to giving up all the poetry of opera as a mere convention, which need not be borne out by any sort of artistic illusion. The first time I was taken to the opera, I was so ignorant of what the entertainment meant that I looked at the circle of resplendently attired persons in the boxes and balcony with a vague expectation that they would presently stand up and sing.

But when I was an experienced young opera-goer, and had seen Titiens—the great Titiens—a dozen times, I believe I was far more hopelessly astray on the subject than I had been on that memorable first night before the curtain so astonished me by going up. For such experience only tended to make me a connoisseur in this pseudo-opera which was nothing but a prima donna show, and to train me to regard the impresario as one whose sole business it was to engage the most famous performers in that spurious *genre*, and to announce them at the beginning of the season in a long prospectus which was equally remarkable for the absence of any allusion to the artistic conditions under which the operas were to be performed, and the presence of names of artists whom the manager had not engaged, and whom he had no reasonable prospect of being able to engage.

Sir Augustus Harris has reformed that prospectus altogether; but for the life of me I can never quite divest myself of a suspicion that the great Wagner Reformation has never convinced him, and that he regards people like myself as heretics and renegades. However, if the Nibelungen tetralogy and Tristan really reach Covent Garden or Drury Lane this year—nay, if even one of them, say Siegfried or Die Walküre, comes off—that will be the best answer to me.

17 *February* 1892

THE first packed audience of the year at St. James's Hall was drawn on Thursday last by the Wagner program, plus the Eroica, at the London Symphony Concert. Wagner, nevertheless, failed to get the room settled by half-past eight. I was late; but that would have made no disturbance worth mentioning had not about a hundred other people been late too. Our struggle, or rather scrimmage, to get into the room when the doors were opened after the first piece, and our persistence in wandering in search of our seats in the wrong direction when we did get in, necessitated a longish interval between the first and second numbers; and later on it became evident that the concert could not be finished by half-past ten without cutting the customary interval between the two parts very short indeed. This Mr Henschel accordingly did, with the result that when, by dint of repeated rappings, he succeeded in getting a perfect "Bayreuth" hush for the Parsifal prelude, he was paralysed by the discovery that the tuba was absent. After a period of intensifying suspense the artist duly appeared, and took his place with the solid calm of a man who knew that we could not begin without him. Up went Mr Henschel's stick again; and we were once more breathless with expectation when the fresh discovery was made that the orchestra lacked its apex in the familiar and conspicuous person of the eminent drummer, Mr Smith. Hereupon the Bayreuth hush, overstrained, broke into ripples of laughter and a chatter of questions from those who did not understand the delay, and explanations by those who did. Finally, Mr Smith hurried in, and was received with an ovation which took him aback for the first time in the experience of the oldest concert-goer. Somehow, the Bayreuth hush seems to be an unlucky institution, even in St James's Hall. In the Bavarian Festspielhaus, of course, it is, and always has been, quite hopeless: somebody inevitably drops an opera-glass, or slams a seat, or rushes in all but late out of the sunshine without, and remarks before the solemn influence has had time to operate, "Oh my, aint it dark! however are we to tell our seats?" But hitherto I have been able to boast that there is never any difficulty in getting the London hush, about which, by the bye, no Briton is patriotic enough to gush. After last Thursday I fear I shall have to confess that the malign influence of Bayreuth has reached and corrupted us at last. What used to be a spontaneous piece of good sense and good manners has now become, when Parsifal is in question, a "put-up" solemnity. Naturally, the Powers that rule over Art are angered by this and have made Mr Smith, formerly the most punctual of drum-players, their scourge and minister to bring the ways of Bayreuth to confusion.

The performance proved afresh that Mr Henschel has now got hold of the art of orchestral conducting, and that the bringing to perfection, humanly speaking, of the London Symphony Concerts is only a question of time and perseverance. The performances come right in the mass; the due balance of tone, the color, and, above all, the intelligent and imaginative execution which is produced by playing steadfastly to fulfil the poetic purpose of the composition, are now so far achieved that Mr Henschel's battle for a place as a conductor is nine-tenths won. The remaining tenth, depending on purity of tone, subtlety of *nuance*, and delicacy and precision of touch in the details, he is not likely to cease striving for, since it was, in fact, a premature attempt to achieve these that caused him at first to worry his band and waste his time at rehearsals by beginning at the wrong end.

At present, whilst this tithe is still in arrear, it is instructive to compare the Henschel band with the Philharmonic band, which exactly lacks what the London Symphony band has, and has what the London Symphony band lacks. For my own part, though I insist on the necessity of the combination of the qualities of both, I cannot understand the taste of the man, if such a one lives, who would not rather a thousand times have the interesting roughness of the new band than the empty elegance of the old. At the same time, it must be understood that the interest does not lie in the roughness, any more than the emptiness lies in the elegance; and my criticism on the performance of the Eroica symphony is, therefore, that it will take five years more work to make the vigorous sketch of Thursday last into a finished picture. The violin work which accompanies the Grail motive in the Parsifal prelude also requires a tremendous application of elbow-grease to make it in the least like the wing-winnowing which it should suggest. For the rest, there was nothing to complain of and much to be thankful for. The Siegfried Idyll, in particular, shewed a huge improvement on last season's performance of it. Madame Nordica, always courageous to the verge of audacity, and strong in that technical skill in the management of her voice which seems to be now almost a monopoly of American prima donnas, attacked Isolde's death-song in superb black velvet and diamonds, and survived it, not without deserved glory; though there is all the difference in the world between Madame Nordica's bright impulsiveness and the seas of sentiment in which Isolde should be drowned.

One of the curiosities of this concert was the analytic program by Mr Joseph Bennett, who, as everyone knows, consecrated his life, rather unfortunately, to the cause of Anti-Wagnerism. Now, when you are engaged to write a program for a concert commemorative of Wagner, you cannot—at least without risking a certain friction with the *entrepreneur*—take the opportunity to demonstrate to the audience that what they are listening to is a series of outrages on all the true principles of musical art. Even the story of Wagner's milliner-made dressing-gowns would hardly be in place on such an occasion, since it is held to be fatal to his pretentions as a composer. Mr Bennett, thus hard put to it, yet came off triumphantly, like a man of resource as he is.

First, he got over the difficulty of singing the praises of the composition under analysis by quoting them from his enemies, thus: "Mr Edward Dannreuther, than whom no one knows better what he is talking about when Wagner comes up for discussion, declares," etc. Or: "The following admirable notes upon the prelude to Wagner's last and, as many believe, greatest music-drama are from the pen of Mr C. A. Barry, than whom no better authority," etc., etc. The ground being cleared in this fashion, Mr Bennett gave the analyses the slip no less ingeniously. Die Meistersinger was eluded by the remark that "technical discussion here of so elaborate an overture would serve little purpose." Of the Siegfried Idyll we were told that "it would serve little purpose, even if confusion could be avoided, were we to follow Wagner's working of the themes through all its elaborate details."

Tristan was treated in the same way. "This music," said Mr Bennett, "evades analysis: indeed, it is intended to be felt rather than submitted to any process of scientific inquiry." In the reference to the prelude there was, for those behind the scenes, a rich double meaning in the following artful passage, which to the outsider appeared remarkable for nothing but its extraordinary recklessness of metaphor. "The movement, as a whole, will be best understood and enjoyed by him who most clearly perceives the connection of its various parts with the theme which is its germ. Mere verbal commentary cannot contribute to this end in the slightest degree, since there is no form to define, and there are no salient features serving as milestones on the road for the identification of stage after stage." Amusing as all this is, it is extremely provocative of a discussion on the modern system under which the critic joins the retinue of the *entrepreneur* as writer of his program, or his catalogue preface, or what not.

When Macfarren used to do the programs for the Philharmonic Society, he allowed his opinions of modern music to appear pretty plainly between the lines, and even openly sneered at Goetz's overtures as examples of the effect of consecutive sevenths. Yet he did not say all that he would have said had his hands been perfectly free, although he was in a stronger position than any critic, and had behind him the PhilharmonicSociety in a stronger position than any private *entrepreneur* like Mr Vert or Mr Henschel. It is not surprising, then, to find the most remarkable difference between Mr Bennett's Wagner programs and those articles of his which contain his whole mind on the same subject. Without pretending to be deeply scandalized by the discrepancy, I still think it sufficiently awkward to make its avoidance desirable if it can be managed. Of course, it is not easy; for if analytic programs are to be written at all, they must come from musicians who can write; and all scribbling musicians now turn an honest penny by criticism. But the same man need not write every article in a program any more than every article in a magazine.

In the Crystal Palace programs the signatures of Sir George Grove, Mr Dannreuther, Mr Manns, and Mr Barry may occur in one and the same Saturday sixpenny book; so that none of these gentlemen need say smooth things about compositions which he dislikes. If Mr Henschel were to ask me to write a program for Brahms' Requiem, for instance, I should as a matter of course send him to Dr Parry, who has an unquenchable appetite for pedal points, of which delicacies this colossal musical imposture mainly consists. Surely that would be better than suppressing my own opinion of the work, and stringing together between inverted commas the opinions of those who differ from me, with a prefatory observation to the effect that they are the people to consult if you want a favorable view of the Requiem. How could I feel sure that they would not resent my annexing their work and getting paid for it, even though they might, as a matter of politeness or magnanimity, consent to the operation at my request? The distribution of the articles among different writers would meet this difficulty, though it would leave untouched the graver question of what musical criticism will be worth when all the men who write it are programists in the pay of the persons criticized.

It seems to me that if we musical critics ever get tired of the irresponsible freedom of odd-jobbing, and make ourselves into a regular guild of workers with a recognized professional status, we shall have to establish a pretty strict etiquette on one or two points of this kind.

Herr Jan Mulder's concert at Mrs Jackson's last week was more important than drawing room concerts generally are, as it brought forward a capital 'cello sonata by the Rev. J. Ridsdale, who composes unambitiously, but with genuine feeling and grace, in the old formal arabesque style, of which Spohr was the last famous exponent.

The Crystal Palace concerts, I may remind my readers, were resumed last Saturday.

24 *February* 1892

THE Stock Exchange orchestra is not, as I firmly believed up to Thursday last, composed entirely of stockbrokers. If it were, probably an orchestral concert by it would be impossible. The performance of the simplest overture requires an immense power of business organization and knowledge of business method on the part of the composer and conductor, as well as absolute punctuality and high efficiency on the part of their staff of players. In fact, the strain on a musician's business capacity tires it out so, that his reluctance to exercise it in the intervals between performance and performance often leads to more confusion in his pecuniary affairs than is common in the case of men of quite ordinary capacity in the City, although City business means chiefly the systematizing of want of system and waste of time. I often pause to contemplate with melancholy amazement the "man of business" wasting the lives of innumerable clerks, at great expense to himself, in counting over his money, as if counting it, even in the most inaccurate manner, could add a single sovereign to the pile, or in making reduplicated records of millions of insignificant and immemorable transactions, knowing well that not five out of each million will ever be referred to again, and that the absence of any record even of these five would not cost a half per cent of what it costs to register the remaining 999,995. The Chinaman burning down his house to roast his pig is nothing to this. One's impulse is to exclaim, "Give these men, not a fiddle, since they could not play it, but at least a big drum or a pair of cymbals, and let them have just one run with an orchestra through the overture to Il Seraglio to shew them what business really means."

But I should not hope to derive any enjoyment from such a performance; and this is the real reason why I have hitherto always steadfastly refused to go to the Stock Exchange concerts. The likelihood of every man, on City principles, making a point of coming in several bars late, and playing thirty notes for every one set down for him, seemed so strong that I pooh-poohed the newspaper accounts of the achievements of Mr Kitchin's band. Yet I had a certain curiosity about the affair, too, which eventually helped a friend of mine to break down my prejudice. This friend is a stockbroker for whom I have always had a great admiration, softened by a feeling of compassion for a chronic affliction which has embittered his whole existence. He is what they call brilliant—imaginative, vivacious, full of humor and dramatic perception, a man who might still make his mark if he pleased, in literature or the drama, who might even have made a good musical critic if he had been caught young and trained to the work. But he is the victim of a chronic successfulness which forces him, in spite of strong social sympathies, to become continually richer and richer, and threatens finally to cut him off from human society, and leave him a solitary Monte Cristo. When I first knew him he was comparatively poor; I doubt if his income was much more than forty times as large as mine; and I think, in spite of his generous temperament, he envied me my poverty. Since then he has struggled with his unfortunate propensity as earnestly as any man could; but his efforts are vain: every time I go to see him he is in a more magnificent house than the former one; and as I glance significantly over the palatial environment he looks at me with a mutely pleading eye, which says plainly: "I know, old chap; but dont reproach me: I cant help it: you mustnt drop me for having failed to stave off an extra thousand or two." What can I do but make myself as comfortable as possible on the spot in order to reassure him? The other day he demanded, as a crowning proof of my undiminished friendship, that I should go to the Stock Exchange concert in order to convince myself that Art does not utterly wither in the atmosphere of Capel Court. I confess I suspected him of having taken secretly to playing the cornet, and of having a design to astonish me by appearing before me as a performer. But, being afraid to refuse him lest I should seem to be casting in his teeth my entire freedom from his complaint, I went; and I do not mind admitting that more than I could have considered possible can be done with a squad of musical stockbrokers if you sandwich them between two thoroughly trustworthy professional veterans. I will go further: I will confess—nay, proclaim—that the combination of the professional steadiness and accuracy with the amateur freshness, excitement, and romance, produces a better result than an ordinary routine performance by professionals alone; and I would rather hear this Stock Exchange band at work than hear the best of our professional orchestras playing under a mediocre conductor.

For, in the profession, the better the men are, the staler they are, and the more formidable and inspiring must be the energy and devotion of the leader who rouses them. The symphony on Thursday was an old one by Gade, the last movement of which was mere filigree-work of the Mendelssohnian pattern, requiring nothing but extreme prettiness and precision of execution, which I can hardly say it got, though the performance was creditable on the whole. Before the symphony Miss Alice Schidrowitz and the leader of the band made a very elegant display with voice and violin respectively in Hérold's Jours de mon enfance, which reminded me of the *jours* of my own *enfance*. It sometimes seems odd that Hérold's sort of music should be going on still, and that there are plenty of young people to whom it is as novel and romantic as ever. After the symphony we had Beethoven's violin concerto; and this proved something of a find for me, the young lady who played the solo part—Miss Lilian Griffiths—being decidedly an artist of considerable talent. Except for a trifling slip or two in the last movement her technical success quite justified her ambitious selection; and her execution was remarkably firm and dainty, all the phrases, besides, being rhythmically placed to a nicety. She should, however, have chosen Mendelssohn's concerto instead of Beethoven's; for she is a graceful rather than a poetic or eloquent player: indeed, her fourth string verges on the prosaic, a bad fault when Beethoven is in hand. Only, as increase of knowledge in this direction generally means increase of sorrow, I am far from grumbling because a young Englishwoman is not absolutely Beethovenian at her début. All I say is, why not choose Mendelssohn? For the rest of the concert I cannot answer, as I left whilst Miss Lilian Griffiths was bowing to the gallant and enthusiastic plaudits with which Capel Court, as one man, saluted her. By that time, I am sorry to say, it was too late to hear Beethoven's posthumous quartet in A minor and Mr Algernon Ashton's new violin sonata at Mr Gompertz's concert over the way in Prince's Hall.

Miss Osmond, who appeared at Steinway Hall on the 16th, is a young English pianist who has studied in England from first to last, which is at present, I am sorry to say, a course rather patriotic than wise. Miss Osmond has exceptional agility of finger; and this has led her, apparently, to depend for success chiefly on her ability to strike all the notes in florid compositions of the Balakireff type with great rapidity. But I recommend Miss Osmond to go abroad for a while, after all. Not that she will find better teachers there; but she will find places where a young lady can, without excessive expense or scandal, spend enough of her life in the opera-house and the concert-room to educate herself musically—an end not to be gained by any quantity of pianism alone. For her fault now is that her pianism has outstripped her musicianship; and it is but too likely that this is due to her misfortune in living in a country where you cannot have even a cheap piano provided for the children to march to in a Board School without some mean millionaire or other crying out that the rates will ruin him.

Messrs Longmans have just published the most interesting book I have opened for a long time—the late Ferdinand Praeger's Wagner as I Knew Him. It is an account of Wagner by a man who was not ashamed of him as he really was, and who was not afraid of being denounced for exposing the failings of a gentleman recently dead, as Sir Augustus Harris would call Wagner. A more vivid and convincing portrait than Praeger's was never painted in words: even the bluntest strokes in it are interesting. No doubt the author, with all his vigor of mind and strong commonsense, was too matter-of-fact to see all the issues that presented themselves to Wagner's very subtle mind. For instance, Wagner wrote in 1876: "In my innermost nature I really had nothing in common with the political side of the Revolution [of 1849]." Praeger's comment on this is simply: "Max von Weber told me that he was present during the Revolution and saw Wagner shoulder his musket at the barricades."

A deeper experience of revolutionary politics would have taught Praeger that the very speech on "The Abolition of the Monarchy," which he quotes, shews that Wagner's vehement hatred of the gross military despotism of that time, though it made a revolutionary orator and a barricader of him, never made him a really able politician. Wagner found this out eventually; and the discovery was sufficient to alter his tone as to his exploits in 1849, of which he had previously been sufficiently vain. No doubt the usual demand for a coat of perfectly respectable whitewash for all great men when their turn comes to be hero-worshipped has led some of Wagner's later disciples to try very hard neither to know nor to let the public know that "The Master" was once a colleague of Bakunin, with whom he helped to organize the barricading affair in Dresden in 1849; and Praeger's flat refusal to countenance any such feeble-minded suppression is altogether to his credit; but he hardly appreciates the grounds Wagner had for coming at last to think of himself as having taken a comparatively commonplace, superficial, and amateurish part in the political side of the Revolution of which, on the artistic side, he was the supreme genius.

But since Praeger has given the facts, it matters little that he has once or twice missed their exact significance; and I only wish I had space to quote a few dozen of the anecdotes and pregnant instances with which he makes us see his extraordinary hero as genius, buffoon, coward, hero, philosopher, spoilt child, affectionate and faithless husband, king of musicians, execrable pianist, braving poverty and exile, wearing silk dressing-gowns and sending for confectionery in the middle of a barricading affray—in short, defying all the regulation categories by which we distinguish admirable from despicable characters, and yet throughout all standing out consistently as a great and lovable man. Praeger, by the bye, mentions an autobiography which Wagner left for publication on his son's majority. Will someone ask Siegfried Wagner, who was born in 1870, how soon we may expect this book, which is likely to prove the most interesting autobiography since Goethe's Dichtung und Wahrheit?

2 March 1892

THE winter series of London Symphony Concerts came to an end on Thursday last; and Mr Henschel celebrated the occasion by making a speech. It was just before the Schumann symphony (in D minor), and what he said was: "Ladies and gentlemen,—I feel it to be my duty to inform you that although any defects in the performance are, no doubt, altogether my own fault, yet the light here is so bad that it is hardly possible for the orchestra to distinguish a flat from a sharp." The band rubbed in this protest with vigorous applause; and the audience smiled vaguely, and fell to counting the incandescent lights above the platform—six to each pendant, five pendants on each side: total, sixty lights, and sharps nevertheless indistinguishable from flats. It seemed hardly reasonable; but Mr Henschel was right for all that.

Most amateurs have found out by experience that in a room which is lighted sufficiently for all ordinary purposes the pianoforte candles are indispensable if music is to be read comfortably. There was certainly not light enough on the orchestral desks on Thursday for any but very young eyes. Of course the parts were read accurately enough; but a first-rate orchestral performance uses up the executants so thoroughly that the slightest uneasiness or preoccupation tells on its artistic quality; and I have no doubt that the mess which was made of the accompaniments to Hugo Becker's last two solos was due to lack of candle power overhead. Becker himself, playing from memory, was sufficiently illuminated from within. The repeated calls which followed his performance were partly due to Stradivarius, who would, I think, be famous on the strength of that violoncello alone, even if he had never made a violin.

I cannot pay Becker a higher compliment than to say that he is worthy to be the trustee of such an instrument. I say the trustee; for I flatly refuse to recognize any right of private property in such a treasure. If he played it badly I should advocate its immediate and forcible expropriation, no matter what it had cost him. I live in constant dread of some Chicago millionaire purchasing the best twelve Strads in the world; having them altered into glove boxes; and presenting them to the bridesmaids at his daughter's marriage with an English peer.

When E. M. Smyth's heroically brassy overture to Antony and Cleopatra was finished, and the composer called to the platform, it was observed with stupefaction that all that tremendous noise had been made by a lady. But the day is not far distant when everything that is most passionate and violent in orchestral music will be monopolized by women just as it is now in novel writing. I shall not say that there is any likelihood of our ever seeing a female Mozart or Wagner, lest I should hurt the feelings of many male composers who are nothing like so clever as Miss Smyth or Miss Ellicot; but surely nobody who is not imposed on by the bogus mysteries of musical composition will deny that there is no reason why we should not have a female Moszkowski, a female Rubinstein, or a female Benoit, and find the change of sex rather an improvement than otherwise.

In fact, if the chief of the Royal Academy of Music does not carefully avoid composing in the style of that *entr' acte* from Colomba which was performed at the close of this very concert, we shall have female Dr Mackenzies by the score. When the whole mass of strings and the harp began that strum! strum! strum! strum! to a tune on the cornet which had all the vulgarity of a music-hall patriotic song without its frankness and simplicity of metre, I distinctly saw the ghost of Sterndale Bennett looking at me just as he looks out of Millais's portrait. And when I told him that the composer of the cornet morceau was his successor at Tenterden Street, he disappeared with a shriek before I could assure him that though the composer once thought this *allegro giovale* (*giovale* is Italian for rowdy) good enough for the theatre, and was, perhaps, even a little proud of the elaborate inconvenience of the rhythm, it is not up to his standard academic mark.

The Schumann symphony might have been more delicately played; but the result, as far as I am concerned, would have been much the same in any case. I cannot understand why we take ourselves and Schumann seriously over a work the last half of which is so forced and bungled as to be almost intolerable. I wish someone would extract all the noble passages from Schumann's symphonies, and combine them into a single instrumental fantasia—Reminiscences of Schumann as the military bandmasters would call it—so that we might enjoy them without the drudgery of listening to their elaboration into heavy separate works in which, during three quarters of the performance, there is nothing to admire except the composer's devoted perseverance, which you wish he had not exercised. We all have a deep regard for Schumann; but it is really not in human nature to refrain from occasionally making it clear that he was greater as a musical enthusiast than as a constructive musician. If he had only had Rossini's genius, or Rossini his conscience, what a composer we should have had! I drag in Rossini because he was born on the 29th of February, 1792, and so gained the distinction of having a concert all to himself on Monday last at the Crystal Palace—too late for description here.

The Saturday concert brought forward Becker again. He was to have repeated the Saint-Saëns concerto; but he thought better of it, and gave us instead a harmless concert piece by Bazzini, which soothed me to such an extent that I have no very clear recollection of the details. Becker was rapturously encored for the tarantella of the inevitable Popper, whereupon he inhumanly sat down again and inflicted on the Popperites an "old master" of the severest type. One of the novelties of the concert was a scena by a Mr Herbert Bunning, being the soliloquy of Lodovico il Moro in prison. Mr Oudin sang this as well and sympathetically as the most sanguine composer could have desired; but as the scena began with a spirited breakdown for the whole orchestra, which recurred whenever Lodovico's dullness, or perhaps the coldness of his cell, drove him to seek relief in the dance, the whole composition acquired a serio-comic flavor which was not, I imagine, intended by Mr Bunning. Still, in the words of Mr Leland's judge, "I like to see young heroes ambitioning like this"; and though I must pronounce Mr Bunning's emotional matter too commonplace, and his modes of expression too cheap and obvious to entitle him to the rank he seems to challenge, yet the same criticism might have been justly made of Wagner himself up to a later period of development than I take Mr Bunning to have reached as yet. Mr Oudin also gave us a piece of the Templar in Ivanhoe.

The overture of The Barber of Bagdad, with which the concert opened, made another step forward in popularity. I should like to hear the whole opera again; and, *a fortiori*, the general body of our amateurs, less jaded than I, must be of the same mind. Why does not Mr Carte turn his attention to Cornelius's most popular work, and to the Beatrice and Benedict of Berlioz, the nocturne from which, by the bye, was sung by Mrs Henschel and Madame Hope Temple at the London Symphony concert? The comparative roughness of Mr Henschel's band on that occasion heightened the effect of the finished execution of Mendelssohn's Italian symphony by the Crystal Palace Orchestra, which was in its best form on Saturday. I am far from having grown out of enjoying the Italian symphony; but I confess to becoming more and more disagreeably affected by the conventional features of the instrumentation, especially the trumpet parts in the first movement.

I think it must be admitted that even in Beethoven's symphonies the trumpet parts are already in many places mere anachronisms. Perhaps the dots and dashes of trumpet which we learn from "the study of the best masters" between the Bach period of brilliant florid counterpoints for three trumpets, and the modern Berlioz-Wagner style based technically on the essentially melodic character of our cornets and tubas, were always ridiculous to ears unperverted by custom and the pedantry which springs from the fatal academic habit of studying music otherwise than through one's ears. People would compose music skilfully enough if only there were no professors in the world. Literature is six times as difficult an art technically as composition: yet who ever dreams of going to a professor to learn how to write? Anyhow, when Mr Manns next performs the Italian symphony, I hope he will either omit the dots and dashes, or else have them played on those slide trumpets which are always produced with such solemnity when that august classic, the pianoforte concerto in G minor, is in the bill.

9 *March* 1892

THE Rossini Centenary passed without any celebration in London (as far as I know) except an afternoon concert at the Crystal Palace, whither I went, partly for the sake of old times, and partly because the concert afforded me an opportunity, now very rare, of hearing Rossini's overtures, not from a military band, or from a careless promenade-concert orchestra with an enormous preponderance of string quartet, but from a first-rate wind-band, balanced by about as many strings as the composer reckoned upon. The program was made up of no fewer than four overtures—Siege of Corinth, La Gazza Ladra, Semiramide, and William Tell—with an admirable arrangement of the prayer from Moses for orchestra and organ by Mr Manns, and two vocal pieces. Di piacer and Una voce, curiously chosen, since one is almost an inversion of the intervals of the other. There was, besides, a selection from William Tell, arranged for the band alone.

This was rather too much for the endurance of the orchestra, which became a little demoralized towards the end. Rossini's band parts consist mostly of uninteresting stretches of rum-tum, relieved here and there by some abominably inconvenient melodic trait; for he was the most "absolute" of musicians: his tunes came into his head unconnected with any particular quality of tone, and were handed over to the instrument they would sound prettiest on, without the least regard to the technical convenience of the player—further, of course, than to recognize the physical limits of possibility, and not write piccolo parts down to sixteen-foot C, or trombone parts up to C in altissimo. Consequently, though the scores of Berlioz and Wagner are in a sense far more difficult than those of Rossini, you do not hear during performances of their works any of those little hitches or hair-breadth escapes which are apt to occur when a player has to achieve a feat, however trifling, which is foreign to the genius of his instrument.

It is true that what I call the genius of the instrument varies with the nationality of the player; so that a French horn, though most refractory to a compatriot of its own, or to an Englishman, will be quite docile in the hands of a German; or twelve violins played by Italians will have less weight in an orchestra than five played by Englishmen, not to mention other and subtler differences. Yet the fact remains that we have at present a sort of international school of orchestration, through which an English player, whatever his instrument may be, finds much the same class of work set for him, whether the composer be the Italian Verdi, the French Gounod or Massenet, the Jew Max Bruch, the Bohemian Dvořák, the Norwegian Grieg, the Dutchman Benoit, and so on to the Irish Villiers Stanford, the Scotch Hamish MacCunn, and the English—well, perhaps I had better not mention names in the case of England. Rossini's scores, especially those which he wrote for Venice and Naples, run off these lines; and the result is, that at a Rossini concert there is more likelihood of actual slips in execution than at a Wagner or Beethoven concert; whilst the eventual worrying, fatiguing, and boring of the executants is a certainty when the program is a long one.

The Crystal Palace band held out brilliantly until the final number, which was the overture and selection from William Tell, in the course of which it occurred to most of them that they had had about enough of the Swan of Pesaro. Yet the Swan came off more triumphantly than one could have imagined possible at this time of day. Dal tuo stellato soglio was as sublime as ever. Mr Manns conducted it as he had arranged it, with perfect judgment and sympathy with its inspiration; and in spite of myself I so wanted to hear it again that after a careful look round to see that none of my brother-critics were watching me I wore away about an eighth of an inch from the ferrule of my umbrella in abetting an encore. Another encore, of which I am guiltless, was elicited by the cabaletta of Una voce, which, however, Miss Thudichum did not sing so well as Di piacer. The repeats in the overtures were, strange to say, not in the least tedious: we were perfectly well content to hear the whole bag of tricks turned out a second time. Nobody was disgusted, *à la* Berlioz, by "the brutal crescendo and big drum." On the contrary, we were exhilarated and amused; and I, for one, was astonished to find it all still so fresh, so imposing, so clever, and even, in the few serious passages, so really fine.

I felt, not without dread, that the nails were coming out of Rossini's coffin as the performance proceeded; and if I had been seated a little nearer the platform, there is no saying that I might not have seized Mr Manns's arm and exclaimed, "You know not what you do. Ten minutes more and you will have this evil genius of music alive again, and undoing the last thirty years of your work." But after the third overture and the second aria, when we had had six doses of crescendo, and three, including one encore, of cabaletta, I breathed again. We have not heard the last of the overture to Semiramide; but we shall not in future hear grave critics speaking of it as if it were first-cousin to Beethoven's No. 3 Leonora. The general opinion, especially among literary men who affected music, used to be that there was an Egyptian grandeur about Semiramide, a massiveness as of the Great Pyramid, a Ninevesque power and terror far beyond anything that Beethoven had ever achieved. And when Madame Trebelli, as a handsome chieftain in a panther-skin, used to come down to the footlights, exclaiming, "Here I am at last in Babylon," and give us Ah quel giorno, with a cabaletta not to be distinguished without close scrutiny from that to Rosina's aria in Il Barbiere, we took it as a part of the course of Nature on the operatic stage. We are apt to wonder nowadays why the public should have been so impressed at first by the apparent originality, dramatic genius, depth and daring of Meyerbeer as to be mystified and scandalized when Mendelssohn, Schumann, and Wagner treated him with no more respect than if he had been an old clo' man from Houndsditch.

But the explanation is very simple. We compare Meyerbeer with Wagner: amateurs of 1840 compared him with Rossini; and that made all the difference. If we are to have any Rossini celebrations during the opera season, the best opera for the purpose will be Otello, partly because the comparison between it and Verdi's latest work would be interesting, and partly because it is one of the least obsolete of his operas. When it was last played here at Her Majesty's, with Nilsson, Faure, and Tamberlik, it proved highly bearable, although Faure was then almost at the end even of his capacity for singing on his reputation, and Tamberlik was a mere creaking wreck, whose boasted *ut de poitrine* was an eldritch screech which might just as well have been aimed an octave higher, for all the claim it had to be received as a vocal note in the artistic sense. The only difficulty at present would be to replace Nilsson, who sang Desdemona's music beautifully.

William Tell, of course, we may have: Sir Augustus Harris's attempts with it have always ranked among his triumphs from the artistic point of view, probably because (like Rienzi) it is an opera not of heroes and heroines, but of crowds and armies. He is therefore able to deal with it as he deals with his pantomimes and melodramas, which he takes so much more seriously and artistically than he is able to take those unfortunate operas in which his spoiled children of the Paris Opera, lazier than Rossini himself, have to be petted at every turn. However, enough of Rossini for the present. I cannot say "Rest his soul," for he had none; but I may at least be allowed the fervent aspiration that we may never look upon his like again.

Before quitting the subject of the opera season, let me express a hope that the statement lately made as to the likelihood of Nessler's Trumpeter of Sakkingen being produced at Covent Garden may not be borne out. The Trumpeter, to begin with, is not a trumpeter at all, but a flagrant amateur of the *cornet-à-piston*. The opera is a pretty but commonplace work of the long-lost-child order of plot and pathos; and there is not the smallest reason why it should be dragged across the frontier, seeing that we have half a dozen native composers who could furnish an opera of equal interest provided some reasonable care were taken to engage the services of a competent librettist. I heard The Trumpeter once at Frankfort, and have no desire to hear it again, especially on a stage which should be reserved for the best of the best, and not for the Adelphi commonplaces of musical melodrama. If it need be heard here at all, it is more in Mr Carte's line than Sir Augustus Harris's. That is, if I rightly understand Sir Augustus Harris as aiming at the consecration of Covent Garden to works of the highest grade, leaving what I may call semi-grand and cottage opera to the house at Cambridge Circus. Nessler's opera is no more a first-class work than The Basoche is; and it is much less witty.

The death of Lady Jenkinson—the Dowager Lady Jenkinson as she had been for only five weeks—ought not to pass without a word of notice from the musical chroniclers. She founded a scholarship at the Royal Academy in memory of her friend Thalberg; and she gave a yearly prize for pianoforte-playing at the Guildhall School, thereby setting an excellent and much-needed example. Lady Jenkinson was an Irishwoman, early famous for her pianoforte-playing and her personal beauty, the tradition of which reached me through my mother, who was a neighbor of hers at Stillorgan Park, near Dublin, in her young days, when she was the beautiful Miss Lyster.

On one occasion I happened to explain in this column, *à propos* of Paderewski's playing of Mendelssohn's Songs without Words, that the real reason why they are so seldom played nowadays is not that they are out of fashion, but that, innocent as they look, they are too difficult for most of our players. It not uncommonly happens that people whose opinions I express in expressing my own, write to me, sometimes assuming that I must agree with them on every other point as well as the one in question. Lady Jenkinson wrote to me on the strength of the word I had put in for Mendelssohn; and her letters shewed that at sixty-five her enthusiasm for music, her good nature, and her belief in her fellow-creatures, even including critics, were as fresh as ever. Many musicians whom she helped will have solid reason to regret her loss. May I suggest to the many women in her social position who are at present busily employing their means in such a way as to render their existence a matter of utter indifference to everyone but themselves and their next-of-kin, that if any one of them happens to be looking about for a vacancy, in filling which she could become of some use in the world, there can be no doubt that Lady Jenkinson's death has just created one?

16 *March* 1892

I AM unable to give any account of Mr Hamish MacCunn's Queen Hinde in Calydon, because the first performance was unreasonably fixed for the day of the polling for the County Council. Municipal bands were at stake at that election, and I threw myself into it with ardor, my candidate having pledged himself not only to vote steadily for municipal music but to agitate for giving citizens a really effective power of moving street pianos out of earshot instead of to the next house but one. His opponents never once alluded to music, confining themselves to political matters of entirely secondary importance. The result was that we brought him in by a most tremendous majority, which will, I hope, serve as a lesson to all politicians and parties who identify their cause with that of the enemies of music. Yet I did not quite neglect Mr MacCunn. I made a dash for the

Crystal Palace between the canvassing of two streets, but arrived just too late for Queen Hinde, and had to be contented with a wantonly dismal Wagner selection. Rienzi's prayer was first sung by a tenor who was much bothered by the *gruppetto* on the second note. The lugubrious prelude to the third act of Tannhäuser followed. Miss Fillunger then extinguished the last ray of vivacity left in us by Elizabeth's prayer; after which the band, with a forced and ghastly merriment, attacked the bridal prelude to the third act of Lohengrin, which sounded like the clattering of bones and skulls. Even canvassing was a relief after it.

For some years past the Wind Instrument Society has been giving concerts for the performance of chamber music for wind instruments, which generally proves attractive whenever it is tried at the Popular Concerts. Last year difficulties arose between the Society and the little group of players known as "Clinton's wind-quintet," consisting of Mr G. A. Clinton, the well-known clarinettist, Mr Borsdorff (horn), Mr Malsch (oboe), Mr Griffiths (flute), and Mr Thomas Wotton (bassoon). Preparation for the Society's performances cost these gentlemen so much time that, to secure an adequate return, they found it necessary to stipulate that they should be engaged for all the concerts.

The Society, naturally wishing to keep its platform open to other wind-instruments players, demurred, and offered Mr Clinton four concerts out of six. The quarrel was a pretty one, as both parties were perfectly reasonable in their demands—Mr Clinton, for concerts enough to make it worth his while to keep his quintet in harness; and the Society, for freedom to engage what artists it pleased at its own concerts. Finally, they agreed to differ; and Mr Clinton has now resolved to give concerts on his own account at Steinway Hall. The first of these was announced for Tuesday the 8th; and I have no doubt it duly and successfully came off. The program included Hummel's septet and Spohr's nonet, pretty works both of them, but no longer magnetic enough to draw me to Steinway Hall in such an abominable east wind as prevailed on the 8th. On April the 6th, when Mozart's clarionet trio in E flat will be in the bill, and on May 3rd, when there will be a Beethoven serenade, not to mention some new works at both concerts, I shall perhaps venture. Meanwhile the Wind Instrument Society's concerts are in full swing at the Royal Academy of Music, mostly on Friday nights, when it is quite impossible for me to attend them.

It is important that both enterprises should receive sufficient support to keep them going, for the sake of the opportunities they afford for turning mere bandsmen into artists. At present the dearth of first-rate wind-players is such that important concerts and rehearsals may be made impracticable by the pre-engagement of two or three players—a ridiculous state of things in a city like London. But men will not, as a rule, face the labor of acquiring extra skill unless there is extra credit and remuneration to be got for it; and there will always be a marked difference between the orchestral routine hand and the artist who has occasionally to step out from the rank-and-file before an audience and acquit himself of a difficult task with all the responsibility and prominence of a soloist. The multiplication of concerts at which this occurs means the multiplication of wind-players of the class of (to name veterans alone) Lazarus and the elder Wotton.

And we want, besides these Wind Chamber Concerts, as Mr Clinton calls them, an awakening on the part of our conductors to the fact that it is rather more important, on the whole, that the best players in their bands should sometimes have a chance of playing a concerto, than that young ladies and gentlemen with a crude relish for instrumentation should have their overtures and symphonic poems tried over in public for them. Not long ago a young player of my acquaintance asked a London conductor for such a chance. The conductor replied that he could not think of allowing a performer who had previously occupied a desk in his orchestra to appear at his concerts as a soloist. If that conductor had realized how very strongly such a declaration was bound to prejudice him in the minds of all the intelligent critics and amateurs to whom it was repeated, it is possible that he would have thought twice before making it.

The Philharmonic, I am glad to say, rose to the occasion on Thursday last, when it devoted its first concert of the season to the works of Mozart, whose bust, wreathed with laurel, had the same dissipated air which I remember seeing a lady instantaneously produce in the living Wagner by crowning him, too, with a wreath which had not been made for him. The concert was a great success. The music had been thoroughly rehearsed; the band was on its mettle, the strings going with extraordinary brilliancy and precision; and Mr Cowen did his very best. The result was one of those performances during which, if you happen to turn to the program of the next concert, as I did, and find that the symphony there announced is Beethoven's seventh, you feel that you really cannot listen to such clumsy and obvious sensationalism after Mozart.

For my part, I heartily wish that the Philharmonic Society would devote not merely one concert but a whole season to the commemoration, with a view to educating our London amateurs. These ladies and gentlemen, having for years known Mozart only by vapid and superficial performances which were worse than complete neglect, or by the wretched attempts made to exploit Don Giovanni from time to time at our opera-houses, have hardly yet got out of the habit of regarding Mozart's compositions as tuneful little trifles fit only for persons of the simplest tastes. I have known people to talk in this fashion whilst they were running after every available repetition of the Walkürenritt, the Lohengrin bridal prelude, or the finale to Beethoven's Seventh Symphony—all of them glorified bursts of rum-tum, which any donkey could take in at the first hearing—firmly believing them to be profound compositions, caviare to the general. Much as if a picture-fancier should consider Gustave Doré's and Leon Gallait's work finer and deeper than Carpaccio's, or a literary critic declare Victor Hugo the great master of masters, and Molière an obsolete compiler of trivial farces.

I do not deny that there has been an improvement in popular taste in the last few years, and that mere musical stimulants, from the comparatively innocent whisky-and-water of the Beethoven coda and the Rossini crescendo to the fiery intoxicants of Liszt and Berlioz, are beginning to be recognized for what they really are—that is, excitements which have their use on the stage, in the dance, and in flashes of fun and festivity, but which are as much out of place in the highest class of music as a war-dance would be at a meeting of the Royal Society. The notion that the absence of such stimulants from the symphonies and the chamber-music of Mozart is to be counted against him as a deficiency, is precisely analogous to the disappointment which a sporting collier might experience at going to the Lyceum Theatre and finding that the incidents in Henry VIII did not include a little ratting. And if no such notion has prevailed among our Wagnerians, how is it that when you turn over the programs of the Richter Concerts you find such an inordinate proportion of Walkürenritt and Seventh Symphony to such a paltry scrap of Mozart? in spite of the fact that Richter's conducting of the E flat symphony was one of his highest achievements—if not his very highest—here as a conductor.

When no demand arose for a repetition of it, I could not help suspecting that if Richter had tried his followers with the chorus of Janissaries from Il Seraglio, or with a vigorous arrangement of Viva la liberta, he might have hit off their Mozartian capacity more happily. On the whole, I have no hesitation in saying that as soon as our Wagnerians (and do not forget that there is no more enthusiastic Wagnerian than I have shewn myself) have had their eyes opened to the fact that Wagnerism may cover a plentiful lack of culture and love of stimulants in music, we shall hear more of Mozart's symphonies and concertos, scandalously neglected now for a whole generation, and yet far more beautiful and interesting than any of their kind produced since, by Beethoven or anyone else.

To return to the performance, I have to congratulate M. de Greef on having come triumphantly through the ordeal of taking Mozart's own place at the pianoforte in the C minor concerto, and in the obbligato to the scena Ch' io mi scordi di te, composed for Nancy Storace in 1786 to words from Idomeneo. Nancy was succeeded on Thursday by Madame Giulia Valda, who sang with her usual vigor and self-possession, but fell far short of the standard of vocal execution and delicacy of style required for Mozart's music. The Philharmonic Society was on its best behavior, and committed only two blunders and one crime. The crime was the singling me out from the general body of critics, and putting me in a seat right between the two doors, in a most glacial draught—a clear attempt to "remove" me from my post in the most permanent and effectual way. Its success will depend on the course taken by the cold from which I am suffering. Blunder number one was the retention of a vulgar old concert coda in the overture to Idomeneo, instead of finishing it as written, with the quiet passage leading into the first act of the opera. Blunder number two was the interpolation of Mr Joseph Bennett's extraordinary valentine to Mozart, which Mr Fry recited at the Albert Hall, and need hardly have recited again at St James's Hall. Perhaps Mr Fry thought so himself; for he began to wander towards the end, expressing his astonishment that "Mars's thunder" did not remonstrate about the cheapness of Mozart's funeral and—if my ear caught the word aright—taking the liberty of transforming Mr Bennett's "strangers" who, "tearless and careless, lay that precious form," etc., into "ravens."

The whole concert, as I have already said, was of notable excellence, though here and there the great excess of string-tone over what Mozart calculated upon caused the violins to enter with a certain *sforzando* effect which was anything but acceptable. On the other hand, Mozart would have been delighted with their vigor and splendor in the broader passages, if somewhat astonished at their screamingly high pitch. The only point which they can be said to have actually spoiled was the demisemiquaver figure in the andante of the G minor symphony. This was much too heavily touched; and the blemish was the more apparent because Mr Cowen took the movement a shade too slowly, as musicians are apt to do on the suggestion of the first bar. At least I thought so; but Mr Cowen is entitled to his opinion on the matter; and I will not urge my own now, lest I should seem to disparage the most satisfactory appearance he has yet made as a conductor.

23 *March* 1892

SOME alarm was created at the Crystal Palace on the 12th by the announcement that "Professor Joseph Joachim" was to play Max Bruch's latest violin concerto. At a time when all the best friends of art are striving to turn our professors into artists, it seemed too bad to turn one of our greatest artists into a professor. However, he did not play in the least like one. His artistic conscience is as sensitive and as untiring as ever; his skill is not diminished; and his physical endurance proved equal to a severe test in a quick movement—practically a *moto perpetuo*—by Bach. Bruch's concerto, like most of his works, is masterly in the most artificial vulgarities of the grandiose, the passionate, the obviously sentimental, and the coarsely impulsive. Those partisans of Joachim who contend for his superiority to all other violinists (that is the worst of your amateur critic: he or she always has a Dulcinea whose charms are to be maintained against all comers) are fond of proclaiming the severity of his taste. He knows, they tell us, all the fantasias and the claptrap to which Sarasate and Isaÿe condescend, and can execute them superbly; but he refuses to play any music in public that is not of the very highest class. Then, I ask, why does he play Max Bruch?

I do not, of course, address the question to Joachim himself, since I know better than to hold any artist responsible for everything that his devotees ascribe to him; but I do ask it of the devotees themselves, with a view to instructing them a little as to qualitative as distinct from formal differences in music. It is true that Joachim does not go down to the Crystal Palace with a set of variations by Ernst, and entertain the audience by mimicking the whistling of the piccolo with his harmonics. But if Ernst's variations were as good as those in a Bach chaconne, Joachim would put them at the head of his repertory. The difference is not in the variation form, but in the quality of the music.

Now, if you overlook the difference in form between Bruch's concertos and the fantasias which Sarasate plays so admirably, and compare the quality of the music only, you will end by exclaiming that a violinist who plays Bruch may play anything—variations on the Carnival of Venice, Home Sweet Home on one string, or what you please. Let us make up our minds comfortably that the writing of a piece in three movements in sonata form does not add a cubit to its stature. Otherwise we shall have every composer who finds himself inspired with barely matter enough for a fantasia, spinning it out into a concerto in order that it may lie upon the same shelf with the work of Beethoven and Mendelssohn, and so come under Joachim's notice. In dramatic literature it is now generally understood that an author is not to rush into five acts and blank verse if he can possibly help it; and the result is that nobody now confuses the born vaudeville writers with the great dramatic poets.

But in music there is still a general impression that the form makes the composer, and not the composer the form. Bruch's Scottish fantasia is much better than his concertos; but it is on the strength of the concertos that he is regarded as a sort of contemporary old master, and played by the severe Joachim. By the way, if we must always have concertos, could we not have a little more variety in them? I seem to be for ever listening to Mendelssohn, Beethoven, Bruch, and Brahms; whilst Mozart, Spohr, and Wieniawski are numbered with the dead.

At the Crystal Palace there is an understanding among the regular frequenters that a performance of Schubert's

Symphony in C is one of the specialities of the place. The analytic program of it is one of Sir George Grove's masterpieces; and Mr Manns always receives a special ovation at the end. The band rises to the occasion with its greatest splendor; and I have to make a point of looking interested and pleased, lest Sir George should turn my way, and, reading my inmost thoughts, cut me dead for ever afterwards. For it seems to me all but wicked to give the public so irresistible a description of all the manifold charms and winningnesses of this astonishing symphony, and not tell them, on the other side of the question, the lamentable truth that a more exasperatingly brainless composition was never put on paper. Fresh as I was this time from the Rossini centenary, I could not help thinking, as I listened to those outrageously overdone and often abortive climaxes in the last movement, how much better than Schubert the wily composer of Tancredi could engineer this sort of sensationalism. It was not only his simple mechanism and the infallible certainty with which it wound you up to striking-point in exactly sixteen bars: it was his cool appreciation of the precise worth of the trick when he had done it.

Poor Schubert, who laughed at Rossini's overtures, and even burlesqued them, here lays out crescendo after crescendo, double after quickstep, gallopade after gallopade, with an absurdly sincere and excited conviction that if he only hurries fast enough he will presently overtake Mozart and Beethoven, who are not to be caught up in a thousand miles by any man with second-rate brains, however wonderful his musical endowment. Much as I appreciate the doughtiness with which Sir George Grove fought Schubert's battle in England, yet now that it is won I instinctively bear back a little, feeling that before any artist, whatever his branch may be, can take his place with the highest, there is a certain price to be paid in head-work, and that Schubert never paid that price. Let that be admitted, and we may play the Symphony in C until we are all black in the face: I shall not be the first to tire of it.

A modern disciple of Schubert—or at least a walker in his ways—is Mr Algernon Ashton, who gave a concert of his own music at Prince's Hall last Wednesday. Mr Algernon Ashton goes in for the delight of creation, stopping short at the point where the intellectual grapple turns that delight into the grim effort which makes the greater sort of creators rather glad when it is over. He is at no loss for pretty themes—who is, nowadays?—and he dandles them in his arms, in at one key and out at another, in a very tender, playful, and fatherly way. This is engaging, and even interesting, for a limited period—usually something short of four movements; but it is not quite the same thing as composing quintets in the sense established by the practice of the greatest masters. It may be that I was lazy and discursive and did not concentrate my attention with sufficient intensity on Mr Ashton's ideas.

Anyhow, I thought the quintet purposeless and extemporaneous, fluent without being coherent, carefully finished in detail without being elegant or striking on the whole, and generally tending to recall that terrible couplet of Mr Gilbert's which so often runs through my head at concerts:

> Though I'm anything but clever,
> I could talk like that for ever.

At the same time, I do not wish it to be inferred that such quintets should not be composed. They give a great deal of pleasure in musical circles where Spohr and Hummel are venerated, and Schubert's violin sonatas not despised. They help to educate the members of such circles in the latest harmonic developments, and to accustom them not to make wry faces in good company when they hear a dominant eleventh in some other form than the venerable four-to-three of the schools. But my business is to declare concerning chamber music offered at Prince's Hall whether it is of the stuff from which Monday Popular programs are made. All I can say is, that Mr Ashton is far from having touched even the Schumann level, without bringing into question the summit marked by Mozart's G minor quintet. He is far more successful in his songs and fantasias, which are pretty, and not lacking in appropriate feeling.

I return for a moment to the Crystal Palace to congratulate the directors on having decided not to waste the thunders of the Handel orchestra this year on Gounod or Mendelssohn. Their selection of Samson was arrived at after some hesitation between Samson and Judas. But why not between Samson and Jephtha? The objection to Samson is that, in its integrity, it depends largely on solos which can only be executed by highly accomplished vocalists. It is humiliating to have always to omit, as a matter of course, such numbers as Then long eternity because no one can sing them, or even understand what Handel meant the singer to do with them.

However, we shall do very well if we hear the choruses in their full splendor; for though Samson is not one of Handel's most deeply felt works, yet it shews him in his brightest, most heroic vein, at the height of his strength, decision, audacity, and mastery. The first four bars of Fix'd in His everlasting seat, are alone worth getting up a performance on the festival scale for; and if it were possible to get an English tenor and an English chorus to catch the ring of pagan joy-worship in Great Dagon has subdued our foe, that too would be a memorable experience.

I have also to congratulate the veteran E. Silas on his success at the last Saturday concert with his new pianoforte concerto in B minor, of the brilliancy and cleverness of which we should hear no end if the composer were forty years younger. Had the technical quality of his playing been equal to its spirit and artistic feeling, the reception of the work would have been warmer than it was. Probably Mr Silas will find no difficulty now in inducing some popular pianist to add it to his or her repertory.

30 March 1892

THAT light-hearted body the Bach Choir has had what I may befittingly call another shy at the Mass in B minor. When I last had occasion to criticize its singing, I gathered that my remarks struck the more sensitive members as being in the last degree ungentlemanlike. This was due to a misunderstanding of the way in which a musical critic sets about his business when he has a choral performance in hand. He does not on such occasions prime himself with Spitta's biography of Bach, and, opening his mouth and shutting his ears, sit palpitating with reverent interest, culminating in a gasp of contrapuntal enthusiasm at each entry and answer of the fugue subject.

On the contrary, the first thing he does is to put Bach and Spitta and counterpoint and musical history out of the question, and simply listen to the body of sound that is being produced. And what clothes his judgments in terror is that he does not, like the ordinary man, remain unconscious of every sound except that which he is expecting to hear. He is alive not only to the music of the organ, but to the rattling and crashing caused by the beating of the partial tones and combination tones generated by the sounds actually played from in the score; and he is often led thereby to desire the sudden death of organists who use their stops heedlessly. He hears not only the modicum of vocal tone which the choristers are producing, but also the buzzing and wheezing and puffing and all sorts of uncouth sounds which ladies and gentlemen unknowingly bring forth in the agonies of holding on to a difficult part in a Bach chorus. And his criticism of the choir is primarily determined by the proportion of vocal tone to the mere noises.

To the amateur who has heroically wrestled with the bass or tenor part in the Cum Sancto Spiritu of the B minor Mass, and succeeded in reaching the "Amen" simultaneously with the conductor, it probably seems, not musical criticism, but downright ruffianism to tell him publicly that instead of deserving well of his country he has been behaving more like a combination of a debilitated coalheaver with a suffocating grampus than a competent Bach chorister. But the more outraged he feels, the more necessary is it to persecute him remorselessly until he becomes humbly conscious that in the agonies of his preoccupation with his notes he may perhaps have slightly overlooked the need for keeping his tone sympathetic and telling, and his attack precise and firm. The conscientious critic will persecute him accordingly, not giving him those delicately turned and friendly hints which a fine artist catches at once, but rather correcting him with such salutary brutality as may be necessary to force him to amend his ways in spite of his natural tendency to question the existence of any room for improvement on his part.

When the critic has duly estimated the quality of the vocal material, he begins to take Bach into consideration. An untrained singer can no more sing Bach's florid choral parts than an untrained draughtsman can copy a drawing by Albrecht Dürer. The attempts of ordinary amateurs to make their way through a Bach chorus are no more to be taken as Bach's music than a child's attempt to copy one of Dürer's plumed helmets is to be taken as a reproduction of the original. The critic accordingly must proceed to consider whether the ladies and gentlemen before him are tracing the lines of the great Bach picture with certainty, mastery, and vigilantly sensitive artistic feeling, or whether they are scrawling them in impotent haste under the stick of the conductor.

In the first case, the master's design will come out in all its grandeur; and the critic will give himself up gratefully to pure enjoyment: in the second, he will sit in implacable scorn, asking how these people dare meddle with Bach when they are hardly fit to be trusted with The Chough and Crow. Need I add, that if they happen to have had the unbounded presumption to call themselves by the name of a great man, he will entertain just so much extra contempt for them as we feel for a bad circus clown who aggravates his incompetence by calling himself The Shakespearean Jester.

Although the facts have fallen, as usual, somewhere between these two extreme cases, I nevertheless might now, perhaps, most mercifully leave the Bach Choristers to their own consciences, and say no more about their last performance. It certainly was a very bad one; for the audience, as their coldness shewed, hardly caught a glimpse of the splendor of the work through the cloud of artistic poverty raised by the execution of it. The principal singers were uncomfortable all through, holding on desperately to their books, and never feeling safe until they came to a cadence, when they invariably perked up and delivered it with a confidence and expression so absurdly different from that with which they had been gingerly picking their way to it, that it says much for the politeness of the musicians in the audience and for the ignorance of the rest that every cadence was not received with an ironically congratulatory laugh.

Miss Hilda Wilson was the steadiest of the soloists. As to Mrs Hutchinson, Mr Watkin Mills, and Mr Borsdorff (who played the horn obbligato in the very funniest performance of the Quoniam I ever heard), they are far too good artists to expect any compliments from me on a performance concerning which they can have no feeling except one of devout thankfulness that it is over. The Choir's worst effort was in the Kyrie, a number requiring the highest sensitiveness in the voices and finesse in the execution. As it was, the tone was horribly common, and the execution slovenly. The Sanctus, being much easier, was much better. And this relation between the easier and harder numbers held good throughout the performance. The brisk, florid, but comparatively mechanical movements, in which no great delicacy or expressiveness is called for, such as the Et vitam venturi, the Hosanna, and the Gloria, all of which are pretty plain sailing, went fairly well; whilst the Cum Sancto Spiritu, the most difficult number in this class, was an undignified scramble, and the Et Resurrexit was only so-so. The slow numbers, though carefully done, were constrained and unhappy; and some of the more beautiful modulations, notably that into G major at the end of the Crucifixus, were spoiled by being made obvious "points" of by the conductor.

The summary of the above criticism of the choruses is that the work only received about one-third of the necessary rehearsal. And until this deficiency is ungrudgingly remedied, the performances of the Mass can never be brought up to the standard which they attained under Goldschmidt, who, although he altogether lacked the vivacity needed to place him in perfect sympathy with Bach, yet approached the work with a deep German seriousness which ensured strenuous preparation, and banished all triviality and vulgarity from the performances he conducted.

Mr Villiers Stanford conducted the Mass much better than last time. At such work, it is true, he is always more or less the round peg in the square hole; and he was at fault here and there, dragging the *tempo*, managing a transition like that from the jubilant Gloria to the solemnly tranquil Et in terra pax without tact, or obtrusively calling on his forces to mark some *nuance* which ought to have quietly marked itself. And he is not to be absolved from his share of the general responsibility for the insufficiency of the preparation. Still, these shortcomings are not irremediable; and if Mr Stanford's next attempt is as much better than this as this is than the last, there will be little to complain of —always provided that he will discard the flippancy with which he at present tolerates the unpardonably low standard of quality of tone and refinement of execution which satisfies the Choir.

Mr Morrow's success with the principal trumpet part was much more complete than in his former attempt. On that occasion, as his lip tired early in the performance, so that many of the notes above A were missed during the latter half of the concert, the result of the experiment was doubtful. This time his lip was in good condition; and though he did not attain the infallibility of Kosleck, he quite settled the question as to the practicability of the original parts. It is all the more to be regretted that the effect should have been two-thirds spoiled by his colleagues, Messrs Backwell and Ellis. These gentlemen used the old slide trumpets, which they blew sedately into their desks whilst Mr Morrow's uplifted clarion was ringing through the hall, the effect being that of a solo trumpet *obbligato* instead of three trumpets *concertante*.

Now, surely, Mr Ellis and Mr Backwell could have procured "Bach trumpets" from Messrs Silvani & Smith without any fear of being unable to play the comparatively easy second and third parts on them. The three instruments would then have been equally well heard, and the characteristic play of the three-part counterpoint fully realized. Until this is done the trumpet parts will in some respects sound actually less like what the composer intended than they used to when played on three clarionets. I believe that it is only in its new-old form that the trumpet has any chance of restoration to the orchestra.

At the Crystal Palace the other day, and at the Philharmonic on Thursday, they played Mendelssohn's Trumpet Overture *without trumpets*, using cornets instead. But who can wonder at the conductors allowing this, in spite of all the protests of the treatise writers, when the choice lies between a cornet of which the player has complete command and a dull hard slide trumpet to which he is so unused that when he has to *filer* a note, as in the opening of the Rienzi overture, he must either fly to his cornet or conspicuously bungle his work? In the hands of a man who can really play it, the slide trumpet is undoubtedly better than the cornet for fanfares, penetrating held notes, and certain florid passages which are meant to ring metallically. But such players, since their skill does not repay the cost of cultivation, are scarce; and even in their hands one never gets even a suggestion of the silvery, carillon-like clangor of the top notes of the clarion. All that is ever required of the slide trumpeter is occasionally to get through the obbligato to Let the bright seraphim or The trumpet shall sound, in an amateurish fashion at a festival.

On all other occasions trumpet parts are played on the cornet; and the scores of Wagner, Gounod, and Verdi abound in cornet effects which would come out villainously on slide trumpets. The way to restore the "Bach trumpet," or clarion proper, is simply to induce composers to write parts for it in their scores, and to agitate for its introduction into military bands. Until this is done it will be hardly better worth a player's while to learn the clarion than it is now to learn the *viol d' amore* or the harmonica.

I greatly regret that my absence from town last Friday prevented me from taking advantage of the discussion on Colonel Shaw-Hillier's United Service Institution lecture on military music to raise the question of clarions in bands. Anyone who has ever noticed how the peculiar bugling tone of an Italian military band using flugel horns contrasts with that of an English military band using cornets, and compared both with the tone of the clarion as played by Kosleck and Morrow, must have felt how far we are from having fully developed the orchestra on this side.

I gave Dvořák's Requiem one more chance on Wednesday last, when it was performed—and very well performed too—for the first time in London, at the Albert Hall, under Mr Barnby. And I am more amazed than ever that any critic should mistake this paltry piece of orchestral and harmonic confectionery for a serious composition.

At the Philharmonic on Thursday, Sapellnikoff, who was received coldly, like a forgotten man, had his revenge after the concert in a series of recalls and an encore which were, for a Philharmonic audience, quite frantic. No doubt we shall have some recitals from him, though the agents have been so timid in that department of late.

6 *April* 1892

THE last place a musical critic ordinarily thinks of going to is a music-hall. I should probably not know what a music-hall is like, if it were not for the transfer of the ballet in London from the Opera to the Alhambra. The effect of this transfer has been to confront music-hall audiences, nursed on double meanings, with an art emptied of all meaning—with the most abstract, the most "absolute," as Wagner would have said, of all the arts. Grace for the sake of grace, ornamental motion without destination, noble pose without *locus standi* in the legal sense: this is the object of the tremendous training through which the classical dancer goes before figuring as "assoluta" in the Alhambra program.

Some years ago, a section of the Church of England made the discovery, then rather badly needed in this country, that "*laborare est orare*" is true of labor devoted directly to the production of beauty—nay, more true of it than of labor devoted to the acquisition of money without regard to ulterior social consequences. This came with the shock of a blasphemous violation of vested interests to the section which had obligingly handed over the whole beauty producing department of human industry to the devil as his exclusive property.

One discovery generally leads to another; and the clergymen who took up the new ideas had no sooner opened their minds resolutely to the ballet than they were greatly taken aback to find that the exponents of that art, instead of being abandoned voluptuaries, are skilled workers whose livelihood depends on their keeping up by arduous practice a condition of physical training which would overtax the self-denial of most beneficed clergymen. Strange doings followed. Clergymen went to the music-halls and worshipped the Divine as manifested in the Beautiful; and a deputation of dancers claimed their rights as members of the Church from the Bishop of London, who, not being up to date in the question, only grasped the situation sufficiently to see that if it is a sin to dance, it is equally a sin to pay other people to dance and then look on at them. He therefore politely and logically excommunicated the deputation and all its patrons, lay and clerical.

Matters have smoothed down a little since that time; and whilst nobody with any pretension to serious and cultivated views of art would now dream of ridiculing and abusing Mr Stewart Headlam as the fashion was in the early days of the Church and Stage Guild, the enthusiasts of that body would not now, I imagine, dispute the proposition that the prejudices against which they fought could never have obtained such a hold on the common sense of the public had not too many music-hall performers acquiesced in their own ostracism by taking advantage of it to throw off all respect for themselves and their art. The ideas of the Guild have by this time so far permeated the press, that the present tendency is rather to pet the halls, and to give free currency to knowing little paragraphs about them, the said paragraphs often amounting to nothing more than puerile gushes of enthusiasm about exploits that ought to be contemptuously criticized off the face of the earth.

Last week I devotedly sat out the program at the Empire; and I am bound to say that I was agreeably surprised to find the "lion comique" and the wearisome "sisters" with the silly duet and the interminable skirt dance quite abolished—for that evening, at all events. Instead, we had Poniatowski's Yeoman's Wedding, I fear no foe, and some of Mr Cowen's most popular drawing room songs. I took what joy I could in these; in the inevitable juggler who had spent his life practising impossibilities which nobody wanted to see overcome; in the equally inevitable virtuoso, who, having announced his intention of imitating "the oboy," seized his own nose and proceeded grossly to libel the instrument; and in "the Bedouins," the successors of the Bosjesmen who turned somersaults round my cradle, and of the Arab tribes who cheered my advanced boyhood in flying head-over-heels over rows of volleying muskets.

I heard also the Brothers Webb, musical clowns who are really musical, playing the Tyrolienne from William Tell very prettily on two concertinas—though I earnestly beg the amateurs who applauded from the gallery not to imagine that the thing can be done under my windows in the small hours on three-and-sixpenny German instruments. The concertinas on which the Webbs discourse are English Wheatstones of the best sort, such as are retailed at from sixteen to thirty guineas apiece. There were two frankly odious items in the program. One was a Hungarian quartet, in which the female performers did their worst to their chest registers in striving to impart the rowdiest possible *entrain* to some Hungarian tunes and to Le Père la Victoire. The other was Ta-ra-ra, etc., sung by a French lady, whose forced abandonment as she tore round the stage screaming the cabalistic words without attempting to sing the notes, was so horribly destitute of any sort of grace, humor, naïveté, or any other pleasant quality, that I cannot imagine any sober person looking on without being shocked and humiliated.

Let me now hasten to admit that as the words of the refrain were perfectly harmless, and the lady dressed with a propriety which none of her antics materially disturbed, the most puritanical censor could have alleged nothing in court against the performance, which was nevertheless one of the least edifying I have ever witnessed. I have not had the pleasure of hearing Miss Lottie Collins sing this ancient piece of musical doggerel; but I should be sorry to believe that it "caught on" originally in the unredeemed condition to which it has been reduced at the Empire.

All this, however, was by the way. What I went to see was the ballet. I have already said that classical dancing is the most abstract of the arts; and it is just for that reason that it has been so little cared for as an art, and so dependent for its vogue on the display of natural beauty which its exercise involves. Now the ballet, as we know it, is a dramatic pantomime in which all sorts of outrageous anomalies are tolerated for the sake of the "absolute" dancing. It is much worse than an old-fashioned opera in this respect; for although the repeated stoppages of the dramatic action in order that one of the principal dancers may execute a "solo" or "variation" is not more absurd than Lucrezia Borgia coming forward from the contemplation of her sleeping son, under thrillingly dangerous circumstances, to oblige the audience with the roulades of Si voli il primo, yet Lucrezia is allowed, and even expected, to wear an appropriate costume; whereas if the opera were a ballet she would have to wear a dress such as no human being, at any period of the earth's history, has worn when out walking.

But this advantage of the *prima cantatrice* over the *prima ballerina* is counterbalanced by the fact that whereas dancers must always attend carefully to their physical training, singers are allowed, as long as their voices last, to present themselves on the stage in a condition ludicrously unsuitable to the parts they have to play. Twenty years ago or so you might have seen Titiens playing Valentine, just as you may today see Signor Giannini playing Radames or Manrico, with a corporal opulence which is politely assumed to be beyond voluntary control, but which, unless it culminates in actual disease—as of course it sometimes does—is just as much a matter of diet and exercise as the condition of the sixteen gentlemen who are going to row from Putney to Mortlake next Saturday. Everything in opera is condoned, provided the singing is all right; and in the ballet everything is condoned, provided the dancing is all right.

But, as Rossini said, there are only twelve notes in European music; and the number of practicable vocal ornaments into which they can be manufactured is limited. When you know half-a-dozen caballettas you have no more novelty to look for; and you soon get bored by repetitions of their features except when the quality of the execution is quite extraordinary. My recollection of Di Murska's Lucia does not prevent me from yawning frightfully over the *fiori-*

ture of the dozens of Lucias who are not Di Murskas. In the same way, since the stock of *pas* which make up classical dancing is also limited, the solo dances soon become as stale as the *rosalias* of Handel and Rossini.

The *entrechats* of Vincenti at his entry in the ballet of Asmodeus were worthy of Euphorion; but the recollection of them rather intensifies the boredom with which I contemplate the ordinary *danseuse* who makes a conceited jump and comes down like a wing-clipped fowl without having for an instant shewn that momentary picture of a vigorous and beautiful flying feature which is the sole object of the feat. In short, I am as tired of the ballet in its present phase as I became of ante-Wagnerian Italian opera; and I believe that the public is much of my mind in the matter. The conventional solos and variations, with the exasperating teetotum spin at the end by way of cadenza and high B flat, are tolerated rather than enjoyed, except when they are executed with uncommon virtuosity; and even then the encores are a little forced, and come from a minority of the audience. Under such circumstances, a development of the dramatic element, not only in extent but in realistic treatment, is inevitable if the ballet is to survive at all.

Accordingly, I was not surprised to find at the Empire that the first and most popular ballet was an entertainment of mixed *genre* in which an attempt was made to translate into Terpsichorean the life and humors of the seaside. Maria Giuri, a really brilliant dancer, condescended to frank step-dancing in a scene set to national airs, which, however, included one brief variation on Yankee Doodle which the most exclusive pupil of the grand school need not have disdained. Vincenti himself had an air of being at Margate rather than in the Elysian fields as usual. I am afraid he is rather lost in Leicester Square, where the audience, capable of nothing but cartwheels, stare blindly at his finest *entrechats;* but that is the fate of most artists of his rank. He confined himself mainly to mere *tours de force* in the second ballet, Nisita, in which Malvina Cavallazzi, as the Noble

Youth, was nobler than ever, and Palladino, who reminded me of the approaching opera season, hid her defects and made the most of her qualities with her usual cleverness.

Perhaps by the time I next visit a music-hall the ballet will have found its Wagner, or at least its Meyerbeer. For I have had enough of mere ballet: what I want now is dance-drama.

13 *April* 1892

AT the Philharmonic Concert last week I went down during the interval to find out from the placards at the door whether the musical season was really so dull as I had gathered from the comparatively few concert invitations which had reached me. For I am never quite certain as to how much music may be going on behind my back. The people who only want puffs have given me up as a bad job; the concert-givers who cannot afford to have the truth told about their performances shun me like the plague; the spoiled children of the public are driven by a word of criticism into fits of magnificent sulking; the soft-hearted, uncritical patrons and patronesses, always regarding me as the dispenser of a great power of giving charitable lifts to hard-up people who have mistaken their profession, see plainly that since I reserve so much of my praise for comparatively well-to-do artists my favorable notices must be simply the outcome of invitations, chicken and champagne, smiles of beauty, five-pound notes and the like (I am far from wishing to discourage such realizable illusions); and the genuine enthusiasts, whenever I do not appreciate their pet artists and composers, will have it that I am an ignorant fellow, writing musical criticism for the gratification of my natural hatred of the sublime and beautiful. In brief, there is always a section of the musical world thoroughly convinced that, like the creditor who detained Sam Weller in the Fleet, I am "a malicious, badly-disposed, vorldly-minded, spiteful, windictive creetur, with a hard heart as there aint no softnin." When a person, in passing through this harmless and transient madness, gives a concert or an opera, I am not invited; and as I never bias myself by reading advertisements or criticisms, I may quite easily, at any given moment, be the worst-informed man in London on every current musical topic except the quality of the performances I have actually attended.

Sometimes it is I who have to stand on the offensive, and exclude myself, in self-defence. The *entrepreneurs* who send me a couple of stalls the week before a concert, and a lawyer's letter the week after it, may be irascible gentlemen who must splutter in some direction from congenital inability to contain themselves, or they may be long-headed men of business who understand the overwhelming disadvantages at which the law of libel places every writer whose subject is completely outside the common sense of a British jury. But the effect on me is the same either way. The moment I understand that the appeal to law is not barred between myself and any artist or *entrepreneur*, I fly in terror from the unequal contest, and never again dare to open my lips, or rather dip my pen, about that litigious person.

No doubt, in the case of an *entrepreneur*, the fact that I dare not allude to the artists he brings forward is a disadvantage to them, to the public, and to myself; but I submit that the remedy is, not for me to defy the law and bring ruinous loss of time on myself and of money on my principals, nor for the artists, who are mostly foreigners and strangers, with no effective choice in the matter, to avoid litigious agents, but for the public, as electors and jurymen, to make criticism legal. Many innocent persons believe it to be so at present; but what are the facts?

Last season an opera-singer, of whom I am reminded by an uncomfirmed report of his death at Malta, had his performance criticized by my eminent colleague Mr Joseph Bennett in a manner which was almost culpably goodnatured. The artist, however, declared that the effect of the criticism was to open the eyes of impresarios to the undisputed fact that he was no longer in his prime; and, the paper in which the notice appeared being well able to pay any amount of damages, he sued it. The case was peculiarly favorable to the critic, as there was no difficulty in making even a jury see that the criticism erred only on the side of leniency. But one of the proofs of its justice was that it had depreciated the market value of the artist's services, as every unfavorable criticism must if it has any effect at all. The jury accordingly gave a verdict for the artist against the critic, putting the damages at a farthing to emphasize the fact that they considered that the critic would have been in the right if his occupation had been a lawful one. And if Mr. Bennett had called on me next day, and asked me in the common interests of our profession and of the public never to mention that artist's name again, he could have been indicted for conspiracy and imprisoned.

In spite of the adverse verdict, some critics expressed themselves as satisfied with the termination of the case, on the ground that the artist had a fine lesson, since he had gained nothing, and incurred both heavy costs and loss of reputation, not to mention such press boycotting as arises spontaneously from the *esprit de corps* of the critics without any express concert between them. No doubt this was so, though it does not offer the smallest set-off to the still heavier costs incurred by the defendants. But let us proceed from what actually happened on that occasion to what might have happened. Suppose the artist, instead of depending on his own resources, had been backed by a rich and influential impresario who had made up his mind to muzzle the press. If I were such an impresario I could do it in spite of all the boasted thunders of the Fourth Estate. First, I would take the young men; cultivate them; flatter them a little; wave my hand round the stalls, and say, "Come in whenever you like—always a place for you—always glad to see you." In this fashion I would make personal friends of them; invite them to garden-parties and introduce them to my artists; make them feel themselves a part of the artistic world of which I was the great solar centre; and give them hypnotic suggestions of my intentions in such a way as to create tremendous expectations of the artists I had in my managerial eye. No young man recently promoted from the uncomfortable obscurity of the amphitheatre or gallery, no matter how conceited he may be, knows enough of the value of his goodwill to suspect that a great impresario could have any motive beyond pure amiability in shewing so much kindness to a mere beginner in journalism. The old men would give me still less trouble. They would have learnt to live and let live: not a fault in my performances would they find that they had not pointed out over and over again twenty years ago, until they were tired of repeating themselves. I should not quarrel with them, nor they with me. What with the foolish critics who would think everything delightful as long as I made them happy, and the wise ones who would call everything beautiful as long as I made them comfortable, the ground would be cleared for my final *coup*. This, of course, would be struck at the few born critics—the sort of men who cannot help themselves, who know what good work is, crave for it, are tortured by the lack of it, will fight tooth and nail for it, and would do so even if the managers were their fathers and the prima donnas their sweethearts. These fellows would presently find their principals figuring as defendants in libel actions taken by my artists. They would learn from bitter experience that they must either hold their tongues about the shortcomings in my theatre, or else find themselves costing more in damages and lawyers' fees than any paper could afford to spend on its musical department alone; and the full accomplishment of this would not cost me a thousand pounds if I managed it adroitly. If one big manager can do this, what could not a ring of managers and concert-agents do by organizing a boycott against any obnoxious critic? They could drive him out of his profession, unless his danger roused his colleagues to the need for a counter-organization, which would not be easy in an occupation which employs so much casual and unskilled labor as musical criticism. In short, then, I pursue my present calling by sufferance—by a sort of informal Geneva convention, which puts actions-at-law in the same category with explosive bullets. When a combatant shews the least disposition to violate this convention, I prudently avoid him altogether. At the same time, I do not object to retorts in kind. The one manager with whom I feel on perfectly easy terms runs a paper of his own; and whenever I libel his enterprises in this column to the tune of £500 damages, he does not meanly take an action against me, but promptly fires off a round thousand worth of libels on me in his own paper. I appreciate his confidence as he appreciates mine; and we write reciprocally with complete freedom, whereas, if we suspected any possibility of litigiousness, we should never dare allude to one another.

I offer this little glimpse behind the scenes partly to explain to a bewildered public how it is that only the most desperate and ungovernable critics say half what they think about the shortcomings of the performances they sample, and partly to complete my reasons for going down to the entrance of St. James's Hall between the parts of the Philharmonic Concert to ascertain whether there was a tremendous eruption of musical activity going on unknown to me under the auspices of the gentlemen who shelter their enterprises from criticism beneath the shield of Dodson and Fogg.

But there was nothing of the sort: the season has not recovered from the discouragement of the failure of the concerts given by the Manchester band, and the recoil after the disastrous over-speculation of the year before last, when the program of each week was as long as the program for the month is now. At the Philharmonic concert in question, the chief attraction was Joachim, who played Bruch's new concerto badly—outrageously, in fact—for the first twenty bars or so, and then recovered himself and played the rest splendidly. The orchestra played Mr. Cowen's *suite de ballet*, entitled The Language of Flowers, very prettily, though the audience must have felt that, in the absence of any dancing, the performance was much as if Mr. Cowen had arranged the accompaniments of some of his songs for the band, and given them without the aid of a singer.

As to the other pieces, I am sorry to say that their execution shewed a relapse into the old Philharmonic faults from the standard reached at the Mozart Concert. The death-song from Tristan, with which Madame Nordica did so well at the London Symphony Concert under Henschel, fell flat: every time the orchestra began to rise at it Mr. Cowen threw up his hand in agony lest the singer should be drowned. There was not the slightest danger of that. And, if there had been, she would probably have preferred to risk it rather than have her only chance at the concert spoiled, as it was, by being handled like a trumpery drawing room ballad. I call it her only chance; for I am quite sure that Madame Nordica will agree with me that she was not up to her highest standard of brilliancy and smoothness of execution in the polacca from Mignon.

For the rest, nothing but the *suite de ballet*, and perhaps the Cherubini overture, had been sufficiently rehearsed; and the old complaints of superficiality, tameness, dullness, and so on, have begun again. The fact is, that the Philharmonic thinks its band above the need for rehearsing as carefully as its rivals. But since superiority in London means superiority to first-rate competitors, it can only be secured by the hardest workers. And that is why the Philharmonic is the worst band of its class in London, and will remain so until it sets to work in earnest, instead of simply getting one of its directors to write Panglossian puffs for circulation among the audience, assuring them and the "bigoted" critics that the Society is the best of all possible societies, and the conductor the best of all possible conductors. It had much better give its conductor a fair chance, by either shortening its programs or multiplying its rehearsals, and insisting on a full attendance at each of them.

At the Crystal Palace concert last Saturday I heard a new note in the orchestra, and traced it to the first flute, Mr. Fransella, whom I have not, as far as I know, had the pleasure of hearing before, but who shewed himself a fine artist, fully worthy of the post he has just taken. Mr. Arthur Hervey's Overture in G has a Fate motive and a Love motive, transformable into one another; this being the latest development of double counterpoint, which used to mean merely that two simultaneously played parts would sound equally well when you turned them upside down. It shewed how easily a man of artistic taste and intelligence, with a dash of imagination, can turn out imposing tone-poems. Mr. Hervey handles the orchestra and manages his themes with such freedom and ingenuity that I hope he will try his hand at something more interesting to me than fate and love, for which, in the abstract, I do not care two straws. The pianist at this concert was Mr Lamond, who played a swinging concerto of Tchaikowsky's in the Cyclopean manner, impetuous and formidable, but a little deficient in eloquence of style and sensitiveness of touch.

Miss Gambogi sang Mercé dilette well enough to justify her in having attempted it, which is no small praise; whilst another singer, a gentlemen who had evidently often brought off Dio possente with applause on the stage, discovered that the only operatic method known to the Crystal Palace audience was pure singing, which unluckily happened to be his weak point.

20 *April* 1892

AT Easter-time there is nothing for the musical critic to do but go to church and listen to Bach's Passion Music. This year, I confess to having neglected my duty for the sake of snatching a few days out of London before the season sets in at its worst.

In speaking of the performance of the Brothers Webb at the Empire recently, I paid the concertinas they used the compliment of describing them as "English Wheatstones of the best sort." Here I unwarily fell into the old-fashioned habit of speaking of the English concertina as the Wheatstone concertina, the instrument having been invented by the late Sir Charles Wheatstone. The house of Wheatstone still flourishes; but the manufacture of Wheatstone concertinas is no more peculiar to it today than the manufacture of saxhorns is to the house of Sax, or of Boehm flutes to the representatives of Boehm. Now Mr Jones, of 350 Commercial Road, East, who manufactured the instruments I alluded to, and who claims the Messrs Webb as his pupils, thinks that my way of putting the case confers the credit due to him upon Messrs Wheatstone of Burlington Street.

Accordingly, he not only asks me to correct my statement forthwith, but, I regret to say, deprives my willing compliance of much of its grace by adding that he will place the matter in the hands of his solicitor if I dont. The oddity of this threat lies in the fact that to mistake any English concertina for one made by Messrs Wheatstone, who have much the same prestige among concertina makers as Messrs Broadwood have among pianoforte makers, is to pay it a very high compliment. Possibly Mr Jones feels on this point much as Mr Whistler did when he uttered his celebrated "Why drag in Velasquez?" But I wonder whether if I had by mistake attributed the portrait of Miss Alexander to Velasquez, Mr Whistler would have threatened to place the matter in the hands of his solicitor? I confess I wonder still more what could possibly happen to me if he did? However, if I cannot quite understand Mr Jones's legal position, I can sympathize with his desire to get full credit for his two fine instruments; and I shall in future take due care not to hark back ambiguously to the father of English concertina makers.

The last Monday Popular Concert of the season came off on Monday week with the usual demonstrations. Joachim and Neruda played Bach's concerto in D minor, and were so applauded that they at last returned to play again with a new accompanist in the person of Hallé, who was received with three times three, but who probably retained his own opinion as to the way his Manchester enterprise was treated by the London amateurs. Mr Plunket Greene sang three songs by Lully, Cornelius, and Schumann admirably in the first part of the concert; but whether he waited for the second part in a draught, or was disheartened by the trashy quality of the Magyar song which he sang afterwards, certain it is that he made hardly anything of his second opportunity. There were two quintets, the great G minor of Mozart, and the E flat of Schumann, one of the best of his works. Miss Fanny Davies, who accompanied Joachim in some of his arrangements of Brahms' Hungarian dances, was full of those curious tricks and manners of hers which so often suggest wicket-keeping rather than pianoforte-playing; and Miss Agnes Zimmermann played the pianoforte part in the Schumann quintet like the excellent artist she is. Piatti gave us Kol Nidrei, and retired covered with glory, as who should say, "Well, ladies and gentlemen: you have been making remarks on my age, and listening to Popper, Becker, Hollman, and all sorts of wonderful people; and yet here I am precisely where I was." Joachim was very warmly greeted indeed; and I am not surprised at it; for he seems to be passing now through a sort of St Martin's summer of his talent. Three or four years ago it seemed to me that he was living more on his reputation than on his current achievements; but this year and last his playing would have made his reputation afresh if it had never been made before.

In answer to a request for my opinion of the new Brahms quintet, I must explain that I did not hear it. Messrs Chappell, probably knowing that I am not to be trusted on the subject of Brahms, forbore to invite me on the occasions of its performance; and I was quite content to know nothing of the important event in progress. If there is one thing of which I am more convinced than another it is the worthlessness of criticisms that have dislike at the back of them. Now I do not exactly dislike Brahms; but I can never quite get over that confounded Requiem of his. Therefore, I am not going to meet the quintet half-way. It will come to me some day, I have no doubt; and I shall do my best to make it prove the validity of the estimate of Brahms as a serious composer which I have so often expressed. Until then, why should we molest one another?

27 *April* 1892

THE Basoche is so good an opera of its kind that I am quite at a loss to explain how it succeeded in getting itself trusted to the mercy of London. The plan of the work is almost perfect: the dainty combination of farce and fairy tale in an historical framework could hardly be more happily hit off. The farce is void of all vulgarity; the fairy tale proceeds by natural magic alone, giving us its Cinderellas and its princesses without any nursery miracles; and the pie-crust of history is as digestible as if it had been rolled by the great Dumas himself. Add to this that the music has a charming liveliness, and that whilst Messager, the composer, has avoided the more hackneyed and obvious turns of the modern operatic stock-in-trade in a fresh, clever, cultivated, and ingenious way, yet he does not presume upon his ability. The man who knows his place as well as this is scarce in French art, where the colder and less humorous talents waste themselves on bogus classicism, and the lighter-hearted throw away all self-respect and take to what polite policemen call gaiety. Paris encouraged Meyerbeer in posing as the successor of Mozart and Beethoven, as it encourages Saint-Saëns and Massenet in posing as the successors of Meyerbeer; whilst it allowed Offenbach and Lecocq openly to play the fool with their art. And London, unfortunately, never had any proper accommodation for the works of Auber, who kept his self-respect without losing his head. Our operatic stages were always either too large or too rowdy for his dainty operas.

Now that Mr D'Oyly Carte has at last given us the right sort of theatre for musical comedy, it is too late for Auber: we have had enough of the serenade in Fra Diavolo and the Crown Diamonds galop, and can no longer stand the Scribe libretto which sufficed to keep our fathers from grumbling. We want contemporary work of the Auber class. The difficulty, so far, has been to find a contemporary Auber. The Gilbertian opera did not exactly fill the vacancy: it was an altogether peculiar product, extravagant and sometimes vulgar, as in the case of the inevitable old woman brought on to be jeered at simply because she was old, but still with an intellectual foundation—with a certain criticism of life in it. When the Gilbert-Sullivan series came to an end, the attempt to keep up the school at second-hand produced the old vulgarity and extravagance without the higher element; and Savoy opera instantly slipped down towards the lower level. Sir Arthur Sullivan, meanwhile, made a spring at the higher one by trying his hand on Ivanhoe, which is a good novel turned into the very silliest sort of sham "grand opera." I hardly believed that the cumulative prestige of Sir Walter Scott, Sir Arthur Sullivan, Mr D'Oyly Carte with his new English Opera House, and the very strong company engaged, not to mention log-rolling on an unprecedented scale, could make Ivanhoe pay a reasonable return on the enormous expenditure it cost. Yet it turns out that I either overrated the public or underrated the opera. I fancy I overrated the public.

Now La Basoche is exactly what Ivanhoe ought to have been. Though it is a comic opera, it can be relished without several years' previous initiation as a bar loafer. The usual assumption that the comic-opera audience is necessarily a parcel of futile blackguards, destitute not only of art and scholarship, but of the commonest human interests and sympathies, is not countenanced for a moment during the performance. The opposite, and if possible more offensive and ridiculous, assumption that it consists of undesirably naïve schoolgirls is put equally out of the question: you can take your daughter to see it without either wishing that you had left her at home or being bored to death. You attain, in short, to that happy region which lies between the pity and terror of tragic opera and the licentious stupidity and insincerity of *opera-bouffe*.

Now comes the question, What is going to happen to The Basoche? The opera-goers who support the long runs upon which Mr Carte depends for the recoupment of his princely expenditure, must be largely taken from the social strata upheaved by popular education within the last twenty years. These novices have only just learned, partly from glimpses of Wagner, but mostly from the Savoy operas, that music can be dramatic in itself, and that an opera does not mean merely the insertion of songs like When other lips into plays otherwise too bad to be tolerated. Only the other day they were encoring The flowers that bloom in the spring, tra la, I forget how many times every evening, with a childish delight in frank tomfoolery and tum-tum which a digger or backwoodsman might have shared with them. In Ivanhoe they found plenty of the old rum-tum, with sentimentality substituted for the tomfoolery, and a huge stage glitter; and it is these, and not the elegance of the musical workmanship or the memories of Scott's story, which have kept the work on the stage so long—for it is still flourishing: it was revived last Friday, with Mr Barton McGuckin in the title-part.

I begin to think that Mr Sturgis was right in concluding that the first thing to do with Scott, in order to adapt him to the Cambridge Circus audience, was to remove his brains. Now, on the plane of The Basoche there is neither tomfoolery nor sentimentality: the atmosphere is that of high comedy, of the very lightest kind, it is true, but still much cooler, wittier, finer, more intelligent than that of either Ivanhoe or The Nautch Girl. It remains to be seen whether the admirers of these works will respond to the new appeal. If they do not—if Mr D'Oyly Carte is forced back on the normal assumption that the respectable opera-goer must be catered for as at best a good-humored, soft-hearted, slow-witted blockhead, void of all intellectual or artistic cultivation, then the critics may as well abandon English opera to its fate for another generation or so. There is no use in our making ourselves disagreeable to the managers by clamoring for higher art, if the managers can simply retort by shewing us rows of empty benches as the result of complying with our demands. Deep as is the affection in which I am held by most of our London impresarios, they can hardly be expected to ruin themselves solely to carry out my ideas.

Mr Carte, in mounting the piece, seems to have had no misgiving about its running powers. He has not only spent a huge sum of money on it, but he has apparently got value for every penny of his outlay. This sort of economy is so rare among managers—for instance, Mr Irving, in a Shakespearean revival, generally contrives to spoil a scene or two; whilst Sir Augustus Harris will occasionally slaughter a whole opera, like poor Orfeo, by dint of misdirected expenditure—I say it is so rare, that I strongly suspect that Mrs Carte comes to the rescue at the Royal English Opera just at the point where the other managers break down. However that may be, the only disparaging criticism I have to offer on the staging of The Basoche is, that the dance at the beginning of the third act is a pointless, poorly invented affair, and that the scene, considering that the audience consent to wait half an hour to allow time for its setting, ought to be a wonder of French Gothic, best of the best, which can hardly be said for it at present, handsome as it is.

However, the fact that things have progressed far enough to set me complaining that the scene-painters have not saturated the stage with the architectural beauty of the Middle Ages, proves the attainment of something like perfection from the ordinary standpoint. Bianchini's dresses are admirable; and the movements of the crowds engaged in the action are free alike from the silly stage-drill of *opera-bouffe* and the hopeless idiocy and instinctive ugliness of our Italian choristers. As the work has been thoroughly rehearsed, and the band is up to the best English standard of delicacy and steadiness, I think it must be admitted that, incredible as it may sound, we have at last got an opera-house where musical works are treated as seriously and handsomely as dramatic works are at the Lyceum. Mr Carte has really put London, as far as his department of art is concerned in a leading position for us; and the acknowledgment of that service can hardly be too cordial. The "dram of eale" in the matter is, that The Basoche is the work of a French author and a French composer. Such drawbacks, however, cannot be helped as long as we abandon high musical comedy to the French, and persist in setting men who are not dramatists to compile nonsensical plays of the obsolete Miller and his Men type, in order that popular musicians, of proved incapacity for tragedy, may pepper them with sentimental ballads, and make royalties out of them when paragraphists have puffed them as pages of grand opera.

For the principal performers in The Basoche I have nothing but praise, as they are all quite equal to the occasion, and do no less than their best. A prodigious improvement in the diction and stage manners of the company has taken place since the opening of the theatre. Even Mr Ben Davies conquers, not without evidences of an occasional internal struggle, his propensity to bounce out of the stage picture and deliver his high notes over the footlights in the attitude of irrepressible appeal first discovered by the inventor of Jack-in-the-box. Being still sufficiently hearty, good-humored, and well-filled to totally dispel all the mists of imagination which arise from his medieval surroundings, he is emphatically himself, and not Clement Marot; but except in so far as his opportunities are spoiled in the concerted music by the fact that his part is a baritone part, and not a tenor one, he sings satisfactorily, and succeeds in persuading the audience that the Basoche king very likely was much the same pleasant sort of fellow as Ben Davies.

Miss Palliser is to be congratulated on having a light, florid vocal part instead of a broad, heavy one, in which she would probably knock her voice to pieces through her hard way of using it; but the inevitable association of the light music with comedy is less fortunate for her, as her dramatic capacity evidently lies rather in the expression of strong feeling. On the other hand, Miss Lucile Hill, who was thrown away as Rowena, has in Colette a part which exactly suits her genuine humor, her quiet cleverness, and her—well, whatever is the feminine of *bonhomie*. And then she affords one the relief of hearing a singer whose method of producing her voice is not also a method of finally destroying it. Nine times out of ten, when a prima donna thinks I am being thrilled through and through by her vibrant tones, I am simply wrestling with an impulse to spring on the stage and say, "My dear young lady, pray *dont*. Your voice is not a nail, to be driven into my head: I did not come here to play Sisera to your Jael. Pray unstring yourself, subdue your ebullient self-assertiveness, loosen your chin and tongue, round the back of your throat, and try to realize that the back of the pit is not a thousand yards beyond ordinary earshot." Miss Hill, far too sensible to need such exhortation, gets her encores as triumphantly as if she shortened her natural term as a singer by two years every time she sang a song in public. And her acting, for the purpose of this particular part, could hardly be bettered. Mr Burgon, Mr Bispham, and the rest, down to the players of the smallest parts, make the most of their tolerably easy work. Altogether, if we do not take kindly to The Basoche, we may make up our minds to ninety-nine chances in the hundred of having to fall back on something worse in its place.

4 *May* 1892

HERR HEINRICH LUTTERS, who gave a pianoforte recital at St. James's Hall last week, is not what one would call a magnetic player. He is accurate and businesslike, reasonably tasteful and intelligent, and altogether the sort of artist you praise when you want to disparage the other sort. His interpretation of Beethoven and Schumann is commonplace; and his technique, though trim and gentlemanlike, is undistinguished in quality, and particularly deficient in dynamic gradation, his changes from piano to forte sometimes sounding more mechanical than those of the best sort of clockwork orchestrion.

I seldom now write a criticism of a player without wondering what impression I am producing upon my readers. The terms I use, though they appear to me to be, taken with their context, perfectly intelligible, must suggest the most unexpected and unintended ideas, if I may judge by the way my correspondents take them. For example, on the occasion of Mr E. Silas's performance of his own concerto at the Crystal Palace, I made, in estimating the work from the performance, a certain allowance for what I called the lack of technical quality in Mr Silas's playing. By which I meant that Mr Silas's touch was not that of the trained athlete of the pianoforte, able to bring out upon every step of a rapid scale the utmost and finest tone the instrument is capable of yielding. This power is the foundation of such techniques as those of Paderewski and Rubinstein.

There are plenty of excellent musicians and good teachers who can play very brightly and neatly with their right hands, and thump away with the greatest vigor and spirit with their left—who, besides, will not play in half a year as many wrong notes as I have heard both Paderewski and Rubinstein play in half a minute, and who are invaluable as accompanists and professors, but who are never classed with the great pianists. Mr Silas is a capital player of this class; and as such he was quite well able to play his concerto without bungling, and with a vivacity and agility which would have done credit to a much younger man; but if Paderewski had played it there would have been all the difference in the world in the ringing of the notes. Yet because I expressed this inevitable shortcoming on Mr Silas's part in technical terms only, without explaining elaborately what I meant, I ran the risk of leading the British mother, upon whose fiat the livelihood of the pianoforte teacher depends, to set him down as a blunderer who plays F natural where he should play F sharp, and does not know how a scale should be fingered.

Let me say then, once for all, that players who are not good enough to be above all suspicion of such musical illiteracy never get themselves brought to my notice by means of Crystal Palace concerts; and that if they challenged my verdict by giving concerts of their own I should either give no opinion at all or else give one about which there could be no possible mistake. I may also state, for the information of those who complain that my standard of criticism is too high, that the population of the world is over fourteen thousand millions; and that to speak of any pianist or violinist in superlative terms in London is to declare him or her one of the half-dozen best in that number. Obviously, to be one of the best thousand requires a very high degree of skill, though it does not entitle its possessor to more than a lukewarm compliment in this column. Always bear the fourteen thousand millions in mind; and you will understand the truth of the remark of Dumas *fils*, that it takes a great deal of merit to make a very small success.

Madame Frickenhaus gave a recital on Thursday, and had a large audience, but she was not in the vein for Beethoven, and rattled through that beautiful last movement of the Les Adieux sonata about twice too fast, as if she had a wager to finish it within a given number of seconds. The effect, of course, was to make that short time seem too long. Knowing that Madame Frickenhaus can do much better than this when she chooses, I retired disheartened at the end of the first part, which concluded with those heavy and barren variations by Saint-Saëns for two pianos, on a theme of Beethoven's. In the meantime Mr Norman Salmond had sung Tyrannic Love, accompanied by his wife, who also took the second piano in the Saint-Saëns piece; and Simonetti, the Italian violinist, had played a couple of pieces by Beethoven and Sarasate in his clever, free-and-easy way, just too free-and-easy to be perfectly classical.

Mr. Manns's benefit at the Crystal Palace was, of course, a huge success, and would have been made so by the unassailable popularity of the beneficiary if it had been the worst concert ever known. Its only fault was that there was too much of it. It began with Mr Hamish MacCunn's overture, The Dowie Dens o' Yarrow, which has a good musical fight in the middle section, but is otherwise a predestined failure, since it is impossible to tell a story in sonata form, because the end of a story is not a recapitulation of the beginning, and the end of a movement in sonata form is. Mr MacCunn has chosen his subject like a schoolboy, and his form like a pedant, the result being some excellent thematic material spoiled, and another example held up of the danger of mixing *genres* in musical composition, a danger already quite sufficiently exemplified by the follies of Sterndale Bennett in overture composition. Mr Manns might perhaps have given the work a more consistent air by a melodramatic treatment of the opening section; but as this would have been an artistic condescension as well as a forlorn hope, it is not to be wondered at that he did not attempt it.

The most noteworthy event at the concert was the first appearance in England of Gabriele Wietrowetz, who bounded into immediate popularity on the back of Mendelssohn's violin concerto. She has been thoroughly trained, and has abundant nervous energy; but her performance of the work was only a highly finished copy of the best models. It left me quite in the dark as to her unaided original capacity. Not that she is a mechanical copyist: she seizes on her model and assimilates it with an intensity which amounts to positive passion. Whether she can interpret for herself at first hand remains to be seen.

Another artist who was new to me was Madame Marie Mely, whose voice, though somewhat worn, is still one of rare beauty. Unfortunately she does not appear to have learned what to do with her middle register, which is veiled and uncertain; and this defect, with a certain languor in her delivery—possibly the effect of indisposition or nervousness—and the characteristically Italian vein of tragedy in the song she chose (Pace, pace, mio Dio! from Verdi's Forza del Destino), rather perplexed the audience, in spite of the peculiarly fine and touching quality of some of the singer's upper notes.

Mr Andrew Black got—and deserved—much applause for Vanderdecken's scene from the first act of The Flying Dutchman, which can only be made effective by one who knows how to handle his voice all over, from top to bottom, like a competent vocal workman. Beethoven's Choral Fantasia, the slenderest measure of justice to which always enchants me, was played by Miss Fanny Davies. To those who cannot understand how anybody could touch a note of that melody without emotion, her willing, affable, slapdash treatment of it was a wonder.

The Philharmonic concert last Wednesday was better than the previous one. The worst of this admission is that the Philharmonic is certain to presume on it by so neglecting its next program that it will be necessary to invent some exceptionally poignant form of insult to flog it up to the mark again. It is the most troublesome of Societies, this old Philharmonic, without conscience, without manners, without knowledge enough to distinguish between Benoît and Beethoven or Moszkowski and Mozart except by tradition, unable to see anything in its own prestige and its great opportunities except a pretext for giving itself airs. We all do our best to keep it going, sometimes by coaxing and petting it, sometimes by cuffing it when it gets too exasperating, not unfrequently by telling the innocent public lies about it, and giving it the credit that is really due to Manns, Richter, Henschel, Hallé, and others.

There is nothing to prevent the band being the best in the world, and the concerts from leading music in Europe, except the belatedness of the directorate, which at the present time includes a clear majority whose ages range from fifty-seven to seventy-one. As none of these gentlemen would have passed as specially advanced musicians thirty years ago, and as since that time there has been something like a revolution in music (the position may be faintly realized by recalling the fact that Lohengrin, now more hackneyed than Il Trovatore, provoked a furious controversy on its production here as a daring novelty in 1875, when it was twenty-eight years old), I think I may fairly say that the placing of them in a majority shews that the Society takes no real thought or trouble about electing its Board, particularly as there are plenty of vigorous and up-to-date members to choose from.

The chief event at this last concert was the playing of Beethoven's E flat concerto by Madame Sophie Menter. Poor Beethoven came out of it better than I expected. When the joyous Sophie lays her irresistible hands on a composer who has anything of a serious turn, he seldom escapes in a recognizable condition. I have seen her leave Weber and Schumann for dead on the platform. To see her play a Beethoven sonata in her puissant, splendid, tireless manner, without any perceptible yielding to its poetry or purpose, and yet presiding over its notes and chords with a certain superb power, is a spectacle that never palls on me. In the concerto, however, Beethoven, though somewhat put out of countenance at first, finally rose to the occasion, and gave her all she could manage of the softly brilliant, impetuous revelry which suits her Austrian temperament and her Lisztian style.

At the end came the usual burst of Menter worship; and the Joyous, exalted by the occasion, returned and played Liszt's Erl King transcription. The symphony was Raff's Lenore, in which a great point was made of the crescendo of the march. The opening pianissimo was certainly successful enough; but the climax ought to have been much more magnificent. It is not enough for an orchestra to be able to coo: it should be able to thunder as well. The Lenore symphony requires rather more study and stage management, so to speak, than a Philharmonic conductor can be expected to give to it unless it has a special attraction for him; and so I do not blame Mr Cowen for having failed to excite the audience sufficiently to conceal the weakness of the work as a symphony, especially in the last movement, which will not bear cool examination, notwithstanding its one really imaginative theme and the clever picture of the night scene before the arrival of William's ghost.

It is odd, by the bye, that the program-writer never points out that William's appearance is preceded by a Wagnerian quotation of the phrase in which Vanderdecken speaks of the resurrection that is to release him from his curse. But your born program-writer is always so much bent on pointing out some marvellous harmonic surprise caused by a masterly resolution of D, F, G, B, into C, E, G, C, that he seldom has time to mention matters connected with the poetic basis of the music. Except in this last movement, which ended rather raggedly, the performance was careful and precise, shewing that its preparation had not been altogether perfunctory. Still, it was far from being as perfect as that of Mr. Villiers Stanford's Œdipus prelude, in which the composer's imagination occasionally gets the better, for once in a way, of his scholarly trivialities. The Rex theme might have been more broadly handled by Mr Cowen, even at the cost of comparative roughness: otherwise, the band made the most of the piece.

11 *May* 1892

ONLY the other day I remarked that I was sure to come across Brahms' new clarionet quintet sooner or later. And, sure enough, my fate overtook me last week at Mr G. Clinton's Wind Concert at Steinway Hall. I shall not attempt to describe this latest exploit of the Leviathan Maunderer. It surpassed my utmost expectations: I never heard such a work in my life. Brahms' enormous gift of music is paralleled by nothing on earth but Mr Gladstone's gift of words: it is a verbosity which outfaces its own commonplaceness by dint of sheer magnitude. The first movement of the quintet is the best; and had the string players been on sufficiently easy terms with it, they might have softened it and given effect to its occasional sentimental excursions into dreamland. Unluckily they were all preoccupied with the difficulty of keeping together; and they were led by a violinist whose bold, free, slashing style, though useful in a general way, does more harm than good when the strings need to be touched with great tenderness and sensitiveness.

Mr. Clinton played the clarionet part with scrupulous care, but without giving any clue to his private view of the work, which, though it shews off the compass and contrasts the registers of the instrument in the usual way, contains none of the haunting phrases which Weber, for instance, was able to find for the expression of its idiosyncrasy. The presto of the third movement is a ridiculously dismal version of a lately popular hornpipe. I first heard it as the pantomime which was produced at Her Majesty's Theatre a few years ago; and I have always supposed it to be a composition of Mr. Solomon's. Anyhow, the street-pianos went through an epidemic of it; and it certainly deserved a merrier fate than burying alive in a Brahms quintet. Quite charming, after the quintet, was Thuille's elegant and well-written sextet for wood, wind, horn, and pianoforte, the slow movement of which begins as if the horn had forgotten itself and were absently wandering into See the Conq'ring Hero. Messrs Griffiths, Clinton, Malsch, Borsdorf, Wotton junior, and Oscar Beringer were the executants. Miss Clara Samuell sang one of Dr Mackenzie's best songs admirably; and I could say the same for her Nymphs and Shepherds if she had not made one of those absurd attempts to turn the final cadence into a cadenza by altering the penultimate note and hanging on to it—a sort of claptrap which one hardly expects to hear at this time of day, except at third-rate concerts or in the provinces. It is only at the Opera that such things are still perpetrated by artists of first-rate pretension.

The performance of Elijah at the Albert Hall last Wednesday was one of remarkable excellence. The tone from the choir was clean and unadulterated: there was no screaming from the sopranos, nor bawling from the tenors, nor growling from the basses. In dispensing with these three staple ingredients of English choral singing Mr Barnby has achieved a triumph which can only be appreciated by those who remember as well as I do what the choir was like in its comparatively raw state some fifteen years ago. Nowadays he gets the high notes taken *piano* as easily as the middle ones; and the sharpness of attack and the willing vigor and consentaneousness of the singing when the music in hand is as familiar to the singers and as congenial to the conductor as Mendelssohn's, are all that could be desired.

I sat out the performance on Wednesday to the last note, an act of professional devotion which was by no means part of my plan for the evening; and I did not feel disposed to quarrel with Mr. Barnby more than twice. The first time was over the chorus Hear us, Baal, which he quite spoiled by taking *allegro molto*. If he had taken it as Mendelssohn directed, *allegro non troppo*, with the quaver accompaniment excessively detached, and the theme struck out in pompous, stately strokes, the result would have convinced him that Mendelssohn knew quite well what he was about; and the chorus would not have discounted, by anticipation, the effect of the startled Hear our cry, O Baal, or of the frantic Baal, hear and answer. The second occasion was of the same kind. The chorus Then did Elijah the prophet break forth like a fire was taken almost twice too fast, in spite of Mendelssohn's instructions. For surely no difference of opinion as to the right *tempo* can extend to making a rattling *allegro* of a movement marked *moderato maestoso*. The consequence was that the unaccompanied phrase And when the Lord would take him away to heaven sounded ludicrously hasty; and there was no sensation at the end like that after Thanks be to God: He laveth the thirsty land, which, taken as Mendelssohn ordered it to be taken, roused the audience to enthusiasm. Madame Albani hardly needed the apology which was circulated for her on the ground of a "severe cold" which she simply had not got, though I have no doubt she was suffering, as we all were, from the abominable east wind. The selection of Mr. Ben Davies and Madame Belle Cole for the tenor and contralto parts could not easily have been improved on; and though Mr Watkin Mills began badly, and did not at any time exactly break forth like a fire, he was not too far over-parted.

The audience was a huge one, shewing, after all deductions for the numbers of the foolish people who only run after the reputations of the solo singers, that there is no falling off in the great popularity of Elijah. This need not be regretted so long as it is understood that our pet oratorio, as a work of religious art, stands together with the pictures of Scheffer and Paton, and the poems of Longfellow and Tennyson, sensuously beautiful in the most refined and fastidiously decorous way, but thoughtless. That is to say, it is not really religious music at all. The best of it is seraphic music, like the best of Gounod's; but you have only to think of Parsifal, of the Ninth Symphony, of Die Zauberflöte, of the inspired moments of Handel and Bach, to see the great gulf that lies between the true religious sentiment and our delight in Mendelssohn's exquisite prettiness. The British public is convinced in its middle age that Then shall the righteous shine forth as the sun is divine, on grounds no better and no worse than those on which, in its callow youth, it adores beautiful girls as angels. Far from desiring to belittle such innocent enthusiasm, I rather echo Mr Weller's plea that "Arter all, gen'lmen, it's an amiable weakness."

At the same time, a vigorous protest should be entered whenever an attempt is made to scrape a layer off the praise due to the seraphs in order to spread it over the prophet in evening dress, who, in feeble rivalry with the Handelian prophet's song of the power that is "like a refiner's fire," informs the audience, with a vicious exultation worthy of Mrs Clennam, that "God is angry with the wicked every day." That is the worst of your thoughtlessly seraphic composer: he is a wonder whilst he is flying; but when his wings fail him, he walks like a parrot.

We have now reached the season at which professional ladies and gentlemen are wont to give what they call their annual concerts, and sometimes to take it very ill on my part that I find so little to say about them. But what can I do when the programs contain nothing that I have not described at least forty thousand times already? No matter how charmingly Madame Belle Cole may sing Sognai and O Fatima, or how featly Tivadar Nachez may play Raff's rigadoon, there must at last come a time when the public will yawn over my opinion of these performances, however wide awake it may remain during the performances themselves. The same observation must cover the case of Mr Plunket Greene's German Lieder, as it soon will, no doubt, that of the irresistible Irish soldier's song which he sang the other night at Miss Shee's concert at Steinway Hall, to an old tune arranged by Mr Fuller Maitland. Having been a Bayreuth flower-maiden (one of the enchantresses of Klingsor's magic garden, and not a vendor of buttonholes), Miss Shee herself rather challenged criticism as an artist of some pretension. She is so young that I am almost afraid to tell her that she has still much to learn—notably two things. Number one, never to sing with that wind pressure which blew out the shake at the end of the Jewel Song like a candle before it was finished, and which is quite able to do for a whole voice in less than four years what it did for the shake in less than four seconds. Number two, to learn the difference between Italian vowels and English dipthongs. "Ei la figlia d' un rei che ognun dei salutarei" is not Italian: neither is "mi troverebbei béla." It is perhaps rather hard on Miss Shee that I should single her out for a fault which sets my teeth on edge almost every time I enter a concert room where English singers are singing Italian songs; but I really must be allowed to break out into protest sometimes, necessarily at somebody's expense. Why on earth cannot they go to my veteran friend, Tito Pagliardini, and get him to set their vowels right? For the rest, Miss Shee's is a pretty talent; and I hope she may succeed in cultivating it to perfection. My evening was divided between her concert and Mr Ernest Kiver's, at which I heard a new string quartet by

Reinecke, full of all the composer's engaging qualities. It might have been better played; but this is an inevitable criticism except where the four players have been able to work together for years.

I took an opportunity the other night of acquainting myself with Miss Collins's interpretation of Ta-ra-ra, etc. It is a most instructive example of the value of artistic method in music-hall singing, and may be contrasted by students with Violette's crude treatment of the same song. Violette's forced and screaming self-abandonment is a complete failure: Miss Collins's perfect self-possession and calculated economy of effort carry her audience away. She takes the song at an exceedingly restrained *tempo*, and gets her effect of *entrain* by marking the measure very pointedly and emphatically, and articulating her words with ringing brilliancy and with immense assurance of manner. The dance refrain, with its three low kicks on "Ta-ra-ra" and its high kick on "Boom" (with *grosse caisse ad lib.*), is the simplest thing imaginable, and is taken in even a more deliberate *tempo* than the preceding verse.

Miss Collins appears to be in fine athletic training; and the combination of perfect sang-froid and unsparing vigor with which she carries out her performance, which is so exhaustively studied that not a bar of it is left to chance or the impulse of the moment, ought to convince the idlest of her competitors and the most cynical of music-hall managers that a planned artistic achievement "catches on" far more powerfully than any random explosion of brainless rowdiness. I do not propose to add to the host of suggestions as to the origin of the tune. As it is only a figuration of the common major chord, it is to be found almost wherever you choose to look for it. In the last movement of Mozart's finest pianoforte sonata in F, in the opening *allegro* of Beethoven's septuor, and even in the first movement of Mendelssohn's violin concerto, it will henceforth make itself felt by all those who continue obsessed by it.

18 *May* 1892

THE other day an actor published a book of directions for making a good play. His plan was a simple one. Take all the devices which bring down the house in existing plays; make a new one by stringing them all together; and there you are. If that book succeeds, I am prepared to write a similar treatise on opera composition. I know quite a lot of things that would be of great use to any young composer. For instance, when two lovers are on the stage together, be sure you make them catch sight of the moon or stars and gaze up rapturously whilst the violins discourse ravishing strains with their mutes on. Mutes are also useful for spinning-wheel business and for fires, as in Marta and Die Walküre.

For dreamy effects, tonic pedals as patented by Gounod and Bizet are useful. When large orchestras are available, broad melodies on the fourth string of the violins may be relied on for a strong and popular impression. When the heroine is alone on the stage, a rapid, agitated movement, expressive of her anticipation of the arrival of her lover, and culminating in a vigorous instrumental and vocal outburst as he rushes on the stage and proceeds without an instant's loss of time to embrace her ardently, never fails to leave the public breathless. The harmonic treatment of this situation is so simple that nobody can fail to master it in a few lessons. The lady must first sing the gentleman's name on the notes belonging to the chord of the dominant seventh in some highly unexpected key; the gentleman then vociferates the lady's name a peg higher on the notes of a more extreme discord; and, finally, the twain explode simultaneously upon a brilliant six-four chord, leading, either directly through the dominant chord, or after some pretty interruption of the cadence, to a flowing melody in which the gentleman either protests his passion or repeatedly calls attention to the fact that at last they meet again.

The whole situation should be repeated in the last act,

with the difference that this time it is the gentleman who must be alone at the beginning. Furthermore, he must be in a gloomy dungeon, not larger at the outside than the stage of Covent Garden Theatre; and he must be condemned to die next morning. The reason for putting the gentleman, rather than the lady, in this situation is to be found in the exclusion of women from politics, whereby they are deprived of the privilege of being condemned to death, without any reflection on their personal characters, for heading patriotic rebellions. The difficulty has nevertheless been successfully got over by making the lady go mad in the fourth act, and kill somebody, preferably her own child. Under these circumstances she may sing almost anything she pleases of a florid nature in her distraction, and may take the gentleman's place in the prison-cell in the next act without forfeiting the moral approval of the audience. Florid mad scenes, though they are very pretty when the lady's affliction is made to take the playful turn of a trial of skill with the first flute, which should partly imitate the voice and partly accompany it in thirds, is now out of fashion; and it is far better, in dramatic opera, to be entirely modern in style.

Fortunately, the rule for modernity of style is easily remembered and applied. In fact, it is one of the three superlatively easy rules, the other two being the rules for writing Scotch and archaic music. For Scotch music, as everyone knows, you sustain E flat and B flat in the bass for a drone, and play at random in some Scotch measure on the notes which are black on the piano. For archaic music you harmonize in the ordinary way in the key of E major; but in playing you make the four sharps of the key natural, reading the music as if it was written in the key of C, which, of course, simplifies the execution as far as the piano is concerned. The effect will be diabolical; but nobody will object if you explain that your composition is in the Phrygian mode. If a still more poignant effect be desired, write in B natural, leaving out the sharps as before, and calling the mode Hypophrygian. If, as is possible, the Phrygian is more than the public can stand, write in D without sharps, and call the mode Dorian, when the audience will accept you as being comfortably in D minor, except when you feel that it is safe to excruciate them with the C natural. This is easy, but not more so than the rule for making music sound modern.

For compositions in the major, all that is necessary is to write ordinary diatonic harmonies, and then go over them with a pen and cross the t's, as it were, by sharpening all the fifths in the common chords. If the composition is in the minor, the common chord must be left unaltered; but whenever it occurs some instrument must play the *major* sixth of the key, *à propos de bottes*, loud enough to make itself heard rather distinctly. Next morning all the musical critics will gravely declare that you have been deeply influenced by the theories of Wagner; and what more can you desire, if modernity is your foible?

But I am neglecting my week's work. Although I repeat that "How to compose a good opera" might be written as easily as "How to write a good play," I must not set about writing it myself in this column, although the above sample will shew every learned musician how thoroughly I am qualified for the task. The fact is, I had been reading the reviews of Mr. Frank Archer's book; and it set me thinking of what are called actors' plays, meaning plays which are not plays at all, but compilations consisting of a series of stage effects devised *ad hoc*. Indeed, stage effects is too wide a term: actors' effects would be more accurate. I thought of how hopelessly bad all such works are, even when, as in the case of Cibber's Richard III and Garrick's Katharine and Petruchio, they are saved from instant perdition by a mutilated mass of poetry and drama stolen from some genuine playwright.

And then I fell to considering which would be the worst thing to have to sit out in a theatre—an actor's play or a singer's opera. Before I could settle the point the clock struck; and I suddenly realized that if I lost another moment I should miss the one-fifty-five train to the Crystal Palace, where I was due at two-forty-five to witness the performance of Mr George Fox's new opera, Nydia. And when I sat down just now to write an account of Nydia, it naturally reminded me of Mr Frank Archer, and led to the above tremendous digression on the subject of operatic composition in general.

Nydia is founded on Bulwer Lytton's Last Days of Pompeii, a novel which I read when a boy. I remember nothing of it except the name Arbaces, and the Roman sentinel, and Pliny—though, indeed, I am not sure that I did not get the last two out of Chambers's Miscellany. At all events, I found the libretto of Nydia as new to me as it is in the nature of any libretto to be to a musical critic of my age. It began with a bustling crowd, singing:

Water melons, rich and rare,
None excel them we declare;
Olives, figs, and honey sweet,
You will find them hard to beat;
Here is game, wild mountain boar,
Oysters too from Britain's shore,
Come and buy, come and buy.

This was out of Carmen, tune and all, except the oysters; and even their freshness must have been severely tried by hawking them in the full blaze of an Italian sun.

Then we had a blind girl with a Leitmotif, also rather like the jealousy motive in Carmen, with a heroine, lover, and villain, in due course. The villain, a Pompeian archbishop, held a service in a temple on the lines of the one in Aïda; and the lover came in and dashed him down the steps of the altar, for which exploit he was haled away to prison—very properly, as I thought—in spite of the entreaties of the heroine. In prison he shared his cell with a Nazarene, who strove hard, not without some partial success, to make him see the beauty of being eaten by a lion in the arena. Next came the amphitheatre, with a gladiator fight which only needed a gallery full of shrieking vestals with their thumbs turned down to be perfectly *à la* Gérome. Then the hero, kept up to the mark by the Nazarene, was thrown to the lion, whereupon Vesuvius emitted clouds of spangles and red fire. A scene of terror and confusion in the streets followed, the crowd standing stock-still, with its eyes on the conductor, and the villain falling, slain by lightning, and then creeping off on all-fours behind the calves of the multitude.

Finally the clouds parted; and we had a pretty pictorial composition of the hero and heroine at sea in a galley with the blind girl, who presently took a deliberate header into the waves, to the intense astonishment of everybody except the hero, who, without making the smallest attempt to save her, set up a thundering Salve eternum just as I was expecting him to break into

Rosy lips above the water,
Blowing bubbles soft and fine;
As for me, I was no swimmer,
So I lost my Clementine.

Mr Durward Lely sustained the tenor part with great heroism; and Madame Valda, after innumerable high C's, finished the third act with a big big D which brought down the house.

Mlle de Rideau did her best with the part of the blind girl; and Messrs Clifford, Pyatt, King, Joyce, and the rest did, I imagine, much what the composer expected them to do. The Crystal Palace orchestra played through the score with deadly skill at a serene *mezzo-forte*, not paying the smallest attention, as far as I could perceive, to any of the composer's numerous *pianos* and *pianissimos*, though some of his *fortissimos*, notably an astounding series of double knocks on the drum in the second act, received rather more attention than I should have bargained for had I been the conductor. On the whole, though I must compliment Mr George Fox on his industry, his ambition, and his energy, I find that the point of view from which he regards operatic composition is so far remote from mine that I shall continue to esteem him rather as a singer than as a composer.

As to the concerts of last week, I have only space to say that Miss Evangeline Florence, an American soprano with the extraordinary range of three octaves from the B natural below the treble stave upward (the same, allowing for the rise in pitch, as that recorded by Mozart of Lucrezia Agujari), made her appearance at a concert given by that clever and cultivated singer, Miss Marguerite Hall. She fully satisfied the curiosity of the audience as to her high notes, which sound like violin harmonics of ordinary quality. She is a pleasant young lady, with a sufficiently strong turn for music; but she did not strike me as being an artist by temperament; and I cannot say that her cheerful, rather domestic kind of musical accomplishment is likely ever to make her independent of her upper octave as a public singer.

Of Elkan Kosman, the new Dutch violinist, and of Sir Charles Hallé, whom I found on Friday in St James's Hall playing Schubert to Mr John Morley (who was listening with quite a vegetarian air) and a happy and perfectly attentive audience, I must take some later opportunity of writing.

25 *May* 1892

JOSEPH SLIVINSKI, the latest rival of Paderewski, would make an unparalleled *maître d'armes*. Everything that can be said of Eugène Pini's wrist is true of each separate joint of Slivinski's fingers. He is prodigiously swift; and that air of deliberate, undistraught purpose which a man can only maintain when he is at something well within his physical power, sits unmoved on Slivinski when he is doing things that Paderewski or Isaÿe (on the violin) could not match without some show of desperation. From the purely gymnastic point of view he, and not Paderewski, is the exponent of the Leschetitzky technique; for in his case it has not, as in Paderewski's, become overlaid by a technique of his own: besides, being natural to him, it does not sound cruel and artistically contradictory from him as it often does from Paderewski. His steely finger is always elastic: it leaves the piano ringing unhurt—indeed, you feel no more pity for the instrument than you do for a sword that has parried a brilliant thrust, Slivinski's feeling for it being a veritable *sentiment du fer*.

Whenever the piece which he has in hand enables him to bring his extraordinary gymnastic powers fully to bear, it becomes transfigured, sometimes quite dazzlingly. Even in cases where he brings it to bear in flat defiance of the obvious intention of the composer, as he repeatedly does, it is often curiously and not unpleasantly novel. Where it is entirely appropriate, as in Chopin polonaises and Liszt rhapsodies, the effect is tremendous. Nevertheless, I am still tempted to dwell on the *maître d'armes* view of him. He is so simply and unaffectedly masculine that the moment the music becomes clearly womanly—as in Schumann's Romance, for instance—he modestly abnegates his supremacy at once, and plays neatly and gently, with the utmost good feeling—much as an athlete might sew on a button—but without any pretence of being in his element. Paderewski, in such moments, brings into action a wealth of feminine power and delicacy which no woman could surpass.

The two men, indeed, contrast at all points, except the high discipline under which both have brought their executive ability. Paderewski has the passionate, nervous, wilful power of the artist in poetry, tonal or other: Slivinski has the cool muscular strength, elasticity, and rhythm that make the artist in bodily exercises. Slivinski is a toughly knit, free-stepping, spare man, with salient cheek-bones and closely cropped black hair. Paderewski is a thin, flat man, with a startling turban of the fluffiest red hair on his head. He moves determinedly, but with his chin down and his ankles feeling nervously for the floor, like one walking in darkness. There is no reason to doubt that Slivinski is quite as ambidexterous as Paderewski, if not more so; but he has not his variety of touch, his sympathy with all phases of music, his comprehensive intelligence—in a word, his powers of interpretation as distinguished from his power of manual execution. Nor has he the exquisite though naïve musical instinct of Sapellnikoff: his plain, exclusively virile talent seems impatient of the luxuries, dreams, and *enfantillages* of art.

On the whole, though he is unquestionably a player to be heard and studied, and one, too, not easily to be forgotten, he takes his place for the present without supplanting Paderewski or indeed any other player of established eminence. I say for the present, because the whole of the foregoing criticism must be taken as provisional in view of the fact that Slivinski is a very young man, certain to develop largely on the sympathetic side as he matures.

A very different player from Slivinski is Mr H. S. Welsing, who combined his forces with Carl Fuchs, the violoncellist, at a concert in Prince's Hall on Wednesday. Mr Welsing is a light-fingered player with a pretty touch. He patters with terrific rapidity over the lighter scales and arpeggios, and presently shoots himself plump into a heavy bit of work at a speed quite beyond its possibilities. His *cheval de bataille* for the occasion was the Waldstein sonata, which is full of such traps; and it is hardly too much to say that he fell headlong into all of them, invariably rescuing himself with great gallantry, but not without moments of confusion during which the notes rolled over one another in the wildest confusion, though I will not venture to assert that any of them escaped him. The fact is, the Waldstein sonata requires a more contemplative and less impetuous temperament than Mr Welsing's to expound it; for in spite of the pernicious old convention to the contrary it is not a mere bravura piece, and has never been really successful when so treated. Mr Welsing had a flattering success as a composer, his setting of Shelley's Love's Philosophy, sung by Marie Brema, being enthusiastically encored. As to Herr Carl Fuchs, I can only say that if his right hand were as skilful as his left, he would rank as a first-rate player.

Sauret had the good sense to make a solid concert of his first "recital" at St James's Hall on Thursday last. The Beethoven quartet (F major, Op. 59) was well worth hearing, which means that it had more elbow grease put into its preparation than is commonly spent on such occasions. Sauret also circulated a translated notice of himself from the Neue Berliner Musikzeitung, explaining, in a free English style, that "there is in him a strong 'violin individuality'—not to be mistaken for 'speciality,' like [*sic*] Sarasate." The public will infer that the thing for a violinist to aim at is specialty rather than individuality. What the critic meant, if he had only hunted down his meaning sufficiently to be able to express it accurately, was that Sauret is less of a virtuoso than Sarasate because he has not sunk the man so completely in the violinist—has not specialized his individuality so devotedly. No doubt he gains in fullness and variety of life what he loses in artistic perfection. The critic goes on to say: "In the power which he exercises over his audience he approaches the great Paganini. Sauret's ease in overcoming every imaginable difficulty is fabulous. [This is the reverse of what the writer means; but the intention is obvious.] Thus may the Italian hero of the violin have played." Now it is true that Sauret's command of the violin *is* extraordinary—so much so that if he had concentrated himself on the career of a virtuoso as Sarasate has, he might have justified his German critic's enthusiasm. As it is, violin playing is with him an accomplishment carried to the most brilliant degree, but not a calling. On Thursday he was in an excellent vein, and displayed his best quality in leading the quartet. His subsequent performance of a movement from a concerto by Ernst pleased me less, partly because I do not see any adequate excuse, in the presence of so much music of the highest class for violin and pianoforte, for giving concertos with the orchestral parts strummed on a piano, and partly because I detest Ernst's music as the most ignoble stuff known to me in that kind. The only other violinist whose concert came into the week was Miss Winifred Robinson. I only got in for a scrap of a trio by Dvořák, which was not going smoothly enough to make me regret having missed the rest of it. I unluckily did not hear Miss Robinson's solos.

Gaston de Mérindol, who gave a pianoforte recital at

Prince's Hall on Friday, is hardly more than a cultivated amateur. He is a fluent executant, and plays with refinement and feeling, but without the trained strength and studied conception which we look for in first-class playing. I had to leave in the middle of his recital to go to Grosvenor House, where Mr John Farmer was shewing what could be done with a choir of young ladies selected from the pupils of the Public Day Schools Company. It may seem a small thing to have made a collection of schoolgirls sing a dozen part songs and canons well; and, no doubt, when the opportunity was once provided, all that was needed was the exercise of Mr Farmer's skill and devotion as a choirmaster. But to provide the opportunity—to carry the musical idea so far into the dense jungle of English middle-class Philistinism as to make such a concert possible—this has meant, in Mr Farmer's case, a life-long struggle with the powers of darkness. However, he seems to enjoy it; and he is certainly so far successful that wherever you find John Farmer, there also you find some respect paid to music, even if it only goes the length of a general qualm of conscience as to its neglect. Some day I shall enlarge a little on this subject, and on the respective shares of the school time-tables allotted to music, and to the comparatively unimportant and revolting subject of mathematics. For the present I can only add that the work done at the concert was unexceptionable as far as I heard it, and that Miss Elsie Hall, who played a couple of movements from an early concerto of Chopin's, and, for an encore, his Berceuse, has improved—I had almost said matured, though she is only thirteen—remarkably since I heard her at Steinway Hall. She is a real, not a manufactured, "wonder child." The concert was for the benefit of the Maria Grey Training College for Teachers. I wonder whether it trains them in the whole duty of a headmistress towards the art on which the college sponges for pecuniary aid.

On Saturday, at Prince's Hall, Mr. J. H. Bonawitz began a Historical Recital, which must, I think, be going on still, as I had to leave after the sixteenth piece, and there were eleven, including the Appassionata Sonata, yet to come. Besides, there was a running commentary by the editor of the Musical Times, Mr Edgar Jacques, who, being clever, popular with his colleagues, and well up in the subject, would have been the very man for the occasion, were he not afflicted with a sense of humor, with which he maintained a cheerful struggle throughout the performance. Not that the recital was uninteresting—by no means; nor was it anybody's fault that the harpsichord jingled like a million bell-wires, or that the effect of the Bach clavichord fugue upon it was execrable, or that the Palestrina *ricercate* had to be played on the most modern of American organs, or that the audience, overcome by the association of reading-desk and organ, was ludicrously solemn. Yet these things were; and when Jacques pleaded that the American instrument was "something between" the organ in the Albert Hall and the portable organs of Palestrina's day, and frankly gave up the harpsichord as a bad job after the audience had listened to it for half an hour with unsuspicious awe, the twinkling of his eye betrayed the suppressed convulsions within. At last he disappeared from the platform for a while; and, as I seized the opportunity to slip out, I was conscious of a seismic vibration in the building, which convinced me that Jacques, hidden somewhere among the foundations, was having his laugh out. It does not do to have too clever a lecturer on these occasions unless you have all the other arrangements to correspond.

1 *June* 1892

L'AMICO FRITZ has one strong recommendation from the critic's point of view: there is no trouble in taking its measure. Some of it is fresh, freehanded, bouncing, rather obstreperous, like Cavalleria—was composed before it, perhaps. The rest is more artificial without being in any way better, except that the orchestra is more knowingly handled. High spirits and audacity are jewels in the crown of youth when they are lucky enough to pass with half the musical wiseacres of Europe as strength and originality; but the imposition is one that cannot be repeated. The most striking example I know of a very young composer astonishing the world by a musical style at once fascinating, original, and perfectly new, is Mendelssohn's exploit at seventeen with the Midsummer Night's Dream overture. One can actually feel the novelty now, after sixty-six years. There was nothing whatever of this sort in Cavalleria. The style was the common Italian style of the day; and Mascagni's "originalities" were simply liberties taken with it, liberties consisting of unconventional—I had almost written cheeky—progressions which were exhilarating in their roughness, and freshened up the old musical material wonderfully.

The exactly parallel case of Massenet in France ought to have shewn every critic what to expect from Mascagni's next attempt. However, all this is an old story with me. I was not taken in by Cavalleria; and now that everybody finds L' Amico Fritz obviously deficient in first-rate promise and first-rate accomplishment, I am in the pleasing position of being able to say, "I told you so." Let us therefore clear the discussion of all nonsense about genius of the highest order, and of the ridiculous comparisons with Verdi and Wagner which were rife last year, and give Mascagni fair play as an interesting young composer with a vigorous talent, and plenty of courage in asserting it, congratulating ourselves meanwhile on the fact that Bellini has at last found a disciple, albeit one far inferior to his master.

L' Amico Fritz, then, is an opera which will pass the evening pleasantly enough for you, but which you need not regret missing if you happen to have business elsewhere. The libretto is as delightfully free from blood and thunder as that of La Sonnambula: it is more an idyllic picture than a story. The cherry-tree duet ought really to be hung in the Royal Academy. The pretty harmonies of the opening line, changing in the most fashionably petted Tosti manner, belong rather to the drawing room; but when Madame

Calvé climbed the ladder with an apron on, and threw down cherries to the tenor on the other side of the wall, I was transported as if on a magic carpet to Burlington House, where I remained in imagination until it suddenly occurred to me that I had paid a guinea instead of a shilling for my stall, when I came to myself in rather a melancholy frame of mind.

For the cherry duet "caught on"; and immediately I had a vision of Mr Worldly Wiseman coming from his strongholds in Bond Street and in the Strand theatres to conquer the Opera with his pretty trivialities, his happy endings, his second-hand morals, and his impotent cowardice and superficiality, offering golden opportunities to intellectual and artistic mediocrity, and cloaked indulgence to the sanctimonious people whose appetite for beauty is of such a character that they are themselves ashamed of it. Goodbye, if my vision comes true, to Gluck, Mozart, Weber, Wagner—even to Meyerbeer. The worst of it was that the invader was so horribly well treated. Sir Augustus had taken the greatest pains with that cherry-tree, and with the well and bucket, the watering-pot, and the inevitable landau and horses. His "unprecedented combination of the first [and laziest] musical talent in Europe" actually contributes one first-rate artist to help out Madame Calvé and Mascagni, although it is so busy with those startling novelties, Faust and Roméo et Juliette, that a comparatively provincial German company has had to be sent for to do the Nibelungen tetralogy. For that, it appears, is the end of loading our favorites with princely salaries and fulsome praise.

The unprecedented combination puts us off for years by pretending that it is going to learn a new work (meaning a work that has been familiar in every second-rate German town for the last ten years); and now, when the limit of our patience is reached, the unprecedented ones tell us that London had better ask Hamburg to come over and help it out of its difficulty, and offer us another performance of

Roméo by way of consolation. I throw the responsibility on the combination rather than on the manager, because I know how helpless he is in the face of his guarantors and their pets, and how, even if this were not so, the progress made with new work would still depend mainly on the devotion of the artists to their work; but, all the same, had I been in his place, I think I could have managed to get at least a Siegfried of my own as well as a Meistersinger and an Otello. If I had in my company such a Siegfried and such a Wotan as Bayreuth never heard, I would make them feel that I was something more than their showman, and that a leading singer should not be content to wallow in the old parts which he picked up by ear when he was a little boy.

However, I am forgetting all about L' Amico Fritz and the cherry tree. The duet, as I said, "caught on" immensely; and there was a frantic encore a little later when Madame Calvé and Signor de Lucia finished a number with a sudden pianissimo on a sustained high note, the effect—a favorite one with Mascagni—being that of a ravishing caterwaul. Next to the cherry-tree episode, the most effective bits in the opera are the recital of the story of Eleazar and Rebecca at the well ("something out of Dante, I think," said one of my neighbors); the procession of orphans to a jolly music-hall tune, said to be an Alsatian march; and the long violin solo played behind the scenes which prepares the entry of Giulia Ravogli so cleverly in the first scene. The last act is preceded by the now inevitable intermezzo, with the equally inevitable and exasperating encore (pure affectation on the part of the gallery), and contains a duet in which there is a touch of the dramatic energy of Cavalleria. The story is too happy and sunshiny for more than the touch; and on the whole I think I may compendiously describe the work as having all the merits of a fine bank holiday.

As to the performance, it was more than good enough for the occasion. Signor de Lucia succeeds Valero and Lubert as artificial tenor in ordinary to the establishment. His thin strident *forte* is in tune and does not tremble beyond endurance; and his *mezza voce*, though monotonous and inexpressive, is pretty as prettiness goes in the artificial school. I cannot say that I like that school; but I must admit that its exponents have hitherto set a good example by minding their business and identifying themselves with their parts; and this, considering the lax discipline of the operatic stage at present, is a considerable merit. Giulia Ravogli has evidently been taking lessons somewhere. Strange to say, instead of having had her voice ruined, she has been led to correct the looseness and raggedness of the upper part of it; so that her vocal style has gained in compactness and force. She is as irresistible as ever: else I might venture to tell her that she has not the remotest idea of how a fiddle should be held, much less a fiddle-bow.

Madame Calvé was so affecting in the simple grace and naïve musical feeling which exhaust the scope of the part of Suzel, that in a tragic rôle I should expect a good deal from her. She has a free, even voice of adequate volume, not of the brightest color, but very sympathetic. As a soprano of innate dramatic force, she is the most notable recruit we have had at the Opera for some years. The orchestra had no difficulty with the score, which is vigorous, and supplies all the usual stimulants and luxuries in profusion. The worst orchestral number is the prelude, which is arrant shop stuff. Bevignani conducted; and there was an enthusiastic ovation at the end: Sir Augustus, coy as usual, being dragged out by main force to share in it.

May I, without offence, suggest to the Italian visitors at the Opera that however backward we may be as a nation in musical culture we have at least got beyond the stage at which we can tolerate strident "Bravas" breaking in on the silence of the audience and the flow of the music after every high note and every salient phrase. To me at least, the jar of such an interruption is as irritating as a slap in the face. The chattering from English ladies in the boxes is bad enough; but it does not usually begin until late in the season, when the owners leave town and sublet the boxes to trippers from the provinces; whereas the "Brava" nuisance is in full swing already. I submit it to the good sense of our visitors whether our insular custom of confining such exclamations to political meetings is not, on the whole, to our credit, musically speaking.

On Wednesday there was a grand operatic concert at St James's Hall for the benefit of those who wished to hear the unprecedented combination without entering a theatre. Sir Augustus hospitably invited me; but after a glance at the program I decided to go and hear Mr Lunn lecture at Prince's Hall on singing. It is now thirty years since I first met a singing-master who was having a discussion with Mr Lunn; and during that whole period I have met fresh cases at intervals of from eighteen months to five minutes. A more hot-headed, pugnacious, intolerant, impossible controversialist than Mr Lunn does not exist. He will tell you that he is nothing if not logical, and then offer you the most fantastic comparisons and analogies as stepping-stones to his conclusions. Although you may be the most sympathetic of his partisans, or the most innocent and humble-minded of his disciples, he will treat you as if you had personally instructed every bad singer who has appeared at the Opera since Grisi's time.

The scientific world for him is divided into ignoramuses who do not know of his discoveries, and plagiarists who have annexed them without acknowledgment. As to the things he says about teachers of singing, I simply dare not describe them, they are so inhumanly true. On this particular occasion at Prince's Hall he was more himself than ever. He had written out an elaborate and surpassingly bad lecture by way of a tramway to keep himself straight upon; but he soon went hopelessly off the rails, to our great relief, and abandoned his manuscript with an appalling threat of publishing it. Do not for a moment suppose, however, that the lecture was not a success. Mr Lunn, in spite of all the difficulties he places in his own way, has the advantage of being desperately in earnest, and of being, in the main, perfectly right. It was, of course, easy for him to ridicule Ravelli's singing of Il mio tesoro at the Opera, and to caricature that hurrying of the accompaniment which is always resorted to in order to get a singer over a long-sustained note. But he also produced a pupil of his own who sang the song far better than the average Covent Garden Don Ottavio.

Nevertheless, I cannot admit Mr Lunn's claim that the crucial passage with the long-sustained F was sung exactly as Mozart meant it to be sung. The singer, though he held the F, took breath in the middle of the fourth bar, which was most certainly a violation of Mozart's intention. Any singer who has been taught to hold back the air-current at the larynx like Mr Lunn's pupils, can, if he also distends his pharynx by rounding the back of it, sing the whole five and a half bars through without taking breath. I have often heard it done; and I have half a mind to offer to do it myself, provided the passage be transposed into G to accommodate a limited baritone, and the quality of the execution left out of account. In the minor section of The trumpet shall sound, in The Messiah, there are phrases of ten and eleven bars, the longest containing notes equivalent to thirty-two crotchets. They can be, and should be, sung in one breath, though they bring a singer nearer to the end of his tether than the twenty-two crotchets, in slower time, of Il mio tesoro. If Mr Lunn's baritone pupil, who sang very well, had vanquished For this corruptible, etc., the feat would have been quite *à la* Farinelli.

However, I do not complain; and I hope Mr Lunn will keep pegging away at his most useful mission. Only I can assure him that as soon as pupils really want to sing well, and the public learns to prefer Mozart's sustained F in Il mio tesoro to the B flat which Ravelli bawls in its place, there will be no difficulty about the supply of teachers. Mr Lunn himself admits that his pupils are apt to go to fashionable teachers to get "finished." That means that he shews them what good singing means; that they dont like it, and dont believe in it; and that they find the public agrees with them.

It needs the authority of genius like that of Sims Reeves to enable a young artist to differ from the public and compel it to admit, for the moment, that fine singing is better than popular bull-roaring. In short, it is the demand, and not the supply, that is lacking; and the quality of the demand, in spite of such aberrations as the revival of the goat-bleat school produced by the success of Gayarre, is improving. Let Mr Lunn, therefore, be of good cheer: he is not quite such an isolated phenomenon as he supposes.

8 *June* 1892

ON Tuesday last week I found myself with tickets for nine concerts and a speech by Mr Gladstone. At this I lost my temper, and declared that I would not stir out of the house all day. But I have never been a man of my word; and at three I began my round as usual. First there was Miss Clara Eissler at Erards', playing the harp, which is a cool, limpid instrument for a hot day, and almost suggests that some stout pianoforte has realized Sydney Smith's aspiration by getting out of its skin and sitting in its bones. The particular harp which Miss Eissler used was a very fine one; and she played it as if she appreciated it, instead of pinching it to make it speak in the professorial manner. Unfortunately nobody seems to think of writing anything but the most old-fashioned sort of filigree music for the harp; and as a little of this goes a considerable distance with a critic, however handsomely executed, I was soon on my way to Steinway Hall, where I found Miss Else Sonntag giving a pianoforte recital.

It was a curious freak of fate that made Miss Sonntag, with her frail physique and her characteristic *naïveté*, a pupil of Liszt. To hear her play a Chopin ballade in her master's way is the oddest of musical experiences. She has appropriated his conceptions in her own fashion, mostly by making fairy tales of them. But she has not been able to appropriate his powers of execution; and when she comes to a passage which, from Liszt's point of view, might be arranged as a duet for a lion and a hurricane, it is almost as if a baby mermaid had got into a whirlpool, or had petulantly insisted on trying to shoot the rapids below Niagara. However, she comes out alive, and disports herself prettily, if sometimes rather quaintly, in the smoother waters. On this occasion she was not at her best; for the weather was warm enough to make anybody play wrong notes—almost warm enough to make me play right ones. Even Slivinski, whose recital I next visited, was all but dissolved by the time I got to St. James's Hall.

It was amazing to see the smallness of the paying part of his audience, considering the extraordinary quality of the performance. Of course this will not last for ever. In about fifteen years' time I shall have people rushing up to me to ask whether I have heard the new pianist Slivinski, for whose recitals there is not a seat to be had. But the danger in this system of deferred results is that the greater a player is, the more apt is he to find something better to do than dancing attendance on English stupidity. If Slivinski meets Rubinstein now, Rubinstein will not ask him whether he has succeeded in England, but simply whether the English have failed, as usual, to appreciate him. To which Slivinski will rightly reply in the affirmative. And Rubinstein will remind him that we failed also in his own case and in Liszt's, and that our comparatively prompt recognition of Paderewski must be accounted for by the fact that every intelligent Englishman could see by his head of hair that he was an exceptional man.

If Slivinski does not come back to London in a hurry, the loss will be ours and not his. He unbent somewhat in his last two recitals, and shewed the most astonishing power of making the pianoforte sing in transcriptions of vocal melodies, so that the older people began to compare him to Thalberg. He also gave us a chance of hearing one of those prodigious opera fantasias of Liszt's which few pianists can play and fewer understand. The one selected by Slivinski, that on Robert, is a pungent criticism of Meyerbeer as well as a *tour de force* of adaptation to the pianoforte. To anyone who knows the opera and knows the composer thoroughly, no written analysis of Robert could be half so interesting as this fantasia in which Liszt, whilst vividly reproducing Meyerbeer's cleverly economized and elaborated scraps of fantasy, grace, and power, picks up the separate themes apparently at random, and fits them to one another with a satirical ingenuity which brings out in the most striking way how very limited and mechanical the Meyerbeerian forms were.

After Slivinski, there remained only six more concerts, and Mr Gladstone on current London politics. It is commonly held that the finest politeness is needed to enable you to listen quietly to a man when he proceeds to instruct you at great length in a subject which you understand and which he does not. Feeling unequal to this strain, I consigned the Gladstone ticket to the waste-paper basket with all the remaining concert tickets except one; and with that one I went off to St James's Hall to the farewell concert of Henry Lazarus, at which everybody sang, or conducted, or did something in honor of the occasion. Lazarus's age was for long an inscrutable mystery; and I have my doubts as to the value of the latest settlement arrived at. As lately as twelve years ago he was the best clarionet player in England: when you were sitting behind Costa at the Opera you listened for certain phrases from the clarionet just as you did from the prima donna, except that you were much less likely to be disappointed in the former case. Lazarus was beginning to look oldish then, though he made no flesh, and was still a trim, neatly proportioned man, with old-fashioned but very unobtrusive whiskers, thin lips, and a perfect mouth for his instrument, with a chronic lift at the corners that looked like a smile, and very readily developed into one. Your neighbor on the right would tell you that he remembered Lazarus as premier clarionet for twenty years. Your neighbor on the left would correct him and say thirty years at least. Some veteran would then pooh-pooh both calculations and declare that he had heard Lazarus before 1840, and that he was then in his prime.

And yet it is only within the last couple of years that Mr Egerton has taken his place at the Monday Popular Concerts when Beethoven's septet is in the program. I may quite safely put it that he has been playing in public for more than fifty years, and that during at least forty of them, dating from the death of Willman in 1840, his pre-eminence was unquestioned, as it would be still if his lip and fingers had their old strength. For, with all due respect for the ability of his successors, I do not know one of them who can pretend to his distinction of tone and style, and his elegant phrasing. He now retires finally, confessing to seventy-seven years. We were all a good deal touched when he came up out of the past, as it were, on to the platform at the farewell concert, and sat down to play us a couple of pieces with fingers that trembled a little, but with something of his old habit of assured competence, his old style, and here and there, especially in the *chalumeau* and middle registers, his old fineness of tone.

At the end the applause was tremendous; and when he returned to the platform for the second time, leaving his instrument behind him, he had perhaps some idea of making a speech. Whether this was so or not, he was taken aback by the appearance of a huge wreath poking itself at him over the platform rail; and when, after a moment of bewilderment, he collected himself and took the offering, there was another green monster lunging at him on his right. By the time he had got hold of both, he had given up all idea of speaking, if he had really entertained any. He put his hand on his heart, as all public performers used to do in the days when he was taught to make a bow, and with many mute acknowledgments edged himself to the steps in a quite sufficiently eloquent fashion, and disappeared. The practical object of the concert was the starting of a testimonial fund, of which Mr Charles Coote, of 42 New Bond Street, is treasurer.

At the Philharmonic last week Miss Macintyre sang Robert, toi que j'aime and Ritorna il vincitor with her usual cleverness, and with that invaluable determination of hers to succeed which can only be appreciated by those who know how much talent is wasted in this world for want of will. The orchestra gave itself no real trouble, and was good only in the accompaniments to the Beethoven concerto. In the symphony (Schubert's unfinished) there was no getting a decent *piano*, much less a *pianissimo*, from the 'cellos; so that the exquisite and quite simple second subject of the first *allegro* was stolidly murdered. The *fortes* in the slow movement were also unsatisfactory, Mr Cowen allowing his attention to be drawn off to the great slashes and accents of the strings, instead of concentrating it on the sustained flow of melody in the wind, with the result, of course, that the melody was not sustained at all, the ends of the notes tailing off in the usual feeble Philharmonic fashion.

Becker played a concerto of Raff's for the violoncello, and was warmly applauded for the first movement. He could do but little with the finale, which is trivial, with an ugly solo part. Mr Lamond was the pianist; and he chose that beautiful fourth concerto of Beethoven's, as great in a feminine way as the fifth is in a masculine way. I thought it a curious selection for so rough a player; but I never dreamt that he, or any musician, could miss the grace and tenderness of the opening phrase, even if Beethoven's "dolce" were erased from the pianoforte copy. However, Mr Lamond saw nothing in it but a mere battery of chords. He smacked it out like a slater finishing a roof; and I paid no more attention. I remember how exquisitely Janotha used to play that concerto in the latter half of the seventies, when she first came over here. Nowadays she is content to gabble over Mendelssohn's G minor concerto like a schoolgirl; and when I went to her recital the other day, I found her idly displaying her rare dexterity of hand and her capricious individuality of style without a ray of thought or feeling; so that I left sorrowfully after sitting out two or three barren numbers.

15 June 1892

LAST Wednesday I was told that Siegfried was to be produced that evening at Covent Garden. I was incredulous, and asked my informant whether he did not mean Carmen, with Miss Zélie de Lussan in the title part. He said he thought not. I suggested Faust, Les Huguenots, even Die Meistersinger; but he stuck to his story: Siegfried, he said, was really and truly in the bills, and the house was sold out. Still doubting, I went to the box-office, where they confirmed the intelligence, except that they had just one stall left. I took it, and went away wondering and only half convinced. But when I reached the theatre in the evening a little late, fully expecting to find notices on the seats to the effect that Siegfried was unavoidably postponed, in consequence of the sudden indisposition of the dragon, and Philémon and Cavalleria substituted, I found the lights out and the belated stall-holders wandering like ghosts through the gloom in search of their numbers, helped only by the glimmer from the huge orchestra and some faint daylight from the ventilators.

The darkness was audible as well as visible; for there was no mistaking that cavernous music, with the tubas lowing like Plutonian bullocks, Mime's hammer rapping weirdly, and the drums muttering the subterranean thunder of Nibelheim. And before I left the house—to be exact, it was at half-past twelve next morning—I actually saw Rosa Sucher and Sir Augustus Harris hand in hand before the curtain, looking as if Covent Garden had been the birthplace of her reputation, and as if he had never heard La Favorita in his life. Perhaps it was all a dream; but it seemed real to me, and does so still. Assuming that I was awake, I may claim that at least one of those curtain-calls was not for the manager at all, but for me and for those colleagues of mine who so strongly urged Sir Augustus Harris to try this experiment in the golden years when money was plenty and there was no Dissolution impending, even at the cost of depriving

London of the opportunity of witnessing the début of Signor Rawner as Manrico.

The performance was vigorous, complete, earnest—in short, all that was needed to make Siegfried enormously interesting to operatic starvelings like the Covent Garden frequenters. The German orchestra is rough; but the men know the work, and are under perfect and willing discipline. In readiness and certainty of execution they are fully equal, if not superior, to the ordinary Covent Garden orchestra. But I cannot say as much for them in the matter of purity and individuality of tone. After making every allowance for the difference between the German orchestral tradition, which is partly popular, and the English, which is purely classic, as well as for the effect, peculiar to the Nibelungen tetralogy, of the rugged and massive ground bass which pervades so much of the score, I still cannot accept this imported orchestra as being up to the standard of tone quality we have been accustomed to expect in London.

In that vast mass of brass, it seemed to me that instead of three distinct and finely contrasted families of thoroughbred trombones, horns, and tubas, we had a huge tribe of mongrels, differing chiefly in size. I felt that some ancestor of the trombones had been guilty of a *mésalliance* with a bombardon; that each cornet, though itself already an admittedly half-bred trumpet, was further disgracing itself by a leaning towards the flügel horn, and that the mother of the horns must have run away with a whole military band. Something of the same doubt hangs over the lineage of the wood wind, the bass clarionet alone being above suspicion. Even in the strings, the 'cellos and tenors lack distinction, though here the thicker and heavier tone is partly due to the lower pitch, which is in every other respect a prodigious relief. I think it will not be disputed that the Covent Garden orchestra, if it had half the opportunities of the German one, could handle the score of Siegfried not only with much greater distinction of tone and consequent variety of effect, but also with a more delicate and finished execution of the phrases which make up the mosaic of leading-motives, and with a wider range of gradation from *pianissimo* to *fortissimo* than Herr Mahler's band achieved, excellent in many respects as its performance certainly was. This is no mere conjecture: we have already heard the Siegfried blacksmith music and forest music played by our own orchestras in concert selections better than it was played on Wednesday last.

And that is why I still complain that Sir Augustus Harris is no more establishing the Wagnerian music-drama in London than Mr Kiralfy is establishing the gondola. When he organized the performance of Die Meistersinger by his own company and his own orchestra, he achieved his greatest feat as an impresario. This time he has only sent for a German impresario and a German company to help him out of the difficulty; and for that I grudge him the smallest exaltation, as I could have done as much myself if I had the requisite commercial credit.

The impression created by the performance was extraordinary, the gallery cheering wildly at the end of each act. Everybody was delighted with the change from the tailor-made operatic tenor in velvet and tights to the wild young hero who forges his own weapons and tans his own coat and buskins. We all breathed that vast orchestral atmosphere of fire, air, earth, and water, with unbounded relief and invigoration; and I doubt if half-a-dozen people in the house were troubled with the critical reflections which occurred to me whenever the orchestra took a particularly rough spin over exquisitely delicate ground, as in the scene between Wotan and Erda. It is not to be doubted that all the women found Brynhild an improvement on Carmen and Co.

I say nothing of the great drama of world-forces which the Nibelung story symbolizes, because I must not pretend that the Covent Garden performance was judged on that ground; but considering how very large a proportion of the audience was still seated when the curtain came down at half-past twelve, I think it is fair to assume that the people to whom Wotan is nothing but an unmitigated bore were in a minority. At the same time, Herr Grengg, with his imposing presence, powerful voice, and perpetual fortissimo, did very little to break that ponderous monotony which is the besetting sin of the German Wotan. Lorent, who was on the stage for a few minutes as Alberich, was also earnest, but pointless and characterless. Fortunately Mime (Herr Lieban) saved the situation by his unflagging vivacity. It would be unreasonable to ask for a cleverer representation than his of the crafty, timid, covetous, and, one must admit, unmercifully bullied old dwarf. His singing shewed remarkable artistic ingenuity—exactly the quality which Mime's music requires.

There are two great points in the part: first, that awful nightmare which comes upon Mime after the question-and-answer scene in the first act, when he curses the shimmering light and falls into a growing terror which is just reaching an intolerable climax when it vanishes as if by magic at the voice of Siegfried in the wood outside; and, second, his attempt to poison Siegfried after the fight with the worm, when he involuntarily talks murder instead of the flattery he intends. Both of these passages were driven home forcibly by Lieban, especially the poison scene, where the effect depends more on the actor and less on the orchestra than in the other. Alvary, though he has something of that air of rather fancying himself in his part which distinguishes some of the most popular impersonations of Mr Wilson Barrett (whom Alvary rather resembles personally), attained a very considerable level of excellence as Siegfried, especially in the forest scene, the remembrance of which will, I think, prove more lasting than that of the first and last acts when we have seen a few rival Siegfrieds and grown a little more critical. Fräulein Traubmann, as the bird, was energetic, purposeful, human, and, in short, everything that a bird ought not to be. For so nice a stage illusion we need wilder and far more spontaneous wood-notes than hers.

As I have already intimated, Fräulein Heink, as Erda, had her scene rather roughly handled by both the orchestra and by Wotan; but she nevertheless succeeded in rescuing something of its ineffable charm by her expressive delivery and her rich contralto tones. As to Rosa Sucher, she was as prompt, as powerful, as vigorous, as perfect in her drill, as solid and gleaming in her tone as ever. Her efficiency, brilliancy, and strength have a charm that is rather military than feminine; and consequently they will fail to rouse the voluptuous enthusiasm of our devotees of that splendid and invariably repentant female, the Womanly Woman; but as Brynhild was no Magdalen, Frau Sucher can hardly be blamed for not making her one. Finally, I have to chronicle several curtain-calls for the energetic conductor, Herr Mahler. He knows the score thoroughly, and sets the *tempi* with excellent judgment. That being so, I hope he will yet succeed in getting a finer quality of execution from his band.

The scenery is of the usual German type, majestic, but intensely prosaic. The dragon, whose vocal utterances were managed jointly by Herr Wiegand and a speaking-trumpet, was a little like Carpaccio's dragon at San Giorgio Schiavone, a little like the Temple Bar griffin, and a little like a camel about the ears, although the general foundation appeared to be an old and mangy donkey. As usual, people are complaining of the dragon as a mistake on Wagner's part, as if he were the man to have omitted a vital scene in his drama merely because our stage machinists are such duffers as to be unable, with all their resources, to make as good a dragon as I could improvise with two old umbrellas, a mackintosh, a clothes-horse, and a couple of towels. Surely it is within the scope of modern engineering to make a thing that will give its tail one smart swing round, and then rear up.

The stage effects throughout were punctual and conscientious (always excepting the flagrant exhibition of Brynhild in the last act as the Sleeping Beauty instead of as an armed figure whose sex remains a mystery until Siegfried removes the helmet and cuts away the coat of mail); but they were not very imaginative. The stithy was lighted like a Board School; and the fires of Loge and the apparition of

Erda might have been ordered from the gas company, for all the pictorial art they displayed. Sir Augustus Harris need not look to Bayreuth for a lead in this direction. Where Bayreuth surpasses us is not in picturesque stage composition, but in the seriousness, punctuality, and thoroughness with which it looks after the stage business, which is mostly left to take care of itself at Covent Garden.

I am compelled by want of space to postpone until next week my notice of Mr de Lara's Light of Asia, which was successfully produced on Saturday evening. If it is repeated in the meantime, Mr de Lara will do well to withdraw the fourth act, unless the establishment can do something better in the way of staging it. It almost eclipses the absurdities of the Tannhäuser *mise en scène* at present.

22 *June* 1892

MR ISIDORE DE LARA, the composer of La Luce dell' Asia, is young and new; he has hardly been fairly in the field as a composer for twenty years. It is remarkable how much faster Italians mature than Englishmen. Mascagni is positively Mr de Lara's senior in the operatic world; and no doubt Mr de Lara will be quite content to survive him. Mr Cowen might almost be Mascagni's father; and yet people still talk of him as "Freddy Cowen," without the smallest sense of incongruity. As to Sir Augustus Harris himself, he is admittedly getting on for middle age; and yet it has taken a knighthood to abolish the general custom of speaking of him by the second syllable of his first name alone. My own immunity from such familiarities I believe to be due less to natural awe than to the fact that my surname is so much easier and shorter than my Christian names, which are happily incapable of abbreviation, that the general use of either of them would involve a serious loss of time to the community. But even I am often described as callow, and impressively lectured for my immaturity and rashness by critics of from nineteen to twenty-five. Hence I am not surprised to find that the younger section of Mr de Lara's friendly critics condescend handsomely to him, by way of encouraging a young man; whilst the hostile ones speak loftily, as responsible persons who do their stern duty to society by rebuking an upstart.

Among the academic section there is the feeling that since Mr de Lara, having always followed his own artistic bent with perfect sincerity and independence, is not a man of scholarships and professorships, it is just like his impudence to attempt to compose at all. Add to this that his achievements as a drawing-room singer have brought about him a remarkably ill-behaved crowd of partisans, consisting, as far as I could judge from what I noticed in the stalls at Covent Garden on Saturday week, of prepossessing and apparently prepossessed ladies who would persist in applauding in impossible places, to the indignation of all beholders and the great prejudice of the unfortunate composer; and you will see that what with patronizing critics, bigoted academicians, and indiscreet adorers, Mr de Lara has much to live down.

It must not be supposed that The Light of Asia is a philosophical opera. It is necessary to say this explicitly, because there are some people who, if I were to write an opera called The Light of Edinburgh, and make Adam Smith the hero, would immediately find that the overture contained a good deal of political economy. Wagner's Nibelung Ring tetralogy may be called a philosophic music drama, because the characters are dramatic personifications of the forces which are the subject-matter of metaphysics, the Pilgrim's Progress itself not being a more unmistakeable allegory. The Light of Asia is a representation of the adventures of the man Buddha and his mistress, with about as much Buddhism in it as an ordinary oratorio contains of Christianity.

Still, The Light of Asia differs in one vital respect from the general run of modern oratorios. These works are mostly written by men who are or have been church organists; and church organists are, as a class, more utterly void of religious reverence than any other body of men in the world. As Mr de Lara has presumably never played the organ in a Buddhist temple, he remains fresh to the impressiveness of the Buddha legend, and has set Mr Beatty Kingston's poem to music which is remarkably free from professional pedantry, deliberate imitation, claptrap, padding, and vulgarity. Naturally, a work so deficient in all that the professors can teach is not likely to be popular with them. The fact that it is conscientiously finished to the utmost of the composer's ability completes his title to be criticized with entire respect.

Mr de Lara's chief disadvantage at Covent Garden is that the best side of the composition is the worst side of the performance. The centre of the opera is the song, Loosen from thy foot the bangle, which made its mark a few years ago when Miss Ella Russell sang it at St James's Hall, and for which Miss Eames was heartily applauded on Saturday week. It is a languorous, dreamy, half mystical, half voluptuous Oriental love-song, as the Oriental love-song exists in the English imagination. This sort of seraglio music pervades the whole work, more or less: the second and third acts consist almost entirely of it. Now, in an opera, the creation of an atmosphere so subtle as this requires not only appropriate music but poetic dancing and delicate stage management. I need hardly say that neither of these luxuries were to be had at Covent Garden.

The principal dancer, Miss Mabel Love, whose chronic expression of tragic indignation replaces this season the smile of Palladino, understands what is wanted for the scene in which she appears, and makes a courageous and interesting attempt to supply it; but her powers are not yet matured, and her physical training is still far from thorough; so that she can do but little to soften the ruinously prosaic effect produced by the *corps de ballet*, which accompanies Mr de Lara's swaying syncopations and incense-breathing consecutive fifths with a feeble modification of its ordinary exercises. If the regular ballet was a failure—as, on the whole, it decidedly was—what could be expected from the passages in the third act, where the movements of the chorus of odalisques (if that is the correct expression) should be subdued from positive dancing almost to the abstract poetry of gliding, weaving motion? With this in view, a group of young ladies wandered about in the prompt corner as if some vivisector had removed from their heads that portion of the brain which enables us to find our way to the door; and though the audience, restrained by the presence of Lassalle and Miss Eames, who might have broken into song at any moment, waited patiently, they probably blamed Mr de Lara for maundering.

But Mr de Lara was not in a position to complain. Everybody on the stage was lending a willing hand to the utmost of his or her knowledge; and the management had been quite princely in the way of expenditure. Unless Mr de Lara had torn out handfuls of his hair and strewn them despairingly on the stage in protest against having his opera stifled with goodwill and hundreds of pounds' worth of silks and precious-looking metals when it was perishing for want of two-penn'orth of skill and fancy, I do not see what he could have done. His feelings in the fourth act must have been particularly unenviable. The persons who appeared therein were mostly supernatural; and this immediately brought out the superstitious side of the Covent Garden stage management. Sir Augustus Harris has been imbued from his earliest years with the belief that the vital distinction between the inhabitants of the other world and of this is that the latter move horizontally and the former vertically. Enter his room through the door and walk across to his chair, and he will recognize you as human. Remove a square piece of the floor and rise slowly into the room on a lift, and he will believe you to be a demon as firmly as if you were a musical critic and had found fault with the Royal Italian Opera. You cannot get this out of his mind: it is part of the faith of his childhood.

No fair-minded critic can doubt that when Signor

Miranda was hoisted on to a lift; shot up like a Jack-in-the-box out of a neutral-tinted canvas cloud resembling a photographer's background of monstrous size; and bathed in the fiery glow of a red limelight, Sir Augustus was convinced that only a hardened atheist could refuse to believe and tremble. And yet everybody laughed except Mr de Lara and Signor Miranda, who was standing giddily on the brink of a precipice some twelve or fourteen feet high. As to the siren's cave business which followed, I really have not the patience to describe it, further than to say that it was as like a kitchen fireplace as usual, and that nobody was surprised at the insensibility to its seductions displayed by Buddha, who had been having a nap under a tree in a heavy shower. When he walked off the stage, and the curtain came down for a long pause just at the wrong time, the fortunes of The Light of Asia reached their lowest ebb. Will no friend of Sir Augustus Harris's open his mind gently to the fact that all this machinery of traps and visions is as dead as Queen Anne?

It will be seen that Mr de Lara cannot be said to have had his work performed to the greatest possible advantage. Still, he had much to be thankful for. Lassalle, who took the part of Buddha, and comported himself with a sublime self-satisfaction which would have put the very smuggest Indian idol out of countenance, sang magnificently. Miss Eames, though a little matter-of-fact, gave sufficient weight to the part of Yasodhara; and Plançon saved the first scene, which is musically the weakest part of the work. The rather empty motive with which it opens is nearly identical with the refrain of Autolycus's song in A Winter's Tale; the song of Atman is only a pretty piece of troubadouring; and the mock-scholastic choral passages beginning For earth's sake, produced a burlesque effect not unlike that of the Amen in Berlioz' Faust.

One or two of the instrumental interludes are too long: they cause stage waits; and it struck me that the material of the funeral march got just a shade more repetition than it can bear with the best effect. The scene in the fields is much the worse for the transformation of the work from a cantata to an oratorio. But the rest is of remarkable merit; and the whole work abounds in vocal melody of exceptional excellence. When I recall the extravagant praise that was lavished on Ivanhoe, with its refractory voice parts nailed down to a perpetual mechanical rum-tum, I cannot but wonder why so little has been said of Mr de Lara's purely musical, well-phrased, and often eloquent vocal writing. What he lacks at present is more intellectual vivacity; an intenser, more symphonic grip of his musical material; greater variety of mood; and a distinct orchestral style as distinguished from mere taste in orchestral effects.

The best point in the score at present is the use made in Yasodhara's song of the instrument known to military bandsmen as "Jingling Johnny"—a point that would not be worth mentioning in a score of Gounod's. It will be noticed that these are all negative failings, and that I have admitted the opera to be throughout sincere and original. I will not go so far as to say that Mr de Lara is the only English composer of his generation whose feeling for his work is calculated to do his country credit; but there is certainly more hope in The Light of Asia than in those things with the pedal points and the mixolydian angels in them which are composed by our professors for the provincial festivals. I hope Mr de Lara will never condescend to take shares in the mixolydian business. Some of the partners in it began, like himself, as musicians. Let him consider what they are now, and take heed that he follows not in their footsteps.

29 *June* 1892

SOME months ago I mentioned that a performance of Handel's Samson, on the festival scale, had been arranged at the Crystal Palace. Then came the news that a substitution of the comparatively hackneyed Judas Maccabæus would save Mr Edward Lloyd trouble. The program was accordingly changed for the worse; and the performance thereby became a gigantic celebration of Mr Lloyd's indisposition to exert himself. Formerly, when musicians wanted to describe the most fatuous depths of stupidity, they used to say "*bête comme un tenor*." Nowadays tenors are clever enough; but they are not energetic. Miss Eames lately told an interviewer, who kept his countenance with heroic constancy, that the severity with which Jean de Reszke studies his work is beyond description. No doubt she was thinking of the fact that he has spent the past year in cerebrating with volcanic intensity over the color of Romeo's beard, as to which he could now probably write us a volume worthy to rank with the famous essay on the character of that master of refined pleasantry, the nurse's husband. A paper upon his old fair theory and his new dark theory, which may yet give place to a shaving theory or even a no-beard-at-all theory, would draw a huge crowd to a meeting of the New Shakespear Society.

In the meantime the years are flying; and we have not yet heard Brother Jean as Siegfried, or Siegmund, or Loge, or Tannhäuser, though his Walther in Die Meistersinger, which is, as far as I know, the best in the world, shews what he could do for Wagner if he had the will. The age is therefore confronted with two problems: (1) to make Edward Lloyd learn Samson, and (2) to make Jean de Reszke learn Siegfried. I wish there were some legal process by which we could lock them both up in Holloway Gaol until they had taught one another the parts. They would get on capitally together; for there is no rivalry between them: to Lloyd, Brother Jean is simply a baritone of exceptional range; whilst to Brother Jean, Lloyd is an admirable *soprano robusto*.

The Judas performance came off last Saturday. The audience was the usual festival crowd, big and extremely barbarous, as the soloists well knew; for unscrupulous alterations of the text in order to finish with the most absurd high notes were the order of the day; and the more outrageous they were the better the audience liked them. The choruses left little to be desired in point of precision and none in point of magnitude. The baritones distinguished themselves specially by the brilliancy and steadiness of their tone. I say baritones advisedly; for there seemed to be very few bass voices among them: the tone, which rose to great splendor above the stave, fell off almost to nothing when they got down below C. The sopranos were very bad: they had a noble opportunity in the first verse of God save the Queen; and all they did was to give us a careless, common, vulgar piece of screaming. The altos were much better; the tenors better still; and the baritones, as I have said, best of all.

Miss Clara Samuell sang some of the soprano music, and made the most of her voice by her good intonation and well-formed tone. As to Albani, Patey, Lloyd, and Santley, it is not necessary to say more than that From Mighty Kings, Sound an Alarm, Arm, arm, ye brave, etc., produced all the customary cheering and clapping. Mr. Manns was not in his brightest and most confident vein; but he was none the less equal to the occasion.

After the performance of Das Rheingold last Wednesday at the Opera, I do not think we shall hear much more about the impropriety of beginning the season with Siegfried, which should have come third instead of first. If it be true that it was Alvary who insisted on the transposition, let us admit now that Alvary knew what he was about. Siegfried was a success because there was hardly a moment in the three acts during which Lieban or Alvary, or both, or Sucher and Alvary, were not on the stage to keep things going. Besides, the defects of the orchestra did not matter so much in a score which admits of a certain degree of roughness of treatment. The dullest moment in Siegfried was the dialogue at the beginning of the second act between Wotan and Alberich.

Now imagine our German visitors setting to at a music drama which contains an enormous percentage of Wotan-cum-Alberich, with a score requiring the most delicate handling, and you will be able to understand that the performance of Das Rheingold was none of the liveliest. The band, no longer braced up by the excitement of the first night, did what I hope was its worst. Its playing of the wonderful water music prelude suggested that the Rhine must be a river of treacle—and rather lumpy treacle at that; the gold music was arrant pinchbeck; Freia's return to heaven brought no magical waftings of joy to the audience; and the rainbow music, with its host of harps (I distinctly heard one, and was not well placed for seeing whether there were any others), might have been pleasant deck music during a steamboat excursion to Hampton Court, for all the success it attained in providing a splendid climax to the prologue of a mighty drama.

Then the stage arrangements were rather hard to bear. There was nothing to complain of in the first scene, since no better way of doing it has yet been invented. The Rhine daughters waved their arms, and floated up and down and round and round in their aquarium; and if I could only have forgotten the scene as it appeared to those behind the curtain—the three fire-escapes being elongated and shortened and raced round the floor, each with a lady fastened to the top and draped with a modest green skirt of prodigious length—I should have been satisfied. But the orchestra did not make me forget it, nor did Alberich, nor anyone except Flosshilde (Fräulein Heink), who quite fulfilled the promise of her Erda in Siegfried. The really difficult part of the stage management in Das Rheingold is the change from the home of the gods to that of the dwarfs, and the business of Alberich's metamorphoses and final capture.

The way in which these were either bungled or frankly given up in despair shewed with brutal directness what I have so often tried to hint delicately: namely, that if Sir Augustus Harris would dismiss a round dozen of his superfluous singers, and give a fifth of what they cost him to an artistic and ingenious stage-manager, he would double the value of the performances at Covent Garden. The attempts of Herr Lissman, who is, to say the least, no harlequin, to disappear suddenly through a trick shutter, the obviousness of which would have disgraced a cheesemonger's shop in a Christmas pantomime, were not made any the more plausible by the piffling little jet of steam which followed. As to the changes into the dragon and the toad, they were simply taken for granted, although Sir Augustus might easily have taken advice on the subject, not from Bayreuth, but from any provincial manager who has ever put the story of Puss in Boots on the stage. The descent from god-home to dwarf-home was avoided by dropping the curtain and making an interval at the end of the second scene; and the change back again, which should be an ascent into the clouds, was a badly managed attempt at the descent which had been omitted. Evidently the scene-plot had got mixed on its way from Hamburg.

The shortcomings in the staging of the work were all the more depressing because, with two conspicuous exceptions, the principal performers were so averagely German that it is only by repeatedly telling myself not to be rude that I can restrain myself from saying flatly that they might as well have been English, so powerfully mediocre were they. Grengg sang his way loudly and heavily through the part of Wotan with both his eyes wide open (one of them should have been removed). Every line he uttered was exactly like every other line. Alberich did not even sing: he shouted, and seemed content if he came within a half-quarter tone of the highest notes he aimed at. His acting, though conscientious, was that of a pirate in a Surrey melodrama: neither in his ghastly declaration to Loge of his ambition to become master of the world, nor in his frantic despair when Wotan wrests the ring from him, did he make the smallest sensation.

Frau Andriessen failed to make Fricka interesting—small blame to her, perhaps, considering the impossibility of getting any variety of play out of Wotan. Fräulein Bettaque, as Freia, was pretty and pleasing enough to disarm criticism; and the giants, having little to do except to appear clumsy and intellectually and artistically dense, took to their parts with considerable aptitude. But they certainly would not have made the performance endurable but for the two exceptions I have alluded to: namely, Lieban (Mime), whose ten minutes on the stage, including his capital singing of Sorglose Schmiede, sent up the artistic level of the performance with a bound during that too brief period; and Alvary, who, as Loge, the northern Mephistopheles, succeeded by his alertness in making the rest of the gods look anything but quick-witted.

On the whole, it was fortunate for the success of the work that most of us are at present so helplessly under the spell of the Ring's greatness that we can do nothing but go raving about the theatre between the acts in ecstasies of deluded admiration. Even the critics lose their heads: you find the same men who are quite alive to the disparities between Jean de Reszke and Montariol, Maurel or Edouard de Reszke and Miranda or De Vaschetti, Calvé or Giulia Ravogli and Melba or Miss de Lussan, losing all discrimination when the German artists come up for judgment; admiring a third-rate Alberich as devoutly as a first-rate Mime; and meekly accepting the German tendency to coarse singing and wooden declamation as the right thing for Wagner, whose music really demands as much refinement, expression, and vivacity as Mozart's.

As to the band, one hardly knows what to say of the revelation it has made of the fewness of the people who know *by ear* the difference between a second-rate German orchestra reinforced by a number of students from the Guildhall College and first-rate ones like those of London and Manchester.

When the public wakes up from its happy hypnotic trance and resumes its normal freedom of judgment, it will inevitably be bored by Das Rheingold, unless it is smartly and attractively stage-managed and well acted in English.

And even then it will remain, like Die Zauberflöte, a mere extravaganza, except to those who see in all that curious harlequinade of gods, dwarfs, and giants, a real drama of which their own lives form part. Herren Wiegand and Litter, raised to gigantic stature on thick-soled boots, and poking at one another with huge cudgels whilst the drum is pounded unmercifully down in the orchestra, may look ridiculous; but the spectacle of good-natured ignorance and serviceable brute force, suddenly roused to lust and greed, and falling to fratricidal murder, is another matter—one that makes the slaying of Fasolt by Fafnir the most horrifying of stage duels.

Wotan is a delicate subject, especially in England, where you do not know whose toes you may tread on if you suggest that the Wagnerian stage is not the only place in which Religion, corrupted by ambition, has bartered away its life-principle for a lordly pleasure-house, and then called in the heartless intellect to rescue it from the consequences of its bargain by hypocrisy, fraud, and force. As to Alberich, renouncing love for gold, and losing all fellow-feeling in his haste to accumulate it, I question whether it is good taste to exhibit him at Covent Garden on "diamond nights." But I am sure that Das Rheingold must either be read between the lines and through the lines, or else yawned at. Siegfried, Die Walküre, and Götterdämmerung may pass as ordinary dramas, barring a little interruption from time to time by the prolixities of Wotan; but Das Rheingold is either a profound allegory or a puerile fairy tale. Consequently it is hardly worth doing at all unless it is done very well, which is precisely why it was so much less successful at Covent Garden than Siegfried.

6 *July* 1892

IT is only fair to the artists whom I have to criticize in this hour of political battle to ask that a large allowance may be made for the deterioration of my character produced by electioneering. A fortnight ago I still had, I will not say a conscience, but certain vestiges of the moral habits formed in the days before I became a critic. These have entirely disappeared; and, as I now stand, I am capable of anything except a findable-out infringement of the Corrupt Practices Act. A collation of the speeches I have delivered would destroy all faith in human nature. I have blessed in the south and banned in the north with an unscrupulously single-hearted devotion to the supreme end of getting my man in, which has wholly freed my intellect from absolute conceptions of truth. I learnt long ago that though there are several places from which the tourist may enjoy a view of Primrose Hill, none of these can be called *the* view of Primrose Hill. I now perceive that the political situation is like Primrose Hill.

Wherever I have been I have found and fervently uttered *a* true view of it; but as to *the* true view, believe me, there is no such thing. Place all the facts before me; and allow me to make an intelligent selection (always with the object of getting my man in); and the moral possibilities of the situation are exhausted. And now I can almost hear some pillar of the great church of Chadband saying, "Faugh! no more of this: let us return to the purer atmosphere of art." But *is* the atmosphere of art any purer? One evening I find myself appealing to the loftiest feelings of a town where many of the inhabitants, when you canvass them, still keep up the primitive custom of shutting the door carefully, assuring you that they are "all right," and bluntly asking how much you are going to pay for their vote. The next evening I am at the Opera, with Wagner appealing to my loftiest sentiments. Perhaps Mr Chadband would call that a return to a purer atmosphere. But I know better. Speaking for myself alone, I am as much a politician at a first-night or a press-view as I am on the hustings.

When I was more among pictures than I am at present, certain reforms in painting which I desired were advocated by the Impressionist party, and resisted by the Academic party. Until those reforms had been effectually wrought I fought for the Impressionists—backed up men who could not draw a nose differently from an elbow against Leighton and Bouguereau—did everything I could to make the public conscious of the ugly unreality of studio-lit landscape and the inanity of second-hand classicism. Again, in dealing with the drama, I find that the forces which tend to make the theatre a more satisfactory resort for me are rallied for the moment, not round the so-called French realists, whom I should call simply anti-obscurantists, but around the Scandinavian realists; and accordingly I mount their platform, exhort England to carry their cause on to a glorious victory, and endeavor to surround their opponents with a subtle atmosphere of absurdity.

It is just the same in music. I am always electioneering. At the Opera I desire certain reforms; and, in order to get them, I make every notable performance an example of the want of them, knowing that in the long run these defects will seem as ridiculous as Monet has already made Bouguereau's backgrounds, or Ibsen the "poetical justice" of Tom Taylor. Never in my life have I penned an impartial criticism; and I hope I never may. As long as I have a want, I am necessarily partial to the fulfilment of that want, with a view to which I must strive with all my wit to infect everyone else with it. Thus there arises a deadly enmity between myself and the impresarios; for whereas their aim is to satisfy the public, often at huge risk and expense, I seize on their costliest efforts as the most conspicuous examples of the shortcomings which rob me of the fullest satisfaction of my artistic cravings.

They may feel this to be diabolically unfair to them whenever they have done the very utmost that existing circumstances allowed them; but that does not shake me, since I know that the critic who accepts existing circumstances loses from that moment all his dynamic quality. He stops the clock. His real business is to find fault; to ask for more; to knock his head against stone walls, in the full assurance that three or four good heads will batter down any wall that stands across the world's path. He is no dispenser of justice: reputations are to him only the fortresses of the opposing camps; and he helps to build or bombard them according to his side in the conflict. To be just to individuals—even if it were possible—would be to sacrifice the end to the means, which would be profoundly immoral.

One must, of course, know the facts, and that is where the critic's skill comes in; but a moral has to be drawn from the facts, and that is where his bias comes out. How many a poor bewildered artist, in the conflict of art movements, has found himself in the position of the harmless peasant who sees a shell bursting in his potato-patch because his little white house on the hill accidentally happens to help a field battery to find its range. Under such circumstances, a humane artillery officer can at least explain the position to the peasant. Similarly, I feel bound to explain my position to those in whose gardens my shells occasionally burst. And the explanation is probably quite as satisfactory to the shattered victim in one case as in the other.

Electioneering notwithstanding, I have been at countless concerts during the past few weeks, and am well content to forget a good deal of what I have heard of them. Some were what I may call Coöperative Concerts, each artist guaranteeing the sale of a certain number of tickets in return for the advantage of appearing before the London public. For further particulars I must refer my readers to my Confessions of a Concert Agent, which is to be published when death has placed me beyond the fear of assassination. It will not contain anything scandalous—at least, anything *very* scandalous; but part of it will be sufficiently surprising to the innocent British public to offer some inducement to our *entrepreneurs* to pay me every possible attention with a view to prolonging my life to the utmost. Besides the Coöperative Concerts, there have been a good many concerts of the annual benefit or one-good-turn-deserves-another description, some of them good of their kind, but not critically interesting. We have had two remarkable examples of the value of great masters to finely receptive pupils. Miss Nettie Carpenter, who played Bruch's first violin concerto at the concert given by her husband, Mr. Leo Stern, shewed that she had caught everything from Sarasate except the extraordinary strength and endurance, the unremitting and exquisite sensitiveness and vigilance of his right hand. And Miss Szumowska gave a pianoforte recital at which she played so beautifully and intelligently that I think Paderewski would have admitted that she gave his interpretations of the works in her program better than he, in his coarser and more headstrong moods, has often given them himself. We are having a visit now from Reisenauer, a most Boanergetic disciple of Liszt, who has acquired a huge superfluity of technical power, which, doubtless after sufficient consideration, he has resolved to take out in speed rather than in thought. The result is satisfactory in compositions which are meant to excite and dazzle; but I fervently hope I may never again hear the last variation in Schumann's Symphonic Studies as it sounded under the Reisenauer treatment. Max Schwarz, another pianist, or rather a professor of the piano, reminded me a little of Heinrich Lutters. He is Director of the Raff Conservatoire at Frankfort.

Among the best miscellaneous concerts I have attended were Miss Palliser's and Miss Gambogi's. Miss Palliser produced a child-fiddler, Arthur Hartmann, small enough to be Gerardy's little brother, but grave, self-possessed, and capable to a degree which four times his years have not enabled me to attain. Another and more mature young violinist is the girl Panteo, who played one of Wagner's few *pièces de salon* at the last Opera Concert, and triumphed over an orchestral accompaniment that would have disheartened an older performer. We shall probably hear more of her. Dutch violinists still arrive in shoals. They almost all play with remarkable neatness, and seem likely to be favorites at miscellaneous concerts and in drawing rooms; but Henri Seiffert remains the only one from whom there is much to be expected. Unlike most of his compatriots, he excels in the power of his cantabile playing, and often executes florid ornaments with reckless roughness. I am bound to add that he never, like some of his smoother competitors, suggests any doubt as to whether he could play his scales if put to it. I return to the subject of Miss Palliser's concert for a moment to say that I was much struck by the singing of Mr David Bispham, who seems to me to be fully qualified to take his place on the stage as an operatic artist of considerable distinction. No doubt this has been known and said long ago; but it so happens that I have only heard him at this concert, and once before, in The Basoche, when I took him to be a drier singer than I now perceive him to be. Miss Marie Brema has sung much this season, and always with success, notably at one of the operatic concerts, where her singing of The Erl King completely eclipsed the clumsy concert-singing of the rank and file of the Covent Garden company; but at present she is an organ with one stop, the quality of which will not be improved if it is too persistently ground at. Miss Brema must be more versatile than she has hitherto shewn herself (as far as I have had the opportunity of observing); and if she succeeds in widening her dramatic scope in the direction of comedy, and also enlarging her purely musical resources by occasionally substituting the attraction of simple beauty of sound in the upper part of her voice for that of dramatic intensity in the lower, she will take high rank as a singer. At present she is narrowing her talent by over-specilization. Miss Gambogi's concert was abruptly finished, for me, by Miss Ellen Terry, who projected herself into a recitation with such superb artistic power that I was quite unable to face the feeble superficiality of ordinary concert business after it, and so hurried out of the room. Miss Gambogi is too young as yet to have much grip of her talent, which is, besides, by no means precociously developed; but she has natural refinement, good looks, and an engaging personality, reminding one occasionally of Trebelli. A young lady named Leonora Clench spiritedly attacked the last two movements of Mendelssohn's violin concerto, and came off with credit. Hollmann also helped, and compelled us to acknowledge his excellence, now so well proved that it is an impertinence to praise it.

I am far from having exhausted my concerts; but space begins to close in, and I have yet a couple of other matters to mention. La Statue du Commandeur is now preceded at the Prince of Wales Theatre by a musical tomfoolery called Did you Ring? which at first moved me to majestic scorn, and afterwards brought me down off my pedestal (like Le Commandeur), and made me laugh with undignified heartiness. It is by Messrs Haughton and Mabson, and is played by Miss Amy Farrell, Miss Kate James, and Mr Templar Saxe. I saw La Statue for the second time, and enjoyed it more than I had done before. The dancing of Mlle Litini is as good as the singing of Miss Alice Gomez, whom she somewhat resembles; and the Don (M. Burguet), though he gives the Commandant no excuse for taking him so very seriously at the end, is a capital comedian and a skilful pantomimist. The piece needs to be visited twice, because on the first occasion one sees hardly anything but the petrified personality, or rather colossality, of Tarride as the Commendatore. You lose all sorts of good things whilst you are gaping at the huge white marble man.

The second act, as a highly organized artistic achievement, is far superior to anything in L'Enfant Prodigue. The music is a clever piece of *rococo* in the most modern taste, just half in earnest, like the dumb show itself. It is quite understood, however, between Adolphe David and his audience that thinking of Mozart is barred.

I must postpone notice of Die Walküre at the Opera until next week, strongly recommending everybody meanwhile to go and hear the first act, which retrieved for the German company all the credit it lost over Das Rheingold. The rest is not so good. The second act is horribly mutilated; and Reichmann is overparted as Wotan. The Valkyries are good; and Frau Andriessen, though she was not dazzling on the warlike side, played Brynhild with a sincerity and depth of feeling that greatly advanced her popularity.

13 *July* 1892

I HAVE just received the most amusingly frank book I have read for a long time—just the thing for any old musical hand who would like to be led back, without too much detail, over the last thirty years. It is the History of the Leeds Musical Festival, by Joseph Bennett and Alderman Frederick Spark. Which of the twain handled the scissors and which the paste is not stated on the title-page; but I think I may venture to guess that Mr Bennett selected the press notices quoted, and supplied most of the pen-and-ink setting for the mosaic of programs, facsimiles, advertisements, letters, balance-sheets, and miscellaneous excerpts of which the volume is composed.

Pray do not suppose that I mention the scissors and paste as a reproach to the authors. On the contrary, they have made the book exactly as it ought to be made. Instead of an essay on the festivals, which would be insufferable, we get all the documents needed to give concert-goers the required information in the form to which they are most accustomed—that of the program and prospectus, which is also the most compact for reference. The statistical particulars are thus packed into a book of 400 pages, which you read easily in two hours, picking out what you are curious about in the programs; skipping the dry records of hours, days, and names of nobodies; abstracting the letters at a glance; and taking the anecdotes and significant bits of narrative at your ease.

Imagine a parcel of Yorkshire manufacturers, trained to go through the world on the understanding that every man with wares to sell is to get as much for them as he can; every man with money to buy to give as little as possible for what wares he wants; and nobody without wares to sell or money to buy with to be considered at all. Conceive these plain dealers suddenly set to bargain with great singers, the highest souled and most sensitive artists of their time, creatures to be approached like princes and princesses, too delicate to name a price, and too proud to endure a bid lower than what they privately think themselves well worth!

Naturally, there was a pretty confusion until Yorkshire discovered that the pursuit of manufacturing profits might pass for disinterested benevolence in comparison with artistic rapacity; that manufacturing competition looked like pure altruism beside musical jealousy; and that manufacturing domineering and push had not a chance against the absolutism of the foreign favorites of the musical public. Prima donna number one coolly demanding (and getting), in addition to her salary, the handsome sum she was to subscribe with queenly charity to the Leeds hospitals; prima donna number two inserting a clause in her agreement that no artist engaged should be paid more than herself; Costa ordering the committee not to write letters but to send an ambassador to see him, as if Leeds lay within ten minutes' walk of London, and browbeating them out of every proposal to get a little ahead of Rossini; impresarios planting unspeakable miscellaneous concerts of operatic bits and scraps on them as choice expositions of the highest glories of musical art: these and cognate matters are recorded with all possible openness in Messrs Bennett and Spark's volume.

The Leeds committee-men do not always cut a very dignified figure in its pages. When Charles Hallé treated them politely, reasonably, and unassumingly, in a thoroughly artistic spirit, they immediately proceeded to insult him, and let him know that his Manchester orchestra was not good enough for Leeds—that they were accustomed to a first-rate article from London, conducted by the great Costa. When Costa treated them with contempt, sneered at their ignorance, personally insulted those who dared to argue with him, publicly brought their Yorkshire novelty (Smart's Bride of Dunkerron) to grief in order, I presume, to have an excuse for refusing to have anything to do with novelties in future, and demanded a hundred guineas more for his services than Hallé, they grovelled before him, and only fell back on Sir Arthur Sullivan when their Neapolitan tyrant finally refused to have anything further to do with them. And yet, while Costa was treating them in this way, they had the assurance to write to Liszt asking him whether he would not like to "submit" a work of his for performance at the Festival (of 1877). Which of course elicited the following snub:

"Messieurs,—En réponse à votre lettre du 22 Décembre, j'ai l'honneur de vous informer que je suis tout à fait en dehors des *soumissions* auxquelles vous avez l'obligeance de m'inviter. Veuillez agréer, Messieurs, mes civilités.
30 Décembre '76, Budapest. F. Liszt."

Down to 1877 the majority of the committee never got beyond the primitive notion that a great musical event was one at which Tietjens sang and Costa conducted. I should myself have been educated in that superstition if it had been possible to educate me at all, which it most fortunately was not. Poor Tietjens herself, I imagine, believed in it devoutly; and so did Costa: it was not until she died and he repudiated the committee that Leeds at last found out that familiarity with The Messiah, Elijah, and the overture to William Tell, was not the climax of nineteenth-century musical culture. Since then, thanks to the tact of Sir Arthur Sullivan, the Leeds Festival has become a really important musical event. The forthcoming performances in October will be welcomed by all except those who incautiously attended the benumbing fourth day of the 1889 Festival, on which occasion the whole West Riding was plunged into listless gloom by an unprovoked performance of Brahms' Requiem.

On one point this book, which may be obtained at Novello's for the considerable sum of twenty-five shillings, has made me somewhat remorseful. A friend of mine asked me the other evening whether the Opera, at which I am so constantly grumbling, is not far better than it used to be under the régime that collapsed so soon after Costa vanished.

And I replied, in the words of Matthew Bagnet, "Yes; but I never own to it. Discipline must be maintained." The memories awakened by the programs in the History of the Leeds Musical Festival bring home to me how great the advance has been, and nerves me to clamor implacably for further progress.

20 *July* 1892

MAUREL'S lecture at the Lyceum Theatre on Tuesday last week was a much more businesslike affair than the crowded and fashionable reception of 1891. Our aims on this occasion were supposed to be exclusively scientific and artistic; and we did our best to look like a select body of critics and savants. I think, on the whole, we kept up appearances fairly well, though a stranger from another planet might have thought it rather a suspicious circumstance that Maurel should have felt it necessary to spend quite half an hour in arranging our ideas for us before he came to the actual business of his lecture. In fact, the first half of his address might have been introduced in the following terms. "Ladies and Gentlemen: Most of you are either musical critics or teachers of singing. A long experience of both classes in the various countries I have visited during my long professional career has convinced me that neither musical critics nor teachers of singing ever think intelligently. It is, therefore, necessary that I should give you a little rudimentary instruction in the art of thinking before I give you something to think about."

Here I think Maurel made a mistake. The attempt was probably entirely unsuccessful in the cases of those who needed it, and was perhaps resented in the cases of those who did not. Besides, in making it, he forgot to allow for the English habit of mind. It is our insular custom to tackle intellectual problems without any preliminary arrangement of the subject-matter; and, however slovenly this may seem to a Frenchman, we find that it serves our turn, and are rather proud of it than otherwise.

We admit that they *order* things better in France, but not that they *do* them better on the whole. Mere order for the sake of order is wasted in London: if Maurel had bundled all his practical points into a sack, brought it in a cab to the Lyceum, and simply emptied it out anyhow on the table before us, we should have been quite satisfied that he was setting about the job in the shortest and handiest way, though he would no doubt have felt guilty of a monstrous want of consideration for our intellectual convenience.

The matter of the lecture—which was so excellently delivered in French that even I, who am the most maladroit of linguists, understood every word of it—consisted of two points. First, an unanswerable condemnation of the *coup de glotte* method of vocal attack, as to which I need say no more than that I doubt whether any practical singer has ever dreamt of using it systematically, though I suppose everybody uses it unconsciously for special effects. Most advocates of the *coup de glotte* mean nothing more than to discountenance the habit of gasping like a grandfather's clock before striking, as many distinguished amateur vocalists do, instead of attacking their notes cleanly and promptly.

The second point excited more curiosity. Every critic knows to his cost that singers take considerable liberties with the vowels which they have to sing, producing the extreme notes of their compass on any sound that is most convenient, without regard to the word they are supposed to be uttering. Singers usually exhort composers not to set unfavorable vowels to high notes; and composers, who want to be as free as possible and not to hear every high A sounding exactly like every other high A, exhort singers to master the art of producing all the vowel sounds on every note, without reference to its pitch.

Maurel declares that it is impossible to do this effectively without injury to the voice; but instead of defending the customary barefaced resort to the Italian *a* or French *â* for every difficult note, he declares that it is possible to modify every vowel so as to accommodate it exactly to the pitch, and yet to deceive the ear so completely that the modified sound will be accepted as unmodified. This art of vocal prestidigitation—of substituting what he calls a *trompe d'oreille* for the true vowel where the pitch is not favorable to the latter, is one of the things that he proposes to explain in his forthcoming book on the art of singing. The need for it is also the main theme of his Le Chant renové par la Science, a report of his lecture at Milan, just published by Quinzard & Cie, of Paris. This little book at least settles the question of Maurel's literary competence; for his style is as clear as Tyndall's. His conspicuous urbanity and good taste, qualities almost as ineligible in a musical controversialist as in a Cossack or a Turco, are fortunately counter-balanced by a conscientious sincerity; so that his determination not to talk about himself or to criticize his fellow-artists—as I should do most unboundedly if I were in his place—is not likely to lead to the suppression of any material scientific points, however hardly their recognition may bear on living singers and teachers.

Quite another sort of musical demonstration is that of Miss Constance Howard, who has just completed a series of three lectures on Die Meistersinger at Steinway Hall. Miss Howard's plan is to give a verbal description of an act of one of Wagner's music dramas, playing the *motifs* associated with the various points as she comes to them. She then plays the whole act straight through on the pianoforte, declaiming the words as she goes along. This sort of analysis is not altogether novel: Mr Carl Armbruster has sent, from his public lectures and private classes, shoals of carefully grounded Wagnerian amateurs to Bayreuth; but Mr Armbruster has never, as far as I know, limited his demonstrations to what one person, not a singer, can do with a pianoforte and a vocal score alone.

One of the truest practical things Wagner ever said was that the masterpieces of music are kept alive, not at the theatres and concert-halls, but at the pianofortes of lovers of music. It is the young people who hammer away at Meyerbeer and Verdi just as other young people read Dumas and Victor Hugo; who get their knowledge of the Bible from Handel and Bach much as Marlborough got his knowledge of history from Shakespear; who, having learnt from Mozart how to appreciate Molière, arrive at the level of epic poetry and Greek tragedy through Wagner, all with the aid of a Bord pianette and a cheap library of Peters editions: these are the people upon the number of whom in a nation its musical prosperity depends.

It is true that the pianette-Peters culture can only be turned to its full account by those who have opportunities of learning by actual comparison the relation the pianoforte score bears to the complete performance. Indeed, pounding through such scores is, with most players, a process that is only tolerable in so far as it suggests or recalls the very different sound of the orchestra; but the fact remains that nobody, not even a critic, can acquire more than a fragmentary musical culture from public performances alone. You may find a veteran who has heard every soprano from Pasta to Calvé, every tenor from Rubini to Van Dyk, every Don Giovanni from Ambrogetti to Maurel, every pianist from Cramer to Paderewski, and yet he may know less of the great composers than the playgoer who never reads knows of Shakespear. There are critics of ten years' experience in London at present who have only just heard The Niblung's Ring performed for the first time, and who have not yet heard two operas by Gluck or Weber, or more than one pianoforte sonata of Mozart's.

Here, then, we have the importance of a lecture like Miss Howard's. It suggests the true use of the pianoforte as a domestic instrument. At present men refuse to learn their notes because they feel that they will never be able to play well enough to be worth listening to. They might just as well refuse to learn to read because they will never be able to recite or declaim the contents of volumes of poetry well enough to delight an audience. Miss Howard illustrates how people may read tone poetry and music drama to themselves for their own enjoyment and culture. I wish, however, that the music publishers, who have most to gain by the spread of this idea, would help it by abandoning the absurd scale of charges now in force for copyright works.

Two pounds fifteen for vocal scores of the four numbers of The Niblung's Ring; twelve shillings for Verdi's Otello: what possible sense is there in maintaining these prohibitive prices after the cream is taken off the sale? It is not conceivable that the restricted circulation involved by such charges brings in the largest attainable profit to the publishers and owners; whilst its crippling effect on musical culture is obvious. If I were Chancellor of the Exchequer, I would devote the proceeds of the tax by which spirits are made artificially dear to making music artificially cheap. I should buy up all the Wagner, Verdi, and Gounod copyrights, and sell vocal scores at the post offices at a uniform rate of half-a-crown.

The Goring Thomas memorial concert was the smoothest of successes. The platform was a perfect bower of white blooms; the room was crowded, and stuffy enough to gratify the most exacting hater of ventilation; and the inordinately long program was drawn out to the utmost by Mr Villiers Stanford, who appropriately converted the *allegro vivace* of the Cambridge Suite into a dead march by taking it at rather less than half its natural pace. The result was that I was unable to wait for the second act of Nadeshda, which is by far the best piece of work Goring Thomas ever turned out for the stage. Goring Thomas's fame will not, I fear, be very long-lived. He always seemed to be dreaming of other men's music—mostly Frenchmen's; so that he spent his life in elaborating, with remarkable facility and elegance, what Gounod and his disciples had done before. Still, there is a good deal to be done in the world by men who are first-rate hands at their work when once they have been shewn how to do it. Goring Thomas, always a little too much of a voluptuary in music, was more completely Frenchified than an islander of grit ought to have been; but he was no bungler:

his work could not have been much better without becoming really original and powerful.

In speaking lately of the operetta Did you Ring? at the Prince of Wales Theatre, I inadvertently put the librettist in the place of the composer, Mr. Landon Ronald, to whom I tender my excuses.

27 *July* 1892

THE season is practically over now as far as music is concerned; and a very bad season it has been for everyone but myself; for had the General Election been complicated by a really active musical season, I should hardly have been here to tell the tale. As it was, my last visit to the Opera terminated tragically. After contemplating Götterdämmerung for over three mortal hours exactly as I usually contemplate the Calais light during the last half of a rough crossing from Dover, I fled in disorder, leaving Siegfried with about a hundred bars still to live. His death-scene and that of Brynhild would have rewarded me for holding out another half-hour; but the limit of human endurance was reached; and the season ended then and there for me. Looking back over it, I am bound to say that it has been a discouraging one to musicians. I have always watched the people who fill the stalls in St James's Hall when serious musical business is in hand, with certain misgivings as to their sincerity. I have asked myself, Is it love of music that brings them here, or merely social pressure, like that which forces little children into church to listen to sermons that they cannot possibly understand? Obviously this question could only be settled by observing their behavior under circumstances which gave them a valid social excuse for staying away without in the least obliging them to do so if they still craved for music. Such circumstances do not often arise; but they were created this year by the death of the Duke of Clarence. The effect was instantaneous and unmistakeable. The music was still there; but the excuse was provided; smart dressing was out of the question; and the audiences vanished.

I do not see how that fact is to be got over. It was sufficiently depressing to have to admit, at the best of times, that St James's Hall sufficed for the morsel of first-rate music required by the largest and richest city in the world; but when even this limited demand turns out to be heavily adulterated with hypocrisy and millinery, I am half driven to drop the subject altogether. We are living, artistically speaking, in a hovel; and yet I am expected to agitate about the condition of the dome.

Undoubtedly the great musical event of 1892 has been the performance in London of Wagner's Niblung's Ring, after an interval of ten years. Das Rheingold, composed thirty-eight years ago, and first performed twenty-three years ago at Munich; Die Walküre, composed thirty-six years ago, and first performed, also at Munich, twenty-two years ago; Siegfried and Götterdämmerung, finished respectively twenty-three and twenty-two years ago, and first performed sixteen years ago at Bayreuth: London has just heard these world-famous works for the *second* time, not as part of the regular repertory of an English opera house, but, as before, by a German company imported for the occasion.

And our new English Opera House, built last year, is lying there, a failure so far, nobody knowing whether it will be pulled down, or turned into a music-hall, or utilized as a carriage repository, like the old Queen's Theatre in Long Acre. I know these dates; I remember these facts; I understand the value of the Manchester orchestra, which we sent back home the other day as not worth its travelling expenses to us. And I ask any reasonable person whether I can be expected to hurrah, and shake hands, and drink healths, and beam, and congratulate, and pay compliments over a state of things which if it existed in the cotton trade would raise a general alarm of national bankruptcy.

I am half inclined to doubt whether I am in my right mind when I see everybody so unconcerned and satisfied merely because Madame Calvé has touched them with her beautiful singing, or because Die Walküre, which I have known almost by heart for years, cuts and all, has thrown its spell on them for the first time. I remember one day visiting a relative of mine who had shewn a considerable power, rather rare in the family, of making money. His doctors had persuaded him strongly to leave his work, and had been even more urgent with his people to attend closely to him. When I called on him in the course of his vacation, he took me aside into the window, and asked me whether I saw those rooms, and the remains of the meal he had just risen from. I said I did. He then informed me in a whisper that his wife was mad, that they had not a penny in the world to pay for all these costly things, that they were stark ruined. I have been wondering these six weeks whether I have inherited his malady—whether the pressure of the season and the election have not made me imagine disaster and failure whilst the reality is that we are passing through a climax of unexampled musical prosperity. If so, I hope the impresarios and concert agents will come forward with their balance-sheets, and have me removed at once to an asylum.

Still, it is considerably to the credit of this season that it has seen the production of Mr Isidore de Lara's Light of Asia, Mr Bemberg's Elaine, Mr George Fox's Nydia, and Signor Mascagni's L'Amico Fritz. The old subscription night routine, with its scratch performances of the worn-out Italian repertory, has all but vanished; and I should be unspeakably grateful for that if I did not know that what Burke said of politics is true also of criticism: there is no room for gratitude in it. And if there were, the gratitude would be due to me, who have so ruthlessly hunted down the old repertory, with its perfunctory Trovatores and slip-shod Traviatas.

This year we have had new works tried and old works let alone to an unprecedented degree. We have also had an opportunity of learning something from the German company. The orchestra played Wagner just as the Manchester band plays Berlioz: it knew the works instead of merely spelling through them at sight in the London fashion; and everybody must have been struck with the difference this made, even when the familiarity of the orchestra degenerated into vulgarity. Among the leading artists the one whose success is likely to have the greatest influence is undoubtedly Alvary. I do not mean that Alvary was the member of the company who had the largest share of direct natural gifts for the stage. In that case, his success would have been no more remarkable than that of Frau Klafsky, Fräulein Heink, or Lieban.

Van Dyk's eminence as a tenor is explained at once by his exuberant force and brilliancy, as Jean de Reszke's is by his romantic grace and distinction both of voice and person. Put either of them into a group of half a dozen barristers, and you would single them out at a glance as confidently as you would single out Salvini. Put Alvary there in his habit as he lives off the stage, and you would accept him without suspicion as a sufficiently barristeristic person, well set up, but with no more of Siegfried about him than there would be of Hamlet about Mr Beerbohm Tree under the same circumstances. His voice is serviceable, but by no means beautiful; and in plucking Nothung from the Branstock, or forging it anew on Mime's anvil, he has no superfluity of physical power with which to exult and play the Titan. And yet he held the attention and interest of the house whenever he was on the stage, and made a smart Loki, a pathetic Siegmund, and a remarkably handsome and picturesque Siegfried.

Wilkes, who was one of the ugliest of mortals, used to boast that he was only quarter of an hour behind the handsomest man in Europe; and I can imagine Alvary boasting that, with nothing exceptional to help him except his brains, he could keep pace all through Der Ring with Van Dyk or De Reszke, perhaps falling five minutes behind the one in shouting over the sledge-hammer, and behind the other in singing Winterstürme wichen dem Wonnemund, but regaining his ground at other points, and holding his audience to the end as successfully as either of them. He has proved to us that as soon as the development of opera into genuine music drama makes the lyric stage attractive to clever and cultivated men, we shall no longer be dependent on prodigies.

Possibly some of my readers may prefer prodigies, thinking, no doubt, that they are all De Reszkes and Van Dyks; but if they had seen as much as I have of the results of picking up any Italian porter, or trooper, or gondolier, or ice-barrow costermonger who can shout a high C; thrusting him into heroic rôles; and sending him roaring round the world to pass in every capital over the prostrate body of lyric drama like a steam roller with a powerful whistle, they would understand the immense value I attach to the competition of artists like Alvary, who could not retain his place on the stage at all if he had nothing but his lungs to recommend him. The career is now opening to the talented; and the demand for artists of the Alvary type will increase with the number of our music dramas.

For you must not for a moment suppose that Wagner is going to be an isolated phenomenon in art. The peasant who, on hearing of Wordsworth's death, said he supposed his son would carry on the business, was not half such a fool as the man who imagines that the list of Bayreuth dramas closed with the death of Wagner. We have produced our Æschylus: our Sophocles and Aristophanes have yet to come; and very handsomely our Wagnerians will abuse them when they do come for violating the classic traditions of Wagner, and dispensing with his continual melody, his careful regard for form, and his effective but simple and quiet scoring.

3 *August* 1892

A LONG string of mishaps prevented me from hearing Mr Bemberg's Elaine until last Saturday week, when the second act somehow got omitted. The oversight passed unnoticed, however; and I cannot say that I was greatly disappointed: indeed, I should not have mentioned the circumstance if it did not form a practical criticism of the opera as distinct from its presentation, with which I shall, by your leave, not concern myself. Mr Bemberg is no English composer, but rather a music-weaver who, having served an apprenticeship to Gounod, and mastered his method of working, now sets up in business for himself. In Elaine we have the well-known Gounod fabric turned out in lengths like the best sort of imitation Persian carpet, the potential supply being practically unlimited.

There is one ballad, L'Amour chaste comme la flamme, which would probably never have been written if Gounod had not supplied the pattern in Mireille, but which is certainly a charming elaboration of the master's suggestions. Mind, I do not hurl Mr Bemberg's want of originality at him as a reproach. One of the greatest artists the world has ever seen began in this very way. Raphael mastered Perugino's style before he developed his own. Mr Bemberg may yet leave Gounod as far behind as Raphael left Perugino. But there are no signs of his doing so yet.

I wonder how soon strong men in England will begin to take to musical composition. It cannot be said that the national genius is for the genteel, the sentimental, the elegant, the superficial. When I am asked to name a composer who is to England what Wagner is to Germany, I do not cite our elderly imitators of Spohr and Mendelssohn, or our youthful imitators of Gounod: I have to go back to Henry Purcell, whose Yorkshire Feast suggests that if he were alive today he might give us an English equivalent to Die Meistersinger.

Again, in what I may call epic or dramatic painting, I do not refer the inquiring foreigner to Mr Frank Dicksee, Mr Herbert Schmalz, Sir Noel Paton, or even Sir Frederick Leighton, as typical English painters: I send them to Mr Ford Madox Brown. And I should certainly never dream of holding up Tennyson's poetry as the verse-mirror of the English spirit. It seems to me quite obvious that if our popular art was really the expression of the national character, England would long ago have been annexed as a convenient coaling station by Portugal. Fortunately, Englishmen take their business and their politics very differently from their art. Art in England is regarded as a huge confectionary department, where sweets are made for the eye and ear just as they are made for the palate in the ordinary "tuck-shop."

There is a general notion that painting tastes better before dinner, and music after it; but neither is supposed to be in the least nutritious. Too great a regard for them is held to be the mark of a weak character, or, in cases like those of Ruskin and Morris, of derangement due to genius. Under these circumstances we are kept well supplied with pretty things; but if we want really national music-dramas we shall have to take art seriously, or else wait for the advent of a genius big enough and strong enough to set himself against us all and cram his ideas down our throats, whether we like them or not.

I am obliged to Elaine for one thing in particular: it reconciled me to Madame Melba, who is to all intents and purposes a new artist this year. I do not mind confessing now that I used not to like her. Whilst recognizing the perfection of her merely musical faculty, I thought her hard, shallow, self-sufficient, and altogether unsympathetic. Further, she embarrassed me as a critic; since, though I was utterly dissatisfied with her performances, I had nothing to allege against them; for you really cannot take exception to an artist merely because her temperament does not happen to be sympathetic with yours.

This year, however, I find Madame Melba transfigured, awakened, no longer to be identified by the old descriptions —in sum, with her heart, which before acted only on her circulation, now acting on her singing and giving it a charm which it never had before. The change has completely altered her position: from being merely a brilliant singer, she has become a dramatic soprano of whom the best class of work may be expected.

A little book on Wagner, just published by Messrs Kegan Paul & Co., should be bound up with every library copy of the late Ferdinand Praeger's very entertaining Wagner as I Knew Him. Mr Ashton Ellis's retort to Wagner as I Knew Him is practically, "Yes; but you didn't know him." Praeger was never at any time able to take in more of Wagner than his natural size enabled him to hold, which was somewhat less than the whole man; and their acquaintanceship began rather later than Praeger, when at the height of his biographic fervor, quite realized.

At any rate, Mr Ellis shews that in the Dresden rising in 1849 Wagner, though he took his share of public duty by managing the business of escorting convoys into the town, and "conducting" the signalling, was not, like Bakunin, what the Fenians used to call a "head centre" in the affair. The sensational incident of the woman falling shot, and Wagner heading a charge on the Prussian soldiers and capturing them, turns out to be just about as true as might have been expected: that is to say, the woman was not shot; the soldiers were not captured; and Wagner was not present; but the story is otherwise founded on fact. Mr Ellis straightens out the whole narrative very completely, and explains, for the benefit of those persons who have not the revolutionary temperament, how the German sovereigns, unable to conceive how monarchy could in the nature of things be constitutionally limited, forced all the best-informed and most public-spirited of their subjects to resist them.

To me Wagner's conduct needs no apology, since it is plain that every man who is not a Pangloss is bound to be in a state of incessant revolutionary activity all his life long if he wishes to leave things better than he finds them. However, there are unaccountable people who think otherwise; and to them I recommend Mr Ellis's Vindication. Indeed, I recommend it to all English Wagnerians, who already owe more to its author than to any other man, except perhaps Mr

Dannreuther. And when Mr Ellis's translation of Wagner's prose works, which has now reached the 1851 Mittheilung an meine Freunde, is complete, even Mr Dannreuther's claims must give way to those of the editor of The Meister.

28 *September* 1892

THE light operas which have been running for some time past at the Lyric and Trafalgar Square theatres did not succeed in moving me to break the autumn silence on their account. Cigarette is a work of uncertain *genre*, melodramatic and farcical in alternate episodes, except during one desperately melancholy moment in the second act, when Messrs Collette and Evelyn have to sing a duet with chorus, intended to be comic, but void to a quite stupefying degree of any passable nonsense or fun, not to say sense or humor. I must say that I like opera-manufacturers to make up their minds as to the plane they are going to work on, and stick to it. The Marquis de Portale, disowning and cursing his son (who wants to marry for love) in a ranting exit speech of the best Wardour Street workmanship, is all very well in his way; and there is, perhaps, a place in the world for recruits comically labelled Benzoline and Nicotine, though I stipulate that the place shall not be in my neighborhood. Again, there is no general objection to church scenes with sacred music sung behind the scenes to the pealing of the solemn American organ. Nor do these exclude the possibility of Gaiety trios with step-dance refrains. But when the Marquis de Portale and Benzoline, the anthems and the step-dances, jostle one another on the same stage on the same evening, the effect to my taste, is unseemly. And that is what occurs in Cigarette. Its aberrations into commonplace melodrama on the one hand, and unsuccessful burlesque on the other, may harmlessly divert our light-opera audiences, which seem to me artistically less intelligent and less cultivated than even the big oratorio audiences at the Albert Hall and Crystal Palace; but they are not worth the powder and shot of serious criticism. The only member of the cast whose performance suggested any comment was Miss Florence Bankhardt, who has apparently had a training as a dancer, and is therefore in a better position than the ordinary comic-opera prima donna who has had no training at all. Her playing as Cigarette was rather spoiled on the first night by restlessness and exaggeration; but if she has sufficient instinct for her profession to tranquillize her abundant energy and turn it to account in pursuit of softness and ease of style, there is no reason why she should not hold her own in parts like Cigarette.

The Wedding Eve, at the Trafalgar, is at least homogeneous in its triviality. It is much more smartly and tastefully mounted than Cigarette; and the leading parts are both better and better cast. Mr Tapley, whose powers as a tenor singer enabled him to gain a prominent position when he was still rather a rough diamond as to his carriage and diction, has now polished himself into one of the best artists in his line in London, and that, too, without losing the freshness and natural humor which put him on easy terms with his audiences from the first. Miss Decima Moore gets on very prettily in the part of Yvonette, her gift of good looks, good manners, facility, and tact carrying her through in spite of an occasional pettiness of touch and emptiness of play which shew how far she is from having attained the skill and breadth of style which mark the fully accomplished artist. The customary humors of comic opera abounded in the portion of The Wedding Eve which I witnessed; and there was no lack of choral young ladies, all dressed and wigged and complexioned alike, according to operatic custom, which seems to me to be stupid and thoughtless on this point. I would fine a chorus-singer half a crown for looking like any other chorus-singer. For the rest, the management of the new theatre is evidently liberal and tasty—if I may use that revolting expression for want of a substitute that will not overshoot the mark. Of the music of both Cigarette and The Wedding Eve I need say nothing except that it is as neat and plausible as anything in the shop windows of Bond Street. Mr Haydn Parry has supplied the score of the former, and M. Toulmouche that of the latter. Some dances in The Wedding Eve are by "Yvolde," a voluminous composer whose aliases are too numerous for mention here.

To a superficial person it may seem that my objection to a mixture of *genres* in opera has been most signally exploded by the huge success of Haddon Hall at the Savoy last Saturday. I do not admit this for a moment. I contend that Savoy opera is a *genre* in itself; and that Haddon Hall is the highest and most consistent expression it has yet attained. This result is due to the critical insight of Mr Grundy. He is evidently a frequenter of Covent Garden; for he has discovered that what Italian opera desperately lacks is the classic element of comic relief. He has sat out the last acts of Lucia, and has felt, as I so often have myself, that what was wanted there was a comic Highlander with a fling, and a burlesque chorus to enliven the precepts of Raimondo.

He has then gone to the Savoy, and has seen that there, too, relief was wanted—sentimental relief generally, but anyhow relief from Mr Gilbert, whose great fault was that he began and ended with himself, and gave no really congenial opportunities to the management and the composer. He exploited their unrivalled *savoir faire* to his head's content; but he starved their genius, possibly because he did not give them credit for possessing any.

Now The Basoche and Haddon Hall prove that Mr and Mrs D'Oyly Carte have unmistakeable genius for management: their stage pictures are as recognizable by the style alone as a picture by Watteau or Monticelli. You do not catch them spending ten guineas on two-penn'orth of show: they are at once munificent and economical, getting their full pound of beauty out of every yard of costly stuff on the stage. As to Sir Arthur Sullivan, he is certainly not a dramatic composer; but he has over and over again proved that in the sort of descriptive ballad which touches on the dramatic his gift is as genuine as that of Schubert or Loewe. In this province he excites a feeling which is as different as possible from the cynical admiration of his adroitness, his tact, his wit, and his professional dexterity, which is all that could ever be evoked by his settings of Mr Gilbert's aridly fanciful lyrics, whether for the stage or the drawing-room.

All these observations have evidently been made by Mr Grundy, who has accordingly devised a unique entertainment, consisting of a series of charming stage-pictures which at once put you in the mood to listen to episode after episode of descriptive ballad music, full of unforced feeling, and tenderly handled down to the minutest detail of their skilful and finished workmanship. After each of these episodes you are let down into indulgent boredom during a brief would-be dramatic number, in which the principals are consciously ridiculous, and the music suggestive of nothing but a storm in a tin pot. And then, just as you are beginning to feel dull and apprehensive of failure, comes the comic relief—the unspeakably outrageous but unspeakably welcome comic relief. The patter song which Mr Kenningham suddenly fired into the house from a masked battery in the form of a futile "dramatic" trio in the first act, produced, by its mere unexpectedness and contrast, an effect beyond the reach of Mr Grossmith.

Later on, the business of Mr Rutland Barrington and the comic Puritans, who are addicted to Stage Socialism (a very fearful variety), created uproarious merriment; and if Mr Rutland Barrington's elaborate japes on the land question fell somewhat flat, it was probably not so much because the joke was at the expense of the audience as because everybody had got accustomed during the late general election to hear better and fresher fun made out of the subject at every political meeting throughout the country. In the second act the comic business was less happy. The act began with it; so that it did not take the form of "relief"; and the hopes raised by the entrance of Mr Denny in a kilt, playing the bagpipes, were speedily dashed by the discovery that his Scotch dialect was spurious, and that Mr Grundy's treatment of the tempting theme of Social Purityism was cheap and witless, the duet, If we but had our way, being the least successful comic number in the opera.

It is always a mistake to undervalue our friend the enemy; and Mr Grundy had better recognize that unless his social satires are at least as smart as Mr Hugh Price Hughes's sermons, Mr Hughes will get the better of him. The real relief in this act occurs when Sir Arthur Sullivan takes up the running with his romantic setting of the elopement scene as a quartet, or rather as a descriptive ballad for four voices. (By the way, in the previous comic trio Hoity toity, the composer has reproduced the exact movement of For a British tar is a soaring soul from Pinafore, the notes alone being altered.) The following few minutes, during which the stage remains a black void, with hammer-and-tongs storm music and patent lightning flashes recurring with unerring precision in the same four spots, is merely an effective dodge to intensify the brilliancy of the ensuing ballroom scene, which is a Cartesian triumph.

It was the last act, however, which swept away all doubts as to the popular success of the opera. First, a sentimental duet for Mr Green and Miss Brandram brought down the house; and then the comic business became irresistible. A song for Mr Rutland Barrington, with a general dance in which he joins after a painful struggle with his conscience, was none the less triply encored because much the same thing had been seen in The Vicar of Bray. Yet it was no sooner over than it was eclipsed by the entry of Mr Denny, in breeks, to sing an absurdly funny musical burlesque of Auld Lang Syne, and to dance, and dance again, and yet again—the encores seemed endless—a Highland fling, in which he was seconded with remarkable grace and *élan* by Miss Nita Cole. All the critics in the house exclaimed as one man that if something of this sort could be done at Covent Garden with the last act of La Favorita, Il Trovatore, etc.,

etc., their lives would be indefinitely prolonged—which, by the bye, is an argument against the innovation.

Of the cast of established favorites I need say little more than that they fully sustained their reputations. Miss Lucile Hill's part is more difficult and less effective than that which she had in The Basoche, but her ability is no less conspicuous. Mr Courtice Pounds, costumed as a harmony in strawberries-and-cream, was nervously screwed up to the tenseness of a compressed spiral spring, in which condition he declared, with convulsive elocution, that Too-Wen'ty cousins should not interrupt his lovemaking. He also took his high notes flat; expressed his emotions facially in a manner extremely disconcerting to the spectators; and generally did himself injustice. These, however, were clearly mere first-night aberrations, the effect of an unblunted artistic sensitiveness; and he is no doubt by this time as good a John Manners as could be desired.

Mr. Rutland Barrington was capital, though his compulsory lapses into melodrama tried the gravity of the audience as severely as they tried his own. If at such moments he were allowed to sing in Italian, the effect would be far finer. It only remains to warn the matter-of-fact theatre-goer that from the hour when, at the beginning of the piece, Sir George Vernon points to the sixteenth-century façade of Hadden Hall, and remarks that it "smiled before the Conquest," to the final happy moment when Charles I, having beheaded Cromwell in 1680, or thereabout, restores the property to the evicted parent of the heroine, Haddon Hall, in history, costume, logic, and everything else of the kind, is perfectly impossible.

5 October 1892

THE recent death of Trebelli must not pass without a word of comment in this column, more especially as so many of the obituary notices contain descriptions of her singing which are purely imaginary. In her best days her voice was extraordinarily rich in the middle. Her tribute to Bella Venezia in the opening chorus of Lucrezia Borgia:

Men di sue notti e limpido
D'ogn' altro cielo il giorno,

sounded better than a ripe plum tastes, though the phrase lies round the middle of the treble stave, altogether above the point at which ordinary singers have to leave their chest register, on pain of displacing and ruining their voices. She produced contralto effects in mezzo-soprano and transposed soprano parts more successfully than in contralto parts, in one of which—Amneris, in Aïda—she ground her lower notes so unmercifully for the sake of "dramatic effect" that their old rich purple-velvety quality vanished irrecoverably.

This was one of many exploits of hers which seemed to prove her natural judgment much inferior to her cultivated taste; but I am afraid the truth was that the public were so obtuse to her finest qualities as an artist, and so appreciative of claptrap, that she either lost faith in herself at times, or else gave up the struggle with the public in despair. At Her Majesty's, as Cherubino or Zerlina, she would sing Voi che sapete, or Batti, batti, transposed, but without a note altered or a phrase vulgarized, only to find herself written of with much less enthusiasm than Pauline Lucca at Covent Garden, whose treatment of Mozart was—well, I have spent five minutes in trying to find an epithet both adequate and decorous, without success. On the other hand, when, as Maffio Orsini, she turned the brindisi into a bad joke by that never-to-be-forgotten shake of hers, which was certainly the very worst shake ever heard in an opera-house (it used to get sharper and sharper by perceptible jerks), she was encored and applauded to the echo. She liked Maffio, as she liked Siebel, Urbain, Arsaces, and all parts which freed her from the tyranny of the petticoat, of which, like most sensible women, she was impatient. She never seemed to lose her fresh enjoyment of these parts.

Once, happening to be behind the scenes at the end of the prologue to Lucrezia, I saw her, the moment the curtain fell, throw herself in a transport of excitement into the arms of Titiens, though the two had played the scene together often enough to make it the most hackeneyed piece of business in the world to them. Trebelli was at her best in the most refined and quiet class of work. It is quite a mistake to suppose that she fell short as an oratorio singer. I have never heard her singing of He shall feed His flock surpassed: her diction alone put many of her English colleagues to shame. Her Cherubino, her Zerlina, and her Rezia in Oberon were criticism-proof. Her Carmen was, vocally, the most finished we have heard. In the tragic, passionate contralto parts in Verdi's operas she was not good: she played them out of imaginative ambition, just as she sang such things as Offenbach's C'est l'Espagne out of high spirits; but the result was commonplace and, by contrast with her fine Mozartean work, vulgar.

Unlike her daughter, she was deficient in agility of vocal execution, and could not manage a shake. She had also a certain mannerism which affected her intonation, and made her one of the many great artists who are always the piquant shadow of a shade out of tune—flat, as I judged it; though I confess that in very minute dissonances I cannot tell flat from sharp. She was, I should say, a much more cultivated musician than most of her colleagues; and she was an eminently good-looking woman, with a ready smile that did full justice to her teeth. The collapse of the old régime at the opera caused the stage to leave her long before she was ready to leave the stage; and she was by no means worn out as a singer when physical infirmity, produced by a paralytic stroke which fell on her some years ago, created the vacancy which remained unfilled until Giulia Ravogli came.

Criticism, of course, knows no gratitude and no regret; but I must say that if all the artists of the Titiens epoch had been as good as Trebelli, my occasional references to that dark age would be much less ferocious than they generally are.

Of the late Emil Behnke I knew just enough to be able

to say that his death is a considerable loss to teachers-in-training, speakers, and singers who find themselves stopped by a difficulty which they cannot get round. He was an exceedingly good demonstrator with the laryngoscope, and would shew you exactly what he wanted done instead of making more or less vague suggestions to your imagination. His scorn of the professors who tell you to sing from the head, or the throat, or the chest, or to pin your voice to your hard palate, was immense: he was justly proud of his ability to name with the exactitude of a watchmaker the movement and action he wished you to produce. He knew a great deal about the physical act of voice production; and his principal achievements were the relief of experienced singers from disabilities which their ordinary training had not overcome (or had created), and his cures of stammering.

Everybody who went to him learnt something, though nobody learnt everything from him; and even those who knew beforehand what he demonstrated to them with the laryngoscope knew it much better afterwards. He was always keenly interested in himself and his work, and would talk about it, rush into controversies about it, and denounce the ordinary commercial singing-master up hill and down dale with unabated freshness at an age which finds most professional men stale routineers. Needless to add, he was not a popular character in academic circles. As to his artistic capacity, I confess I had and have my doubts about it. Besides his scientific interest in voice production, he undoubtedly had a strong practical turn, and hated to hear voices spoiled or wasted or only half turned to account. He wanted to have every throat in first-rate working order.

But whether he had that passion for perfect beauty of vocal tone and perfect dignity and expressiveness of delivery in singing which is the supreme attribute of the greatest singers and teachers of singing, I do not know, though I guess with come confidence that he had little more than the ordinary appetite for them. He once "sang" the notes of the common chord for me when shewing me the action of lifting the soft palate. He then got me to "sing" the same notes whilst he observed that action in me. I use the inverted commas because laryngoscopic vocalism can only be called singing by courtesy: as a matter of fact we simply bawled the syllable "Haw" at one another in a manner which would have created the utmost consternation in the theatre or on the platform.

I remember being struck by the fact that though he seemed interested by my success in managing my soft palate, he did not make any comment on the extreme unloveliness of the noise with which I had responded to his invitation to sing, which he had not qualified by any allusion to the impossibility of my complying in the artistic sense under such conditions. The incident by itself proved nothing; but it put me on the track of further observations, which finally left me under the impression (possibly a mistaken one) that his authority was limited to the physical acts involved by ordinary voice production, and did not extend even to the modifications of those acts which have no reasons for their existence except purely artistic ones.

For instance, he had made an elaborate study of breathing, and could teach people to use their diaphragms; but I once heard a pupil of his who had her diaphragm under perfect control, and who yet blew away her voice in the most ineffective way as she sang, because she had not been taught to acquire that peculiar steadying and economizing of the air column which is the first condition of beauty of tone in singing. I am therefore sceptical as to Behnke's having ever trained a complete artistic singer or speaker; though many singers and speakers learnt a good deal from him. I was so convinced on the latter point that at the moment of his death I had arranged with him to take in hand a class of about twenty political speakers, some of whom had already acquired sufficient skill and experience to enable them to teach an ordinary elocution professor his business.

Perhaps the most important thing to make known about Behnke is, that though he elected to take his differences with the majority fighting instead of lying down, and so made enemies of many whose countenance is supposed to be indispensable to musical success, he prospered, as far as I am able to ascertain, quite as well as his more compliant rivals. Although his terms were higher than any but first-rate teachers can venture to ask in these days of Guildhall Schools and Royal Colleges, he was overworked. His Voice Training Exercises sold at the rate of over eight thousand copies a year; and his Mechanism of the Human Voice got into a seventh edition, whilst the better advertised book which he wrote in collaboration with Dr Lennox-Browne nearly doubled that record.

It may be, of course, that London, according to its custom with professional men, gave with one hand and took back with the other, and that all the return he got for his labor over and above his bare subsistence was the privilege of collecting money for his landlord, his servants, his tradesmen, and so forth. But this is the common lot of the orthodox and the heterodox alike. My point is that he had not to pay any more for his self-respect than less courageous men have to pay for being humbugs and nonentities. It is a mistake to be too much afraid of London merely because it is much stronger and much stupider than you are, just as it is a mistake to be too much afraid of a horse on the same ground. Behnke, I imagine, was shrewd and resolute enough to know this.

His death is a real loss; for on his weak side (as I judge him) he at least did no mischief, whilst on his strong side he undid a great deal. Besides, he ventilated his profession, which is, if I may say so in a whisper, rather a stuffy one.

12 *October* 1892

NOW that we have five comic operas running, London perhaps feels satisfied. I, for one, do not want any more. Sufficient for me the privilege of living in the greatest city in the world, with five comic operas within easy reach, and not a symphony to be heard for love or money. However, it is a poor heart that never rejoices; and I have been doing my best to rejoice at the Royalty over The Baroness, and at the Lyric over Incognita. To Incognita especially I must be civil; for is it not financed by that great syndicate which has set about buying up the London press as the Viennese press has been bought up? Do not expect outspoken criticism from me in such days as these: I cannot afford it: I must look to the future like other journalists. Therefore the utmost I dare say against Incognita is that the more you see of it the less you like it, because the first act is better than the second, and the second much better than the third, which produces the effect of being the first act of some other comic opera. The piece has a plot turning upon some maze of Portuguese diplomacy; but I speedily lost my way in it, and made no attempt to extricate myself, though I was conscious of its boring me slightly towards the end of the performance. The music is quite Lecocquian: that is to say, it is cleverly scored, rises occasionally to the level of a really graceful chansonette, is mechanically vigorous in the finals, and calculatedly spirited in the frequent Offenbachian rallies, for which the old quadrille and galop prescription has been compounded with the old remorseless vulgarity. It is also Lecocquian in the speedy running dry of its thin fountain of natural grace and piquancy, and the eking out of the supply with machine-made *bouffe* music more and more as the opera proceeds. This remark does not apply to the third act, which is not by Lecocq at all, but by Mr Bunning, who, if I recollect aright, recently had a most tremendous tragic scena performed at the Crystal Palace; by Mr. Hamilton Clarke; and by the composer who conceals his identity under the exasperating name of Yvolde. I may add that the pretty stage pictures of the first act degenerate into the pecuniary garishness of the second in sympathy with the degeneration of the music; and with this I abandon all attempt at formal criticism, and proceed to discuss the affair at random. To begin with Miss Sedohr Rhodes, she made all the usual American mistakes. First, by a well-worked battery of puff, she led us to expect so much from her that an angel from the spheres would have disappointed us; and then she arranged an elaborate handing up of floral trophies across the footlights, in spite of the repeatedly proved fact that this particular method of manufacturing a success invariably puts up the back of an English audience. I have never seen the American flower show turned to good account by any prima donna except Miss Macintyre. One evening at Covent Garden, when she was playing Micaela to the Carmen of an American *débutante*, the two ladies appeared before the curtain simultaneously; and the contractor's men set to work at once to deliver bouquets and wreaths. Carmen, overwhelmed with innocent surprise at this spontaneous tribute from the British public, gracefully offered a nosegay to Micaela, who quietly turned her back and walked off the stage amid signs of thorough and general approval which ought to have settled the question of flowers or no flowers for all future American prima donnas. On Thursday night Miss Rhodes, though she entirely failed to make herself first favorite on the merits of her performance, got so overloaded with trophies that she had to ask Mr Wallace Brownlow to carry the last basket for her. He, being good-natured, did not there and then inform her publicly that he was not her florist's porter; but if he had done so he would, I imagine, have had the entire support of the house. The puffs and the flowers were the more ill-judged in Miss Rhodes's case because she has exactly that degree of talent which playgoers, with cheap generosity, like to discover and encourage when it is modestly and friendlessly presented to them, whereas if it be thrust pretentiously upon them as first-rate, they delight in taking it down a peg. When Miss Rhodes stepped out of her sedan chair in the first act she was for a few moments a complete success; for, with her delicate skin, fine contours, slender fragile figure, small hands and feet, and perfect dress, she was sufficiently near the perfection of the ladylike ideal of beauty. Unfortunately, it presently appeared that she not only looked like a Court beauty, but sang like one. Her voice, thin, and with a flexibility which is only a quality of its fault, could not be fitted by her warmest admirer with any stronger adjective than prettyish. In order to substantiate her pretentions as a vocalist she had to attempt a florid vocal waltz which was much too difficult for her, and which was only encored from a chivalrous desire to console her for the opposition of a party of malcontents who were, I must say, musically in the right, though they would have done wiselier to have kept silent. Her dancing, again, was rather pretty, but not extraordinary. She speaks in the American dialect, which I do not at all dislike; but her diction, though passable, has all the amateurish deficiency in force and style which we tolerate so weakly in our operatic prima donnas. On the other hand, the assurance with which she carried off her part in spite of her want of technical grip, and the courage with which she faced the opposition from the gallery, shewed that she is not lacking in force of character. I therefore conclude that she will improve with experience up to a certain point. To pass that point she will require something of the genius for her profession which is displayed so liberally by Miss Jenoure, who quite fulfilled the promise of her performance in The Mountebanks. Her singing, from the purely musical point of view, is commonplace enough; but her dancing and pantomime are capital. Mr Wallace Brownlow made a very decided hit as the hero. He is a vigorous and handsome young man of the type which Kemble made fashionable in "the palmy days"; his voice is a genuine baritone, of good tone all over his range; he sings with fire and feeling, without any suicidal shouting; and he has abundant freshness, virility, humor, and activity. What he lacks is training in speech and movement: he is always off his balance, and is therefore only comfortable when he is hard at work at some stage business or other; and his diction is rough and ready, audible and intelligible certainly, but no more artistic than the diction of the Stock Exchange. Happily, these are eminently remediable faults; and when they are vanquished, Mr Haydn Coffin will have a rival all the more formidable because of the wide difference of style between them. The tenor is Mr John Childs, whose vigorous B flat will be remembered by the patrons of Carl Rosa. It is still in stentorian condition; and though Mr Childs has a strong provincial tendency to bawl occasionally (if he will pardon the expression) and to concern himself very little about his tone and style when using the middle of his voice, the encore he won for the catching soldier's song in the first act was the heartiest of the evening. The opera is so strongly fortified by a squadron of comedians of established drollery and popularity that a great deal of thin and childish stuff becomes amusing in their hands. Mr Monkhouse, who has gained remarkably within the last two years in quietude and refinement of play without losing an inch of the breadth of his humor, was seconded by Miss Susie Vaughan in a stale and odious duenna part which she contrived to make not only bearable, but for the most part genuinely funny. The attempt to double the harlequinade in the third act by the introduction of a second comic king (Mr Fred Kaye) and a second comic old woman (Miss Victor) was not a success. Mr Kaye was certainly laughable in his surpassingly silly character; but Miss Victor, who had really no function in the piece at all, and had been engaged solely that she might repeat the vulgar business of her part in Miss Decima—a part entirely unworthy of her—cannot be congratulated this time. The whole third act, however, is such a desperate and obvious makeshift that it would be mere affectation not to accept it, with its serpentine dance, pastoral symphony with transformation scene, and comic turns for Mr Monkhouse as a gipsy-girl, etc., as a brilliant variety entertainment. The band is good, as it usually is at the Lyric; and the chorus, though not up to the Savoy level of refinement, would pass with credit if some of the men could be induced to refrain from shouting. Finally, let me say that the Lord Chamberlain, by licensing the second act of Miss Decima has completely cleared himself of all suspicion of Puritanical intolerance. When I saw the audience laughing at the spectacle of a father, in nightcap and bedgown, chuckling as he listened at the door of his daughter's bridal chamber, I could not help feeling how vast an advance we had made since last year, when all London was supposed to have shuddered with horror at the wickedness of that scene in Ibsen's Ghosts, where the mother in the drawing room overhears her son kissing the housemaid in the dining room.

Mr Cotsford Dick's Baroness, at the Royalty, is not so well staged as Incognita, the management having evidently been compelled to accept what recruits they could get for the rank and file in the face of a heavy competition. On the whole, they have made the best of their circumstances; and the opera gets a tolerable chance. The book, which begins as a burlesque of King Lear, and proceeds on the lines of the Who's who? pattern of farce, is funny enough, especially in the Turkish-bath scene, until the third act, in which the tangled threads of the plot are unravelled in a rather butter-fingered way. The fact is, Mr Cotsford Dick, who is his own librettist, takes matters too easily and genially to turn out distinguished work; but he always manages to keep on pleasant terms with his audience. The music is lively and pretty, with plenty of Cotsford-Dickian ballads, and much unblushing borrowings from The Mikado and Trial by Jury, not to mention a vocal waltz of which the honors are divided between Gounod and Weber. The verses I need not describe, as Mr Dick's powers in that field are familiar to all my readers. The cast has been selected with a view to having the music sung rather than to having the opera played. Miss Giglio, who makes a considerable display as a vocalist, and is evidently quite conscious of being able to sing the heads off most comic-opera prima donnas, hardly seems to know that speech and action on the stage are arts not a whit less important and less difficult than fluent vocalization. Mr William Foxon, too, though rather above the usual stage mark as a tenor singer, is, to speak plainly, such a stick that it is difficult to believe that he has ever seriously studied and practised the business of the stage with a competent instructor. The principal tenor, Mr Charles Conyers, is an agreeably robust and good-looking young gentleman, no great artist dramatically, but a pleasant singer of ballads. Mr Magrath, familiar to us as the old knight in Cosi fan tutti and the venerable barber of Bagdad in Cornelius's opera, flashes out in The Baroness as a dark-eyed handsome youth who might serve the President of the Royal Academy as a model for a young Italian noble. He was much more nervous over this comparatively trivial job than he shewed himself in his former far more difficult exploits; and his air of melodramatic exaggeration was not always humorously intentional: there was a touch in it of that traditional penny-plain-and-twopence-colored style which has left so many promising young artists fit for nothing better than the boundless absurdities and artistic shams of "English Opera" in the provinces. His drinking song in the last act was loudly applauded; but it would have been a much greater success if it had been sung with the easy self-possession of a gentleman at a ball, and not with the heroic stress of John of Leyden's Versez in the last act of Le Prophète. I take Mr Magrath the more specially to task on this point because he has improved in every other respect, and is likely to have an honorable career if he shuns the burnt-cork path along which I have seen so many well-equipped aspirants go down to their destruction. The fun of the opera was kept up vigorously by Mr Lionel Brough, Mr Fred Emney, Mr George Grossmith, junior, and Mr Charles Stevens, a comedian whom I last saw, if I mistake not, at Bristol, where he was for some years a leading member of Mr Macready Chute's company.

I am informed that three other comic operas are in contemplation, in addition to the five already in full swing. I can quite believe it. The one business notion that theatrical managers have is that when the bank flourishes, then is the time to make a run on it.

19 *October* 1892

ON Saturday last the Crystal Palace concerts came to relieve the musical famine. Before saying anything about the music, I may point out that a move has been made at last in the direction of reducing the expenses of attending these concerts. Hitherto the bill has been made up in the following way: railway ticket, two shillings first-class (saving by second-class not worth making, and third-class barred on special concert train); program, sixpence; admission to Palace, half-a-crown; admission to concert-room, one shilling, or for a numbered stall half-a-crown, reducible to two-and-a-penny-fifthing by booking in advance for the whole twenty concerts: total, five-and-sixpence at least, and seven-and-sixpence at most, without counting a probable visit to the tea-room for persons addicted to that deleterious fluid. These charges are absolutely prohibitive for four out of five Londoners; and regular frequenters of the concerts are, consequently, very scarce outside the ranks of the season-ticket holders resident in the neighborhood of the Palace.

In general social value the free orchestral concerts given on other afternoons, with a smaller band, are probably much more important than the Saturday ones. This season, however, the railway companies have consented to issue twenty first-class return tickets from London to the Palace, available on concert Saturdays only, for a guinea to holders of the two-guinea serial stall tickets. By this arrangement I shall save nineteen shillings if I go to all the concerts; and even if I only go to one more than half of them, I shall still save a shilling. A further concession has been made in favor of those families who take one or two serial stall tickets and transfer them from one member of the household to another according to tastes, circumstances, and the fortunes of the weekly war for their possession. By paying an additional guinea the transferable stall ticket can be made to carry with it admission to the Palace, which formerly involved twenty separate half-crowns, since the ordinary guinea season ticket is not transferable.

I make no apology for dwelling on these financial arrangements. It has always been evident to people who understand the importance of these concerts, that their utility is far too much restricted by the necessity of making charges which cut off, not only the shilling public, but the half-crown public as well. If Mr Irving, Mr Tree, Mr Hare, etc., were to raise the prices at their theatres to a minimum of five-and-sixpence, the stupidest citizen would see that we should have either to endow a theatre or else face the consequences of leaving the mass of the people without any higher dramatic recreation than such as they might extract from the excitement of playing the very mischief by using their votes without the smallest regard to the vital necessity of maintaining a high general level of artistic culture in a country rapidly becoming entirely democratized.

Even as it is, with the Lyceum gallery accessible daily for a shilling, people are asking for an endowed theatre, because the social need for art of the highest order is so inadequately expressed by the effective commercial demand for it: our Philistines being able easily to outbid our Idealists and Realists combined for the use of all the capital that is available for dramatic enterprise. Still, London is never left absolutely without dramatic performances, as it so commonly is without concerts. You can go to the theatre every weekday all the year round; but when there is an orchestral concert once a fortnight in St James's Hall, music is supposed to be in full swing, whilst such a concert once a week indicates the height of the season.

What we want in London is an orchestral concert *every day*, with permanent engagements and pensions for the conductors and players, among whom there should be, in each division, competent soloists, each playing solo once a week or so. Concertos should, on all ordinary occasions, be played by members of the orchestra, and not by wandering "stars" who pay an agent a lump sum to foist them off for three or six months on givers of concerts and parties as distinguished virtuosos. All masterpieces should be rehearsed up to that point of intimate knowledge which the Manchester band has attained in its Berlioz repertory; and this should be insisted on whether the work in hand were a trifle by Grieg, requiring two or three days' attention, or the Ninth Symphony, requiring two years (*à la* Habeneck).

I say this with deep feeling; for I protest that if there is anything of which I am heartily sick, it is the London no-rehearsal system, under which, with the best players in the world, equipped with the best instruments in the world, we have orchestras that read everything and know nothing; so that the moment we are confronted by works which can only be played properly by a band thoroughly obsessed with every melody and every accent in the score, we are beaten and disgraced not only by our provincial rivals from Manchester, but by a second-rate German band from Hamburg, which supersedes us in our own leading opera house.

I do not make these remarks *à propos de bottes*. A gentleman of benefactorious disposition has offered to endow the Albert Palace to the tune of £10,000. Let us suppose that the Vestry, the County Council, etc., rise to the occasion and complete the endowment of the Palace. It will then remain for some musical millionaire to eclipse all the rest by endowing an Albert Palace orchestra on the lines I have suggested. Who speaks first?

Meanwhile I am forgetting the Crystal Palace concert, which introduced to us two novelties: to wit, Mr C. A. Lidgey's Ballade for Orchestra, Op. 7, after Doré's picture A Day Dream, and Les Lupercales, by André Wormser, the composer of L'Enfant Prodigue. M. Wormser's "symphonic poem" (save the mark) occasionally rises, at second hand, to the level of Offenbach's Orphée. There is one little dance tune in the style of L'Enfant which is tolerable: the rest, with its sham Greek modes which are simply minor scales without leading notes, is vulgar, noisy, and, except in the dance tunes, ingeniously ugly. Mr Lidgey's Ballade is much better. The first section is very successful in point of form (in the real as distinguished from the common, academic sense of the term). It is well balanced, all of one piece, with gathering movement and a strong climax. But it has no special originality or distinction—if it had, Mr Lidgey would have ranked as an eminent composer after its performance. When the double bar is passed the composition falls off, the working out containing a good deal of stale imagination and instrumentation, and the tremendous outlay of organ and orchestra on the peroration adding nothing to the value of the theme on which it is lavished. Vladimir de Pachmann, pianist and pantomimist, played Beethoven's third concerto and some Chopin, including a juvenile scherzo which nobody wanted to hear at full length at five o'clock in the afternoon. De Pachmann is unquestionably a very able pianist, and by no means an insincere one; but now that I have seen, in La Statue du Commandeur, a lady sing a song in dumb show, I want to see a pianoforte concerto played in the same way; and I think there can be no doubt that de Pachmann is the player for that feat. The concert opened with Sullivan's In Memoriam overture, substituted for a number from one of Bach's suites.

Now that the new English Opera House is about to be turned into a music-hall, and that the Theatre of Varieties is supposed to be swallowing up all other theatres, I have resolved to keep myself up to date by visiting the halls occasionally. The other evening I went to the Empire, where I immediately found myself, to my great delight, up to the neck in pure classicism, *siècle de Louis Quatorze*. To see Cavallazzi, in the Versailles ballet, walk, stand, sit, and gesticulate, is to learn all that Vestris or Noblet could have taught you as to the technique of doing these things with dignity.

In the stage management too—in the coloring, the costuming, the lighting, in short, the stage presentation in the completest sense—an artistic design, an impulse towards brilliancy and grace of effect, is always dominant, whether it is successful or not; and in some scenes it is highly successful. Now is it not odd that at a music hall to which, perhaps, half the audience have come to hear Marie Lloyd sing Twiggy voo, boys, twiggy voo? or to see Mr Darby jump a ten-barred gate, you get real stage art, whereas at the Opera the stage is managed just as a first-rate restaurant is managed, with everything served up punctually in the most expensive style, but with all the art left to the cook (called "primma donna"), helped by the waiters (otherwise the chorus).

Wagner noticed long ago that the supremacy of the ballet-masters, who are all enthusiasts in the ballet, made it the most completely artistic form of stage representation left to us; and I think that anyone who will compare Versailles at the Empire with Orfeo at Covent Garden from this point of view, will see what Wagner was driving at, and what I have driven at pretty often without any further effect so far than to extract from my friends many goodnatured but entirely irrelevant assurances that our operatic impresarios are the best fellows in the world when you come to know them. As to which I may observe that I am a capital fellow myself when you come to know me.

One performance at the Empire exhibited the audience to pitiful disadvantage. A certain Señorita C. de Otero, described as a Spanish dancer and singer, danced a dance which has ennobled the adjective "suggestive" for me for ever. It was a simple affair enough, none of your cruel Herodias dances, or cleverly calculated tomboyish Tararas, but a poignant, most meaning dance, so intensely felt that a mere walk across the stage in it quite dragged at one's heartstrings. This Otero is really a great artist. But do you suppose the house rose at her? Not a bit of it: they stared vacantly, waiting for some development in the manner of Miss Lottie Collins, and finally grumbled out a little disappointed applause. Two men actually hissed—if they will forward me their names and addresses I will publish them with pleasure, lest England should burst in ignorance of its greatest monsters.

Take notice, Oh Señorita C. de Otero, Spanish dancer and singer, that I wash my hands of the national crime of failing to appreciate you. You were a perfect success: the audience was a dismal failure. I really cannot conceive a man being such a dull dog as to hold out against that dance. Shall it be said that though Miss Collins could stimulate us cleverly but mechanically, Otero, an immeasurably greater artist, cannot touch us poetically? If so, then let the nations know that dancing in England is measured simply by the brightness of the scarlet and the vigor of the kicking. But I wax too eloquent.

There was a second ballet, called Round the Town, mostly mere drill and topical spectacle, plus a few excellent pantomimic episodes in which Cavallazzi again distinguished herself, as did also Mr W. Warde, a skilful and amusing comic dancer, who played the swell (archaic name for a Johnny). Vincenti has given up the British public in despair, and treats them to unlimited cartwheels and teetotums instead of to the fine classic dancing he used to give us in Asmodeus. Both ballets, I may remark, became tedious at the end through the spinning-out of the final scenes by mechanical evolutions involving repeats in the music almost beyond endurance.

One other performer must not go unnoticed. Miss Marie Lloyd, like all the brightest stars of the music-hall, has an exceptionally quick ear for both pitch and rhythm. Her intonation and the lilt of her songs are alike perfect. Her step-dancing is pretty; and her command of coster-girls' *patois* is complete. Why, then, does not someone write humorous songs for her? Twiggy voo is low and silly; and Oh, Mister porter, though very funnily sung, is not itself particularly funny. A humorous rhymester of any genius could easily make it so.

I am greatly afraid that the critics persisted so long in treating the successes of music-hall vocalism as mere impudent exploitations of vulgarity and indecency (forgetting that if this were more than half true managers could find a dozen Bessie Bellwoods and Marie Lloyds in every street) that the artists have come to exaggerate the popularity of the indecent element in their songs, and to underrate that of the artistic element in their singing. If music-hall songs were written by Messrs Anstey, Rudyard Kipling, W. S. Gilbert, etc., our best music-hall singers would probably be much more widely popular than they can ever become now. Twiggez vous, Miss Lloyd?

26 *October* 1892

IT is impossible not to sympathize with the devotion of Signor Lago to the romance and adventure of opera management. When I was a boy I took that view of opera myself: the wildest pirates and highwaymen in fiction did not fascinate me more than the prima donnas in Queens of Song, nor could the pictures of their deeds and the tales of their exploits please me as did Heath's gift books with decorative borders and operatic tableaux, or the anecdotes in that quite inimitable work, Sutherland Edwards's History of the Opera, which I take to be the most readable book of its kind ever written. I have lived to become the colleague, and to all appearances considerably the senior of Mr Sutherland Edwards; and I tired long ago of paying at the Opera doors and then supplying all the charm of the performance from my own imagination, in flat defiance of my eyes and ears.

Yet I still remember the old feeling of the days when the Opera was a world of fable and adventure, and not a great art factory where I, with wide open eyes and sharpened ears, must sit remorselessly testing the quality of each piece of work as it is turned out and submitted to my judgment. I read Wagner now, and take the theatre seriously to make amends for my youthful profligacy; and I am tremendously down on the slovenly traditions of the old school when they survive apart from its romantic illusions and enthusiasm; but when it survives in such integrity as is possible under existing circumstances, I cannot always bring myself to be hard upon it.

And that is why I always approach a Lago season in an indulgent humor. I know that the atmosphere of the stage will be one of perfect freedom; so that every individual thereon, down to the hindmost chorister, will be welcome, released from control or direction of any kind, to give the rein to his or her individual genius. I also know that the choristers, hindmost and foremost, will have no individual genius to give the rein to, and that they will stand and look on at the principals, criticizing their solos, and trusting to me as one who has known many of their faces for years, and who ought therefore to be glad to see them all there again, not to try to get the bread taken out of their mouths by a lot of new-fangled girls from the Savoy with Cambridge certificates.

I know, further, that the treasury will not run to downright splendor in the way of dresses and scenery, and that the ballet will have to be made the best of by kind friends in front. In short, that, as in the old times, unless the principal singers are good enough to triumph for the moment over surroundings which at every turn defeat the efforts of the imagination to produce a gratuitous illusion, there will be virtually no opera. I am not sorry to see that the power of the younger generation of critics to put up with these hard conditions is comparatively small, leading them to greatly underrate the value of the Italian operas of the old repertory which they more especially associate with such conditions; but to me submission is not so difficult; for I was broken in to the system when young, and can get back only too easily to my old attitude and concentrate my attention wholly on consent to do this at Covent Garden, where the public position of the enterprise, its pretensions, and the prices charged entitle me to demand that the performances shall in all respects set the highest European standard; but with Signor Lago, playing to his two-shilling pit and shilling gallery, and frankly offering his entertainment on the old lines, I do not feel bound to be so strict.

Besides, Signor Lago discovered Giulia Ravogli and Cavalleria, and in due course had these trumps annexed by his rival, and played against him on his opening night. Who would not sympathize with him under such circumstances?

Eugene Onegin, his latest card, reminded me, I hardly know why, of The Colleen Bawn. Something in the tailoring, in the scenery, in the sound of the hero's name (pronounced O'Naygin, or, to put it in a still more Irish way, O'Neoghegan) probably combined with the Balfian musical form of the work to suggest this notion to me. There is something Irish, too, as well as Byronic, in the introduction of Eugene as an uncommonly fine fellow when there is not the smallest ground for any such estimate of him. The music suggests a vain regret that Tchaikowsky's remarkable artistic judgment, culture, imaginative vivacity, and self-respect as a musical workman, should have been unaccompanied by any original musical force. For, though I have described the form of the opera as Balfian, it must not therefore be inferred that Tchaikowsky's music is as common as Balfe's—ballads apart—generally was. Tchaikowsky composes with the seriousness of a man who knows how to value himself and his work too well to be capable of padding his opera with the childish claptrap that does duty for dramatic music in The Bohemian Girl. Balfe, whose ballads are better than Tchaikowsky's, never, as far as I know, wrote a whole scene well, whereas in Eugene Onegin there are some scenes, notably those of the letter and the duel, which are very well written, none of them being bungled or faked (factitious is the more elegant expression; but the other is right). The opera, as a whole, is a dignified composition by a man of distinguished talent whose love of music has led him to adopt the profession of composer, and who, with something of his countryman Rubinstein's disposition to make too much of cheap second-hand musical material, has nothing of his diffuseness, his occasional vulgarity, and his incapacity for seeing when to drop a worn-out theme.

The performance, as far as the principals are concerned, is by no means bad. Signor Lago was particularly fortunate in finding to his hand, in Mr Oudin, just the man for Onegin, dark, handsome, distinguished, mysterious-looking—in short, Byronic, and able to behave and to act in a manner worthy of his appearance, which is not always the case with the Don Juans and Corsairs of the stage. Miss Fanny Moody achieved a considerable dramatic success as Tatiana; and it may possibly interest her to learn, on the authority of no less critical a Russian than Stepniak, that she so exactly represented the sort of Russian woman of whom Tatiana is a type, that he is convinced that she would make a success in the part in Russia, even if she sang it in English. To my mind, however, it is a pity that Miss Moody's gifts are so exclusively dramatic. If she were only musical—if she could give that hard, penetrating voice of hers the true lyric grace of execution and beauty of sound as unerringly as she can give it convincing dramatic eloquence, she would be a prima donna in a thousand. Happily for Signor Lago, he could not have chosen a part better calculated than Tatiana to emphasize her power as an actress and cover her want of charm as a vocalist. Mr Manners scored the hit of the evening in a ballad in the last act, the audience being, to tell the truth, greatly relieved after a long spell of Mr Oudin's rather artificial style by the free, natural, sympathetic tone of Mr Manners's voice, which is as sound and powerful as ever. Mr Ivor McKay, having been shot with a terrific bang, produced by a heavy charge of anything but smokeless powder, by Mr Oudin, retired from the tenor part, which is now filled by Mr Wareham: how, I know not. Madame Swiatlowsky is good and very Russian as the nurse; and Mlle Selma fits well into the part of the mother. Miss Lily Moody, a vigorous young lady with a strong mezzo-soprano voice which has not been sweetened by her work as a dramatic contralto, is a somewhat inelegant Olga.

The stage management was, I submit, rather worse than it need have been. Granted that there is nobody capable of making the willing but helpless chorus do anything in the quarrel scene except make it ridiculous, and that the two capital dances are utterly beyond the resources of the establishment, I still think that the gentleman, whoever he was, who loaded that pistol with so fine a feeling for the stage effect of the duel, might, if promoted to the post of chief gasman, manipulate the lights so as to make the change from dark to dawn in the letter scene rather more plausible than on the first night. The dresses were quite good enough for all purposes; but the supply ran short, the dancers at Madame Larina's in Act II reappearing in the same costumes at Prince Gremin's in Act III. Onegin fought the duel in a dark coat with two rows of blazing golden buttons, which made him a perfect target; and he would most certainly have been slain if he had not fired first. Years afterwards he came back, a grey-haired man, to make love in that same coat. In fact, Signor Lago might have made a "missing-word competition" out of Onegin's exclamation, "I change from one land to another, but cannot change my ——." The missing word is "heart," but would be guessed as "coat" by nine-tenths of the audience. This scrap from the book reminds me that Mr Sutherland Edwards, who knows Russian, has expiated that unnatural accomplishment by translating the libretto, the most impossible of literary tasks, but one which he has managed, with his usual tact, to accomplish without making himself at all ridiculous. Onegin is now being played three times a week; and it is to be hoped that it will pay its way for the better encouragement of Signor Lago in his policy of bringing forward novelties.

La Favorita was played on the following night; but I forbore it. I saw an act and a half of Lohengrin on Saturday, and can certify that the pit got handsome value for its money, although they would do it differently at Bayreuth. Signor Zerni, the tenor, is a representative of that modern Gayarrean school which has raised bleating to the rank of a fine art throughout Europe. He has been carefully warned to keep his voice as steady as the nature of his method will permit; and this he does with sufficient success to save himself from the fate of Suane, Signor Lago's last venture in that manner. Mr Manners will make a good king when he has become thoroughly familiar with the part; and Signor Mario Ancona, as Telramund, is exceptionally good as Telramunds go in London.

Mr Worlock, too, is by no means an everyday herald; and on the whole, if there were only somebody to make the chorus look alive occasionally, especially at the entry of Lohengrin; if Signor Lago would urge the choristers to either let their beards grow or not, but by no means to shave only once a week; and if, further, some of the band would follow the example of Albani, who plays Elsa as scrupulously and carefully as ever she did on the most brilliant night at Covent Garden in the regular season, Signor Lago would be able to boast of having pulled the biggest opera on his list very creditably off. Arditi conducted. Onegin, by the bye, was conducted by Mr Henry J. Wood, who did his work steadily, and, as far as my acquaintance with the music enabled me to judge, chose the *tempi* well; but he did not succeed in getting any really fine execution out of the band, which does not play at all as well as it could if it liked.

Slivinski, who stepped in to replace Paderewski (laid up with rheumatic fever) at Manchester, gave a recital last week at St James's Hall. The altogether extraordinary degree of technical accomplishment displayed by him during his last visit has had its edge very perceptibly taken off by, as I guess, too much drawing room playing, and perhaps by yielding to squeamish complaints of the swordsmanlike quality of his touch.

However that may be, he has certainly been cultivating the feathery execution which Paderewski sometimes uses for Chopin studies; and though he is too skilful a player to attempt any style without some success, he has lost more in force and distinction than he has gained in softness and prettiness. Also he has contracted a habit of slurring over—

indeed, all but dropping—the unaccented notes in rapid passages. This was more or less noticeable all through the recital; but when he came to Liszt's transcription of Schubert's Auf dem Wasser zu singen, with its exquisite accompaniment of repeated semiquavers, the ticking of the second semiquavers was not heard until they were played as chords instead of single notes. His deficiency in eloquence of style was very apparent in his playing of that touching and dignified piece of musical rhetoric, Schubert's Impromptu in C minor, which he quite misconceived.

In Schumann's Fantasie Stücke, which he played right through all the numbers, he was very good, except in the first, which he gave with a *rubato* which had the worst fault a *rubato* can have—that of sounding as if the pianist, vainly trying to play in strict time, were being baffled by the sticking of the keys. But on the whole the Schumann pieces proved that Slivinski has advanced as an interpreter. One or two of them were perfectly played; and the whole program was full of evidences of his exceptional powers.

2 *November* 1892

THE young English composer is having a good time of it just now, with his overtures and symphonies resounding at the Crystal Palace, and his operas at the Olympic. Mr Granville Bantock's Caedmar is an enthusiastic and ingenious piece of work, being nothing less than an adaptation of all the most fetching passages in Wagner's later tragic music dramas to a little poem in which Tristan, Siegmund, Siegfried, Hunding, Isolde, and Sieglinde are aptly concentrated into three persons. The idea is an excellent one; for in the space of an hour, and within a stone's-throw of the Strand, we get the cream of all Bayreuth without the trouble and expense of journeying thither. There is also, for the relief of anti-Wagnerians, an intermezzo which might have been written by the late Alfred Cellier or any other good Mendelssohnian.

The plot, as I understood it, is very simple. A pious

knight-errant wanders one evening into the garden of Eden, and falls asleep there. Eve, having had words with her husband, runs away from him, and finds in the sleeping warrior the one thing lacking to her: to wit, somebody to run away with. She makes love to him; and they retire together. Elves appear on the deserted stage, and dance to the strains of the intermezzo. They are encored, not because the audience is particularly charmed, but because Cavalleria has put it into its head that to recognize and encore an intermezzo shews connoisseurship. Then the pair return, looking highly satisfied; and presently Adam enters and remonstrates. Ten minutes later the knight-errant is the sole survivor of the three, whereupon he prays the curtain down.

The whole affair is absurdly second-hand; but, for all that, it proves remarkable musical ability on the part of Mr Granville Bantock, who shews a thorough knowledge of the mechanism of the Wagnerian orchestra. If Caedmar had been produced as a newly discovered work of Wagner, everyone would have admitted that so adroit a forgery implied a very clever penman. After Caedmar, Signor Lago put up the third act of Ernani. Strange to say, a good many people did not wait for it.

Just imagine the situation. Here is a baritone singer, Signor Mario Ancona, who has attracted general notice by his performance of Telramund in Lohengrin and Alfonso in La Favorita. Signor Lago accordingly mounts a famous scene, the classic opportunity for lyric actors of the Italian school (baritone variety), a scene which is not only highly prized by all students of Italian opera, but which had its dramatic import well taught to Londoners by the Comédie Française when they crowded to see Sarah Bernhardt as Doña Sol, and incidentally saw Worms as Charles V. In the play Charles is sublime in feeling, but somewhat tedious in expression. In the opera he is equally sublime in feeling, but concise, grand, and touching in expression, thereby proving that the chief glory of Victor Hugo as a stage poet was to have provided libretti for Verdi.

Every opera-goer who knows chalk from cheese knows that to hear that scene finely done is worth hearing all the Mephistopheleses and Toreadors that ever grimaced or swaggered, and that when a new artist offers to play it, the occasion is a first-class one. Yet, when Caedmar was over there was a considerable exodus from the stalls, as if nothing remained but a harlequinade for the children and the novices. "Now this," thought I, "is pretty odd. If these people knew their Ernani, surely they would stay." Then I realized that they did not know their Ernani—that years of Faust, and Carmen, and Les Huguenots, and Mefistofele, and soi-disant Lohengrin had left them ignorant of that ultra-classical product of Romanticism, the grandiose Italian opera in which the executive art consists in a splendid display of personal heroics, and the drama arises out of the simplest and most universal stimulants to them.

Il Trovatore, Un Ballo, Ernani, etc., are no longer read at the piano at home as the works of the Carmen *genre* are, and as Wagner's are. The popular notion of them is therefore founded on performances in which the superb distinction and heroic force of the male characters, and the tragic beauty of the women, have been burlesqued by performers with every sort of disqualification for such parts, from age and obesity to the most excruciating phases of physical insignificance and modern cockney vulgarity. I used often to wonder why it was that whilst every asphalt contractor could get a man to tar the streets, and every tourist could find a gondolier rather above the average of the House of Lords in point of nobility of aspect, no operatic manager, after Mario vanished, seemed to be able to find a Manrico with whom any exclusively disposed Thames mudlark would care to be seen grubbing for pennies. When I get on this subject I really cannot contain myself. At the thought of that dynasty of execrable impostors in tights and tunics, interpolating their loathsome B flats into the beautiful melodies they could not sing, and swelling with conceit when they were able to finish Di quella pira with a high C capable of making a stranded man-of-war recoil off a reef into mid-ocean, I demand the suspension of all rules as to decorum of language until I have heaped upon them some little instalment of the infinite abuse they deserve. Others, alas! have blamed Verdi, much as if Dickens had blamed Shakespear for the absurdities of Mr Wopsle.

The general improvement in operatic performances of late years has taken us still further away from the heroic school. But in due time its turn will come. Von Bülow, who once contemptuously refused the name of music to Verdi's works, has recanted in terms which would hardly have been out of place if addressed to Wagner; and many who now talk of the Master as of a tuneful trifler who only half-redeemed a misspent life by the clever artificialities which are added in Aïda and Otello to the power and freedom of his earlier works, will change their tone when his operas are once more seriously studied by great artists.

For the present, however, it is clear that if Signor Mario Ancona wishes to interest the public, he must depend on character parts instead of heroic ones. His offer of Charles V could hardly have been less appreciatively received. This was certainly no fault of his own; for he sang the opening recitative and cavatina well, and the solo in the great sestet, Oh sommo Carlo, very well. As a piece of acting his performance was a trifle too Italian-operatic; his fold of the arms and shake of the head when Ernani insisted on being beheaded was overmuch in the manner of Mr Lenville; and there was too constant a strain throughout, since even in the third act of Ernani there are moments which are neither stentorian nor sentimental. But one does not expect a revolution in operatic acting to be achieved in a single night, especially in a part which is, to say the least, somewhat inflated; and, on the whole, Signor Ancona was more dignified and sincere than any experienced opera-goer had dared to hope.

The applause at the end was only moderately enthusiastic; but this was largely due to the carelessness of the management, which, instead of providing a book of the triple bill, left the audience entirely in the dark as to what the Ernani excerpt meant, and tried to effect separate sales of vocal scores of Caedmar and shilling books of L'Impresario to elucidate the rest of the program. After which you felt that Signor Lago deserved anything that might happen to him in the way of the performance falling flat.

And the chances of Ernani were not improved by the modesty of Charles's coronation arrangements, or by the unkempt staginess of the conspirators, or by the fact that though the music had been rehearsed sufficiently to secure accuracy, no attempt was made to color and enrich the sombre depths of the orchestra. As to the choristers, they were allowed to bawl away in the old slovenly, rapscallionly fashion, on the easy assumption that, if the time came right and the pitch right (or thereabouts), the quality of tone and style of delivery did not matter two straws. When will Signor Lago pay a visit to our comic-opera houses with their English choruses, and realize that Queen Anne has been dead for some time now?

Der Schauspieldirector, in the version known as L'Impresario, of course put all the rest of the entertainment into the shade. Every number in it is a masterpiece. The quartet would make a very handsome finale for any ordinary opera; the overture is a classic; the air Quando miro quel bel ciglio will last as long as Pergolesi's Tre giorni son che Nina, or Gluck's Che faro senza Euridice? How far its finest qualities are above our heads, both before and behind the curtain, I need not say. The overture was scrambled through post-haste in the old exhilarating slapdash style, expressive of the idea that Mozart was a rattling sort of drunkard and libertine, tempered by the modern and infinitely more foolish notion that he was merely a useful model of academic form for students.

Mr G. Tate sang Quando miro in the person of Mozart himself. To shew how thoroughly he grasped the character he altered the last phrase so as to make the ending more "effective," much as, if he were a sculptor instead of a singer, he might alter the tails of the Trafalgar Square lions by sticking them up straight in order to make *their* endings more effective. This public announcement on Mr Tate's part that he considers himself a better judge of how a song should end than Mozart is something that he will have to live down. Unless, indeed, the real explanation be that Mr Tate is too modest, and succumbed, against his own better sense, to the bad advice which is always thrust upon young artists by people who have all the traditional abuses of the stage at their fingers' ends, and know nothing about art. And that is why, on the boards as off them, eminence is only attained by those whose strength of conviction enables them to do, without the least misgiving, exactly the reverse of what all the non-eminent people round them advise them to do. For naturally, if these non-eminents knew the right thing to do they would be eminent.

Of the performance generally, I have only to say that it has been well prepared and is really enjoyable. Mlle Leila, who played Mlle Herz, has a naturally good voice, which has been somewhat squeezed and wire-drawn by an artificial method; but she managed to hold her own in her very difficult part, which is worth hearing not only for its own sake, but for the very fine Mozartean aria which she introduces when asked by the Schauspieldirector (Mr R. Temple) to give a sample of her powers.

I have to chronicle the resumption of the Monday and Saturday Popular Concerts, and to congratulate Señor Arbos on his playing in the adagio of Beethoven's quartet in E flat (Op. 74) at the opening concert, and Mlle Szumowska on her neat handling of the last three movements of the Pastoral Sonata. The first movement came to nothing, perhaps because Mlle Szumowska had a cold, perhaps because she has not a pastoral turn. Mlle Wietrowetz succeeds Señor Arbos this week as first violin.

9 November 1892

TO Dvořák's Requiem, which was performed last Wednesday at the Albert Hall, I could not be made to listen again, since the penalty of default did not exceed death; and I had much rather die than repeat the attempts I made, first at Birmingham, and then at Kensington Gore, to sit it out. It is hard to understand the frame of mind of an artist who at this time of day sits down to write a Requiem *à propos de bottes*. One can fancy an undertaker doing it readily enough: he would know as a matter of business that in music, as in joiners' work, you can take the poorest materials and set the public gaping at them by simply covering them with black cloth and coffin-nails. But why should a musician condescend to speculate thus in sensationalism and superstition?

When I hear Dvořák's weird chords on muted cornets (patent Margate Pier echo attachment), finishing up with a gruesome ding on the tam-tam, I feel exactly as I should if he held up a skull with a lighted candle inside to awe me. When, in the Dies Iræ, he proceeds, as who should say, "Now you shall see what I can do in the way of stage-thunder," to turn on organ pedal and drum to make a huge mechanical modern version of the Rossini crescendo, I pointedly and publicly turn up my nose, and stare frigidly. But the public, in spite of Charles Dickens, loves everything connected with a funeral.

Those who are too respectable to stand watching the black flag after an execution, take a creepy sort of pleasure in Requiems. If Sir Joseph Barnby were to conduct with a black brass-tipped baton; if the bandsmen wore black gloves and crape scarves; if the attendants were professional mutes (*sordini*), and the tickets edged with a half-inch jet border, I believe the enjoyment of the audience would be immensely enhanced. Dvořák seems to have felt this. Mozart's Requiem leads you away from the point: you find yourself listening to the music as music, or reflecting, or otherwise getting up to the higher planes of existence. Brahms' Requiem has not the true funeral relish: it aims at the technical traditions of requiem composition rather than the sensational, and is so execrably and ponderously dull that the very flattest of funerals would seem like a ballet, or at least a *danse macabre*, after it.

Dvořák alone, mechanically solemn and trivially genteel, very careful and elaborate in detail, and beyond belief uninspired, has hit the mean. One almost admires the perseverance with which he has cut all those dead strips of notes into lengths, nailed and glued them into a single structure, and titivated it for the melancholy occasion with the latest mortuary orchestral decorations. And then, the gravity with which it is received and criticized as a work of first-rate importance, as if it brought the air of a cathedral close with it, and were highly connected! Whereas, if the same music had been called "Ode to Revolution," or "The Apotheosis of Ibsen," or "Dirge for the Victims of Vaccination," it would have been found out for what it is before the end of the first ten bars, as I found it out at the Birmingham Festival.

That is the way things go in England. Some few years ago Peter Benoît, a much-in-earnest Dutch composer, who is almost as great in music as Haydon was in painting, made his début here with an oratorio called Lucifer, containing one pretty song (by Schumann), but otherwise a most barren colossus of a work. The public felt that Lucifer was an integral part of the Church of England, most Englishmen being persuaded that Milton's Paradise Lost is a poetical paraphrase of the book of Genesis; and Benoît was received with deep respect as a too long neglected Dutch Beethoven. Presuming on this success, Peter laid a work called Charlotte Corday at the feet of the Philharmonic Society. That infatuated body, feeling itself traditionally committed to the discovery and encouragement of foreign Beethovens, allowed him to conduct it at one of its concerts. He promptly found out that in England, though Lucifer is respectable, Charlotte Corday is quite out of the question.

The Corday revolutionary scenes were not a whit more mechanical and shallow than the oratorio, and were nearly as bulky, besides being twice as lively (thanks to Ça ira, The Marseillaise, etc.); but the British public would have none of them; and Benoît has not since been heard of in London. I mention the matter to illustrate how easy it is to get taken seriously as a composer if you begin with an oratorio. But if you want to make assurance doubly sure, begin with a Requiem. After Dvořák every musical agent and publisher in Europe will give, as the straightest of tips to foreign composers, the word to write Requiems. I foresee the arrival of shiploads of such compositions on these coasts. When that day comes, I shall buy a broom; select some crossing out of earshot of the muffled drums; and earn my bread in a more humane and less questionably useful occupation than that which I now follow. It is true that even then I shall have to see a funeral go past occasionally. But a funeral goes past in less than two minutes, whereas a Requiem takes a matter of two hours. Besides, it is generally understood that funerals are to be avoided as long as possible, whereas Requiems are offered as a sort of treat, whether anybody is dead or not.

I have myself, however, to sing the requiem of Signor Lago's opera season, which expired on Thursday after a performance of Die Zauberflöte, which I did not attend, partly because of the London Symphony Concert, and partly because the disappearance of Signor Lago's advertisements from the morning papers had led me to believe that the end was already come. It is impossible not to sympathize with the defeated impresario, who has given us so much fresh music during his brief struggle.

From my personal point of view, I hugely appreciated his unspoiled condition. He had the courage of his profession as well as the enterprise of his business, and always stood up without wincing to the hardest hitting in the way of criticism. He never raised the cry of "personal attack," or invited me to discharge my duties with the pistol of the law of libel held to my ear. He did not expect me to gorge him with impossible flattery, nor did he keep a critic and a paper of his own to supply me with weekly examples of what he considered fair and becoming notices of his enterprises. He may even, for all I know to the contrary, have attained the superlative managerial wisdom of seeing that the only criticism which really helps operatic enterprise is criticism which creates and sustains public interest in music, even when it deals with impresarios almost as severely as they generally deserve; and that however agreeable it may be to be extolled daily in terms which would be considerably over the mark if applied to the management of Liszt at Weimar or Wagner at Bayreuth, the end of that must be the same as the end of the old experiment of calling Aristides "the Just" about a thousand times too often.

He belongs, does Signor Lago, to the old days, now for ever fled, it appears, when no critic ever dreamt of alluding to the legal conditions under which his work was carried on, much less to the relations between himself and the managers. The public assumed that there was an unwritten understanding by which its representative was to be absolutely free to pursue his occupation unmolested, both in its legal phase of applauding and its illegal phase of finding fault. Whilst that understanding was observed, every public allusion to it from either side was an impertinence.

But now that it is cast to the winds, and that such verdicts as the one given in favor of the late Signor Ciampi against the Daily Telegraph have proved that even in the cases most favorable to the critic, the public, through its juries, will generally console adversely criticized persons at the expense of newspaper proprietors on the general ground that they can well afford it, I, for one, am forced to remind the said public from time to time that since they will neither protect themselves in the jury-box nor pay enough for their papers to provide for the huge cost and worry of continual litigation, a critic must either give up his work and fall back on some safer branch of literature, or else absolutely refuse to criticize the undertakings of agents and impresarios who resort to the law whenever they are dispraised.

Great artists and most interesting performances pass, and must continue to pass, unnoticed in this column because they are under the auspices of gentlemen who have threatened me with actions when I have pointed out imperfections in their enterprises, though, most inconsistently, they never sent me a ten-pound note when I praised them. I do not blame them in the least, as they are by no means bound to observe the old truce longer than they see the advantage of it: only, I insist on the public being warned that the truce is no longer general, so that it may be understood that I neither neglect my duties nor slight the artists whose visits I pass by silently; and I also wish artistic *entrepreneurs* of all sorts to know that if they want mere advertisements they must pay for them, and if they want criticism they must take the rough with the smooth.

So, you see, I pay Signor Lago no small compliment when I say that the above observations, the bearings of which lie in the application thereof, need never have been obtruded on the public if his fortitude in facing severe criticism, even when followed by heavy losses, were quite as much a matter of course as it once was.

At the first London Symphony Concert last Thursday the band was very rough; and there must have been something exceptionally unfavorable in the atmospheric conditions, for the wind was badly out of tune. Even the drums could not catch the pitch accurately. Berlioz' King Lear overture sounded positively music-hally. I was curious to hear it; but I did not know it or care for it enough to have found out the right way to play it; and I venture to guess that Mr Henschel and the band were in exactly the same predicament. Anyhow, it made a great noise and gave no sort of satisfaction. At the end of the concert the orchestra had a lively game of football with Wagner's celebrated American Potboiler, the second and last of his short series of efforts in that fascinating *genre* (the first was Rienzi).

Mrs Henschel sang Liszt's setting of Kennst du das Land

cleverly, but without anything approaching the requisite depth of feeling. Szumowska played Weber's Concertstück, which she has apparently picked up, not quite accurately, by ear, with fewer slips than she made when she played it at the Crystal Palace a fortnight ago. The most successful item in the program was the C minor symphony, in which Mr Henschel shewed sound conductorial instinct by boldly roughing it for the sake of a powerful general effect instead of giving us smoothness and prettiness of detail with no general effect at all. But it is not to the credit of the band that such an alternative should be forced on him.

I especially protest against the way in which those first three notes of the symphony, forming a gigantic appoggiatura to Fate's knock at the door, were executed. Some of the band regarded them as a triplet of quavers, some as three ordinary quavers, and some as a quaver and two semiquavers, whilst doubtless there were other views represented which I was not quick enough to catch. The coda to the first movement was spoiled by want of crispness; and the second section of the trio was too slow and heavy-footed. However, Mr Henschel has the root of the matter in him. The concerts are interesting and of reasonable length; and the shortcomings are shortcomings of detail which are certain to be remedied in time, and which do not meanwhile interfere seriously with the value of the performances, which is high enough to make it a matter of public importance that they should be well supported.

16 *November* 1892

LAST season appears to have been a favorable one for specialists in singing, for volumes and pamphlets on voice production have been hurled at me from all sides; and this, I suppose, indicates a wave of interest in the subject. All such treatises used to be practically identical as to their preliminary matter, which invariably dealt with the need for a new departure, so as to get away from the quackery of the ordinary singing-master and rediscover the lost art of Porpora. Nowadays, the new departure is still advocated; but there is a tendency to leave Porpora out of the question, and to claim for the latest methods a modern scientific basis, consisting mostly of extracts from Huxley and Helmholtz. With all due respect, however, I beg to remark that there is no sort of sense in attempting to base the art of singing on physiology. You can no more sing on physiological principles than you can fence on anatomical principles, paint on optical principles, or compose on acoustic principles.

Sir Joshua Reynolds painted none the worse for believing that there were three primary colors, and that the human eye was one of the most exquisite and perfect instruments ever designed for the use of man; nor have his successors painted any the better since Young exploded the three primary colors for ever, and Helmholtz scandalized Europe by informing his pupils that if an optician were to send him an instrument with so many easily avoidable and remediable defects as the human eye, he would feel bound to censure him severely. Again, half a century ago every singing-master firmly believed that there were in the human body three glands—one in the head, immediately behind the frontal sinus; one in the throat; and one in the chest: each secreting a different quality of voice.

Nowadays even an Italian singing-master must, on pain of appearing a gross ignoramus to his pupils, know that all voice is produced by the same organ, the larynx, and that the so-called three voices are "registers" made by varying the adjustment of the vocal cords. This advance in scientific knowledge does not alter the position of those teachers of singing who study their profession *by ear*, or of the painters who paint *by eye*—who are artists, in short. But it has a good effect on the gentlemen whose methods are "scientific." In the days of the three primary colors, there were teachers of painting who held that the right color for a scarf across a blue robe was orange, because blue is a primary color, and the proper contrast to it was a compound of the other primary colors, red and yellow. The Divine Artist had colored the rainbow on these principles; therefore they were natural, scientific, and orthodox.

There are still gentlemen who teach coloring on natural, scientific, orthodox principles; and to them the discovery that the doctrine of the three primary colors will not do, and that Shelley's "million-colored bow" is nearer the truth than Newton's tricolored one, no doubt has its value, since their daubs are more varied than before, though the artist-colorist remains no wiser than Bellini or Velasquez. In the same way, the scientific vocal methods based on the latest observations of the laryngoscopists are, on the whole, less likely to be dangerous than those based on the theory of the three glands, although the artistic method is just the same as ever it was.

Now, I am hopelessly prejudiced in favor of the artistic method, which is, of course, the genuinely scientific method according to the science of art itself. On behalf of my prejudice I plead two chapters in my experience of "scientific" methods. When the study of the vocal cords first began, it led straight to the theory that the larynx was a simple stringed instrument, and that singing was, physically, a mere question of varying the tension of the vocal cords, and throwing them into vibration by a vigorous current of air. This was duly confirmed by an experiment, of the physiological-laboratory type, by Müller; and then we had the "tension-of-cords-and-force-of-blast" theory of singing, which all the violent and villainous methods prevalent in the middle of the century, to the ruin of innumerable pupil-victims, claimed as their "scientific" foundation, and which every true artist was able to explode to his or her own satisfaction by the simple experiment of listening to its results.

The second chapter concerns composers more than singers. When it was discovered that musical sounds, instead of being simple, are really enriched by a series of "partial tones," and that the most prominent of these "partial tones" correspond to the notes of the commonest chords, all the professors who could not distinguish between science and art jumped at the notion of discovering a scientific method of harmonizing which should quite supersede the barbarous thoroughbass of Handel and Mozart. A stupendous monument of ingenious folly, in the form of a treatise on harmony by Dr Day, was installed at the Royal Academy of Music, where it reigns, for aught I know, to this day; and the unhappy pupils who wanted certificates of their competence to write music could not obtain them without answering absurd challenges to name "the root" of a chord, meaning the sound that would generate the notes of that chord among its series of "partial tones."

Now as, if you only look far enough through your series, you can find every note used in music among those generated by any one note used in it, the professors, though tolerably unanimous as to the root of C, E, G, or C, E, G, B flat, could not agree about the chromatic chords, and even the more extreme diatonic discords. The result was that when you went to get coached for your Mus. Bac. degree, the first thing your coach had to ascertain was where you were going to be examined, as you had to give different answers to the same questions, according to whether they were put by Ouseley and Macfarren, or Stainer. (Sir John Stainer finally succumbed to an acute attack of common sense, and invested Day's system with that quality in the only modern treatise on harmony I have ever recommended anyone to open.) Sterndale Bennett was a convinced Dayite, and sometimes spoiled passages in his music in order to make the harmony "scientific."

Meanwhile Wagner, working by ear, heedless of Day, was immensely enlarging the harmonic stock-in-trade of the profession. Macfarren kept on proving that the Wagnerian procedure was improper, until at last one could not help admiring the resolute conviction with which the veteran professor, old, blind, and hopelessly in the wrong, would still rise to utter his protest whenever there was an opening for it.

Here, then, we have science, in the two most conspicuous cases of its application to musical art, doing serious mischief in the hands of the teachers who fell back on it to eke out the poverty of their artistic resources. Yet do not suppose that I am an advocate of old-fashioned ignorance. No: I admit that a young teacher of singing, if he cannot handle the laryngoscope, and knows nothing of anatomy or physics, deserves to be mistrusted as an uneducated person, likely to offer fantastic and ambiguous suggestions instead of exact instructions.

But I do declare emphatically that all methods which have come into existence by logical deduction from scientific theory can only be good through the extravagantly improbable accident of a coincidence between the result of two absolutely unrelated processes, one right and the other wrong. Practically, they are certain to be delusive; and this conclusion is not the anti-scientific, but the scientific one. And in all books on the subject which I may happen to review here I shall concern myself solely with the practical instructions offered, and criticize them in the light of my own empirical observation of singing, without the slightest regard to the hooking of them on to physiology or acoustics.

First comes the redoubtable Mr Lunn with a reprint (Forster Groom—a sixpenny pamphlet) of the lecture he delivered last May at Prince's Hall, which I noticed at the time. I disagree with him flatly in his denunciation of the vowel *oo* for practice, and am quite of the opinion of the sensible and practical author of Our Voices, and How to Improve Them, by A Lady (Willcocks—a two-shilling manual), who recommends practice on *oo* in the middle of the voice, and points out that the traditional Italian *a* is invariably translated here into the English *ah*, which would have driven the old Italian masters out of their senses.

Mr Lunn's objection is that *oo* sets people "blowing," against which vice his pamphlet gives effective and valuable warning. But if Mr Lunn will teach his pupils to round the back of the throat (the pharynx) as they sing—and this is a trick of the old school which he does not seem to know—he will find that they can "compress the air," as he puts it, just as effectually on *oo* as on Italian *a*; and his well-taught tenor pupil, Mr Arthur, will be able to do in one breath that passage in Il mio tesoro which cost him one and a quarter at Prince's Hall. A Lady might learn something from Mr Lunn as to the importance of not wasting the breath (the skilled singer, in rounding the pharynx, has an imaginary sensation of holding the breath back—of *com*pressing it at the larynx, though the control really comes from the diaphragm). She says, "The voice should be directed forward, always forward, until the vibrating air is felt right on the lips."

This is both fanciful and misleading. The phrase "direction of the voice" means really shaping the cavity of the mouth by the disposition of the lips, tongue, and jaw, the voice being immovable; and the attempt to carry out the precept as to feeling the air on the lips would lead in practice simply to "blowing." Dr J. W. Bernhardt, the author of Vox Humana (Simpkin, Marshall—a five-shilling book), gives the proper word of command for this particular emergency in the ten quite invaluable paragraphs (94 to 103) in which he urges the necessity of putting no strain on the genio-hyoid muscles—in other words, of keeping your chin loose whatever you do. By his emphasis on this point and his knowledge of the importance of the pharynx, he is able to give some excellent advice; but in suggesting the vowel *o* for practice, he forgot that it would be read as ah-oo, ow, aw-oo, etc., by different readers, Mr Irving being the only living Englishman who makes it a pure vowel.

Dr Bernhardt's plan of beginning it with an aspirate and an *n*, thus, *h'n'o*, is a clever trick as far as the *n* is concerned; but the *h* belongs to his notion (also Mr Lunn's) that the air should be compressed by the vocal cords as by a safety-valve. He carries this so far as to advocate attacking a note, not merely by the *coup de glotte*, as Mr Lunn does, but by nothing short of an explosion. I quite agree with Maurel, that the *coup de glotte* is objectionable; and I never heard a good singer who attacked notes explosively. I am convinced that both Mr Lunn and Dr Bernhardt have been misled by the imaginary sensation, described above, of pressing back the air with the vocal cords.

Any good singer can touch a note gently, reinforce it to its loudest, and let it diminish again, without the least alteration of the pitch, and consequently without the least alteration of, or pressure downwards of, the glottis, the *crescendo* and *diminuendo* being visibly effected by the diaphragm. The explosive process produces bawling, not singing; and Dr Bernhardt virtually admits this when he says that the ladies who, when asked to sing louder, plead "I really have no more voice," would scream loud enough to awaken the echoes a mile away if any sudden fright came upon them. If one of Dr Bernhardt's pupils were to apply this remark practically, by beginning to scream instead of singing (as many prima donnas do), he would, I have no doubt, pull her up with a remarkably short turn.

But at this point I must pull myself up with equal sharpness, leaving unnoticed many points in these three interesting books, for which I beg Mr Lunn, Dr Bernhardt, and A Lady, to accept my best thanks.

23 *November* 1892

"I BELIEVE," says Santley in his Reminiscences, just published by Mr Edward Arnold, "I would have preferred being an actor of moderate fame to being the most renowned singer on earth." That is the beginning. Now listen to the end. "The stage had proved my great *illusion perdue*, my own enthusiasm and love for it had not abated; but I could not fight almost single-handed against the lack of earnestness, except for pecuniary gain, which I encountered turn what way I might, and I resolved to quit it." Let me quote a few of the steps of the disillusionizing process:

"I essayed the part of Don Giovanni for the first time at

Manchester on September 14th, 1865. As usual, I had one rehearsal the morning of the day of performance. Mario, who was always a late riser, did not come in until we were half-way through the rehearsal.

. . . .

"Tannhäuser was not produced at all during my Italian career. I always regret this, as I had a great desire to play Wolfram.

. . . .

"Queen Topaz might have proved a fair success if some care had been taken in its production. Swift, who played the hero, never knew his part—neither music nor words. There was no attempt at stage-management: we all wandered on and off and about the stage as we pleased. The effect produced was very curious: neither players nor audience seemed to have the remotest notion what it was all about. The stage-management throughout was the most perfect—of its kind—I ever knew. At one performance of Fra Diavolo matters were so well arranged that principals, chorus, supers, etc., were all left outside the curtain at the end of the first act. At one of the rehearsals of The Amber Witch, the stage-manager shewed off to peculiar advantage. In the last act, the so-called witch, finding herself menaced by a number of peasants, conceives the idea of acting on their superstitious fears, and sings or recites a Latin prayer. This they take for a spell, and hurry away, leaving her in peace. Mr Stage Manager, hearing the prayer, called out, 'Dont you hear? she's praying: down on your knees.' I happened to know the situation from Chorley, the author of the libretto, and took upon myself to point out the mistake. The stage-manager merely remarked, 'How the devil should I know anything about it? I have never read the book. Here, you Chorus, it's a spell to frighten you; so, as soon as you hear the first words, clear off as fast as you can.'

. . . .

"We had (at La Scala, Milan, 1865) a rehearsal for the stage business with the stage-manager, Piave, the author of several of Verdi's librettos, including that of Il Trovatore. I was highly amused; for the old gentleman wandered about the dark stage with a coil of wax-taper, directing us. He had evidently forgot all about his own work. He told me to come on from the wrong side for my first entrance, and was highly indignant when I suggested he was mistaken; but he begged my pardon when he found his mistake led to a muddle. . . . For Il Templario we had several rehearsals on the stage with the full orchestra and with a multiplicity of directors—Cavallini directing the orchestra with his fiddlestick, and taking the time from Mazzucato, who, seated in front of the stage, beat the time with his hand, whilst the chorus-master stood in front of his regiment, also beating time. Altercations between the conductor and the principal instruments were not uncommon. I remember one which amused me very much. Cavallini turned to the principal 'cello and bass, and remarked that a certain B ought to be natural, not flat. The professors replied that he was mistaken, upon which a long argument ensued, ending in the double bass requesting the conductor to 'shut up,' as he did not know what he was talking about."

I make these extracts because I have been so often told that my criticisms of the opera are "too cynical," and I am so fully aware of how improbable the truth seems to the innocence of the ordinary opera-goer that I am not sorry to be able to call as a witness to the state of things of which we are at present enjoying "the traditions" our chief baritone, one who has achieved all that is as yet possible for a great English singer, and who speaks, nevertheless, as a disappointed man, driven from the stage by the impossibility of getting any honest work done there.

When my witness says, "I can conscientiously say that I never had money-making for an object; my aim and ambition have always been to make the best use of the talent God entrusted to me," I believe he carries conviction of his sincerity to all who remember any considerable portion of his career; and it is not necessary for me or anyone else to supplement that statement by any compliments. The impression he made on me years ago, under the Mapleson régime, was that he was not a ready-made artist for stage-work, and had never been able to get thoroughly finished.

As to his singing, I cannot say how long it took him to perfect that; for the first time I ever heard him (it was as Di Luna in Il Trovatore) he was already fully accomplished vocally. But as an actor he was blunt, unpractised, and prone to fall back on a good-humored nonchalance in his relations with the audience, which was highly popular, but which destroyed all dramatic illusion. He was always Santley, the good fellow with no nonsense about him, and a splendid singer; but never (except as Papageno) was he the character in the opera, who was usually a person with a very great deal of nonsense about him. The nonchalance was really diffidence: one could see that a man of his straightforward temperament could only acquire the art of impersonation by years of unremitting and severe practice.

If he had been on the staff of a National Theatre, working his way steadily on to an unassailable position and a secure and sufficient pension, he would have had plenty of thorough rehearsal to train him; and his earnestness and vigor would have been transmuted into dramatic intensity of feeling and grip of character. A National Opera could hardly have had better material to work up. But there was no National Opera; and the opportunities he actually got were of the kind described in the typical passages I have quoted. For example, he may be said to have created Valentine in Faust, as it was considered a minor part until he made it a leading one; yet I heard him, when he was about forty, play it in an unfinished, hail-fellow-well-met way, even to the extent of rattling off Dio Possente at the rate of a hundred crotchets per minute or thereabouts; and though he was tremendously in earnest in the death scene, the earnestness was by no means fully incorporated with the part.

Later on, in Vanderdecken, Mikéli, Claude Melnotte, and the Porter of Havre, his dramatic grip was much surer;

and at the present moment, on the verge of his sixtieth year, he is a more thorough artist than ever. There can be no doubt that his sincerity of temperament, developed by the Philistine atmosphere of his native Liverpool into bluffness, and his sensitiveness, with nothing to exercise it but the snubs and checks which fall to the lot of a young clerk in a commercial town, were hindrances to him on the stage, where, under honest artistic conditions, they would have helped him. It is noteworthy that when he went to Milan to study, he brought thither a Lancashire eye to which the showy cathedral and beautiful church of Sant Ambrogio were absolutely indifferent. He describes the services at both without a word to indicate any consciousness of the artistic gulf which separates the one building from the other; and he adds, "Picture-galleries, museums, libraries, or exhibitions never possessed much attraction for me."

And yet he is beyond a doubt a highly imaginative man. If he had been a romantic humbug and *poseur*, he would perhaps have educated himself in the artifices of the stage by his efforts to look picturesque in private life; but being the very reverse of that, he started as an awkward masquerader, and was received with the usual nonsense about his not being a born actor—a convenient evasion for the critic who feels that there is something wanting, and does not know his business well enough to be able to say what the something is. If Santley's eyes and limbs had been educated from his childhood as his ear was, he would have been as much a born actor as a born singer; for Nature had been as kind to him in the matter of face and figure as in that of voice. As it was, one remembers his performances far better than those of the numerous "born artists," "thorough artists," "artists to the tips of their fingers," and so on, who have played his parts here.

There is much more in Student and Singer which I should like to quote and moralize upon if I had space—all the more freely, as Mr Santley declares that, as a rule, he does not read criticism. His self-criticism is extraordinarily frank; and after reading such remarks as he permits himself on his fellow-artists I should set a good deal of store by his opinion if he were to set up in my business. On the subject of singing he says little, explaining that he intends to deal fully with it in a separate work, which will be awaited with interest by many young singers who are curious to know how a man can sing for forty years and then appear at a Handel Festival with a much fresher voice than most baritones have after forty week's run of their first comic opera. I conclude with an extract which may be useful to students bound for Italy:

"I had letters of introduction to several musical and other influential people in Milan, three of which I delivered, and this I regretted having done, as they were the cause of no little persecution for loans, gifts, etc. . . . But I had no need of letters of introduction to make the acquaintance of similar gentry, all bent on plunder. I had journalists, or people who called themselves such, who wanted subscriptions to papers I had never heard of and did not wish to see," etc., etc., etc.

Ma mie Rosette, produced last Thursday at the Globe by Messrs Lart and Boosey, is refreshingly free from the stale vulgarities without which no comic opera is supposed to be complete. It is positively elegant, and appeals throughout to the tastes of people who have not a deliberate preference for baseness in art. Therefore it may very possibly fail. M. Paul Lacome's music is taken from good sources; his reminiscences are those of a fairly cultivated musician and not of a mere music-hall frequenter. The numbers interpolated by Mr Caryll fall considerably below this standard: they are thin and trivial, and might have been composed by Mr Solomon in an uninspired moment. The cast is good. Mr Oudin is not mellow and humorous enough for Henri Quatre; but he brings down the house by his singing, especially in an air in the second act, founded, apparently, on Vincent Wallace's "Why do I weep for thee?" Miss Nesville, whose voice is no larger than the point of a very small pin, is clever enough to please the audience, though, for all her undoubted stage talent, I do not feel disposed to admit that she is in her place as a prima donna. Miss Jessie Bond, Mr Wyatt, and Mr D'Orsay are amusing and not oppressive in the comic parts; and Miss Jennie McNulty shews some capacity as Corisande. The opera is prettily mounted; but the electric candles in the second act so dazzle the spectator and kill the costumes in front of them, that their miraculous extinction half-way through is a relief. And Mr Courtice Pounds' second dress, which makes him look like Tavannes in Les Huguenots pretending to be a Highlander, is simple inconceivable, even by those who have seen it.

30 *November* 1892

BY far the most important musical event in London last week was the annual competition of the Board School choirs at Exeter Hall for a Challenge Medallion. I spent three mortal hours listening to eight choirs singing, first, See the chariot at hand, then a "sight test," and finally, whatever part-song was the *cheval de bataille* of the particular school in hand. The audience consisted of the judges, Sir John Stainer and Mr McNaught, of a few critics to judge the judges from the reserved seats, and of the Lord Mayor and Lady Mayoress in great honor and glory on the platform, supported by a contingent of the London School Board, including at one extreme the Reverend Chairman Diggle, who listened moderately, and at the other the Reverend Stewart Headlam, who listened progressively. There was, besides, a vast audience of friends, relatives, and partisans of the competitors, who followed the points of the competition with an intelligence unknown at St. James's Hall.

Some young ladies behind me were eagerly scanning the choristers to find "the angel," who, as I gathered from the context, was a boy of seraphic beauty and goodness. I sought him eagerly, but entirely failed to identify him. There were dreamy, poetic, delicate-featured boys and girls; docile, passively receptive ones (with medals—I despised them); little duchesses whom I should have liked to adopt, little dukes who would have been considerably enriched if anyone had cut them off with a shilling; and a sprinkling of Miss Morleena Kenwigs and Bailey junior, all making points of interest in a crowd of the children of Voltaire's wise friend, Monsieur Tout le Monde. But angel there was none, except all our good and bad angels, who, being two to each member of a crowded audience, must have been kept pretty constantly on the wing to avoid being crushed. Then there were pupil-teachers' choirs, large bodies of picked young women, all of them survivals of the fittest, resolute, capable, and with a high average of good looks. When I look at a fashionable audience of ladies at a recital I always feel, in spite of my profession, as if I were an honest, useful, hard-working citizen; but before the pupil-teachers I quailed, and knew myself for what I really am—that is to say, a musical critic.

The competition, like all competitions, was more or less a humbug, the Elcho shield going eventually to the conductor who had trained his choir single-heartedly in the art of getting the highest marks, which is not the same thing as the art of choral singing. His pupils performed with remarkable vigor and decision, and were the only ones who really succeeded in reading the "sight test" all through; but Mr Casserley's choir from the Great College Street school shewed more artistic sensibility; and Mr Longhurst's boys from Bellenden Road were not further behind than all choirs of one sex alone are inevitably behind mixed choirs, both in quality of tone, in which the difference is enormous, and in the address with which girls pull boys out of difficulties, and boys girls, according to their special aptitudes. The decision shewed that the "sight test," which is the most mechanical part of the business, was five-sixths of the battle. And it was not even fairly conducted. I concluded that it was not possible to keep all the later competitors quite out of earshot of the earlier ones; for the reading of the upper part got better as the afternoon wore on, the little pitchers using their long ears to pick up the tune; whilst the reading of the middle and lower parts in the harmony shewed no such improvement. Thus, the winners of the shield, who, as it happened, sang last, must, unless they had been carefully plugged with cotton-wool for some two hours or so, or else kept outside the building, have heard the "sight test" sung no less than seven times before they tried it. This was sufficient to prepare them completely for the chief difficulty presented by the dotted crotchet and five quavers in the ninth bar, which so bothered the early competitors; as well as by the trap into which even the conductors fell, to their great credit, in the tenth, the composer, Mr Roston Bourke, having deliberately truncated the metre by leaving out a bar at that point. If I had been one of the judges I should unhesitatingly have given twenty marks to every choir which made the mistake Mr Bourke intended it to make, and struck twenty off the unintelligent plodders who passed unconsciously and safely through the danger. As to the senseless syncopation on the word "death," I am ready to head a deputation of ratepayers to the School Board about so perfect an instance of the evil inherent in all competition.

Mr Roston Bourke, instead of acting as a musician desirous to write beautiful music for children, acted as a Jack-o'-Lantern, and did his worst to mislead them. If Haydn had written that "sight test," I believe that the very first symptom of confusion among the children would have sent him out into the Strand to publicly kneel down and beg forgiveness of Heaven for his crime. The sight test was otherwise bad in respect of the minor section, where the greatest difficulty was experienced in reading the notes, being also the only episode calculated to test a choir's power of catching a change in the sentiment of the music.

As might have been foreseen, the result was that the choir which caught the change in sentiment bungled the notes; whilst the winning choir, which alone vanquished all three parts in this section, absolutely disregarded the change in sentiment. As I have already said, the conductor of that choir, Mr J. Harris, a very competent gentleman, knew that if his children came out right upon matters of fact, they might safely disregard matters of taste. And this brings me to the injustice to the children of a competition which depends more on their instructor than on themselves. This is more or less true of all school competitions; but it is especially true of choral singing, the difference between one school and another being mostly a difference in the ability of the conductors, since children, in the lump, are all alike. There is, however, an element of luck in the matter as well, arising out of the existence of specially gifted children.

Every practical musician knows that sight reading is a very rare accomplishment, and that the champion exponents of the Tonic Sol-fa, the Chevé method, Hullah's system, and so forth, are usually persons who have what is called a sense of absolute pitch, and who, in reading from the ordinary staff notation, are guided neither by the intervals from one note to the next, nor by the "mental effect" of the note in the scale, but simply remember the pitch of every separate note, and sing it when they see it written down. These tuneful mortals, if you met them in the middle of the Great Sahara, and asked them to give you B flat, would strike it up like a tuning-fork. The easiest and commonest method of sight reading is to sit next to an absolute pitcher, and sing what he or she sings.

The sense of absolute pitch is rather commoner among children than among adults; and here the school conductor's luck comes in. If he happens to have one absolute pitcher in each division, he may, without having taught a single child to read at sight, get his choir to sing a test on the follow-my-leader plan more successfully than a rival whose singers are all consciously calculating their intervals or sol-faing. Obviously, this possibility introduces an additional element of chance into the competition. On the whole, I think it would be well to discard the challenge shield from the annual exhibition, and so get rid of the senseless game of winning marks. There is quite incentive enough in the presence of the audience and the Lord Mayor to secure all the benefits which are supposed to accrue from an invidious award of the custody for one year of an absurd signboard to the choir which does the ill-office of humiliating all the rest.

The really tragic feature of the exhibition, however, was not in the pedagogic method, but in the little snatches of sweet and delicate singing which occasionally came from the mass of sound of which, in the main, no musical adjustment could disguise the vulgarity. It was not quite so bad as an ordinary oratorio chorus—the remnants of the charm of childhood saved it from that extremity; but already every child's voice was in far better training for slang and profanity than for poetry.

Children become adepts at what they hear every day and what they see every day; and the notion that you can educate a child musically by any other means whatsoever except that of having beautiful music finely performed within its hearing, is a notion which I feel constrained to denounce, at the risk of being painfully personal to the whole nation, as tenable only by an idiot. Imagine a country teaching its children for half the day how to read the police intelligence, how to forge, and how to falsify accounts, and the other half how to tolerate, and eventually prefer, uncouth sights, discordant sounds, foul clothes, and graceless movements and manners.

However, I am gratified to be able to announce, by special request, that the Duke of Westminster, who so firmly protested against the extravagance of furnishing each Board School with a pianoforte, has presented the Westminster Orchestral Society with a life-membership donation of ten guineas.

As to Mr Cliffe's new symphony in E minor, composed for the Leeds Festival, and performed some weeks ago at the Crystal Palace, I am disqualified from any fruitful criticism of it by finding that I do not like it. This is not Mr Cliffe's fault: neither is it mine. The general mood of the work is too sentimental for me; and the orchestration, to my taste, is particularly cloying. Mr Cliffe seems to have no respect for the instruments: instead of giving them real parts, or at least firm virile touches to lay in, he uses them only to rouge his themes up to the eyes, and to hang rings on their fingers and bells on their toes, so to speak.

The themes themselves have no backbone: they languish along by diminished intervals whenever they get a chance of leaning on chromatic progressions; and it is quite a relief to come to some commonplace but straightforward prettiness, like that of the serenade, with the affectionate reminiscence of one of Mendelssohn's Songs without Words in the first phrase. Another reminiscence, which is very conspicuous among the thematic materials of the opening movement, is the first bar of Siegmund's spring song in Die Walküre, extended by a sequence through a second bar, and with its intervals altered, but still unmistakeable. As to the program of Sunset, Night, and Morning (I need not mention the inevitable Fairies' Revel scherzo), all I can say is that sunset, night, and morning never make me feel like that. Evidently a case of deficient sympathy, on which account I do not lay any stress on my impression of the work. Mr Cliffe has apparently done exactly what he aimed at, and done it with great skill and industry, though also, I must reproachfully add, without the least regard for my idiosyncrasy.

Last Saturday we had a new symphonic poem, The Passing of Beatrice, by Mr William Wallace, a young Scotch composer with a very tender and sympathetic talent. I would cite the prelude to Lohengrin as an instance of the successful accomplishment of what Mr Wallace tries to do in his poem, which, if cut down by about nine-tenths, and well worked over, would make a pretty *entr'acte*. The orchestra, by the bye, has rubbed off the rustiness of the beginning of the season, and has been playing admirably these last few weeks.

7 *December* 1892

AT the London Symphony Concert last Thursday, Mr Henschel staked the capacity of his orchestra for refinement of execution on Raff's Lenore symphony, and won. The crescendo of the march, from *pianissimo* to *forte*, was admirably managed. It did not quite reach *for-*

tissimo—not what I call *fortissimo*, at least—and it fell short of the final degrees of martial brilliancy which Mr Manns has sometimes achieved in it; but it was enormously superior to the recent attempt of the Philharmonic band, which began moderately *piano*, tumbled into a *mezzoforte* in the second section, and stuck there for the rest of the movement. The second movement was perfectly executed: it held the attention of the audience from the first note to the last, as slow movements very seldom do. The quick movements would have been equally perfect but for a certain unpunctuality of attack in the vigorous touches, especially in the bass, and an occasional want of weight when the fullest power of the band was needed.

I should explain, however, that I heard the performance, not from my usual seat, but from the extreme back of the room, where, as I went in, I spied a few empty benches suitable for a secluded nap. A long work by Brahms was in the program; so I thought I would go and sit there in case of accidents. It was a concerto for violin and violoncello, with one or two glorious beginnings in it in Brahms' vigorous, joyous, romantic style; but they did not hold out; and there was nothing for it, most of the time, but resignation or slumber. Gorski, the violinist, had not come to much of an understanding with Fuchs, the 'cellist; and neither of them had come to an understanding with Brahms—at least, it seemed so to me; but then my attention wandered a good deal. Miss Evangeline Florence sang the balcony scene from Lohengrin; and the concert wound up with the overture to Die Meistersinger.

Violoncellists who want to play like Gerardy will be interested by the Cours Préparatoire de Violoncelle of his master, Alfred Massau, of the Verviers school of music. There is an abominable custom among agents of persuading young and unknown artists, however admirably they may have been taught, to prepare for their début by taking three months' lessons from some celebrated player, in order that they may be announced and puffed as pupils of the eminent

So-and-so. Thus they are taught to begin by being ashamed of their own talent, and ungrateful to the master to whom they owe its cultivation. The master is robbed of the credit due to him; and the eminent one finds Europe full of players claiming to be his pupils on the strength of perhaps a dozen lessons.

Think of the legion of pianists, good, bad, and indifferent, who, because they once loafed about Weimar for a few months, and managed to obtain the not very difficult entry to the famous music-room there, are now "pupils of Liszt." The system is not only a dishonest one, but stupid into the bargain; for the public, as far as it concerns itself with an artist's antecedents at all, judges the master by the player, and not the player by the master. I therefore give Alfred Massau as Gerardy's master neither on his own claim nor on that of his famous pupil, but on the authority of an official certificate from the Communal Administration of Verviers, duly stamped with the town seal, whereon a lion ramps in a meat safe, with a crown above him, and the motto *L'Union fait la force* below.

The document, dated November, 1891, runs as follows:

"I subscribe, declare, and certify that Mr Jean Gerardy, violoncellist, has gone through the regular violoncello course at our establishment (professor, Alfred Massau), from October 1st, 1885, to August 15th, 1889. He has carried off the following distinctions: Competition of 1886 (2nd division), 1st *accessit*; 1887 (*idem*), 1st prize; 1888 (1st division), 1st prize, with distinction; 1889 (higher competition), silver-gilt medal, with the greatest distinction.

"The jury for these last competitions was composed of MM. L. Kefer, Presiding Director; Van der Heyden, violoncellist from Paris; J. de Swert, violoncellist, Conductor at Ostend; Ed. Jacobs, violoncellist, Professor at the Brussels Conservatoire; and Jos. Mertens, Government Inspector of Schools of Music."

[Here follow the signatures of M. Louis Kefer and the

President of the Communal Administration, solemnly affixed in "our" presence. That is, the presence of the Burgomaster, whose signature, as becomes that of a man with a plural pronoun, is wholly illegible.]

I give this document for the sake of its suggestiveness as to the state of affairs in the musical profession. Verviers is a small Belgian town; its school of music is not widely famous; and Massau, though his reputation as a teacher is first-rate, is not known as a virtuoso in London and Paris. The consequence is that Verviers and Massau, instead of finding themselves made famous by the brilliant European success of Gerardy, actually have to place official certificates in my hands in order to make it known in London that the five years' training which made Gerardy what he is were not the work of Herr Bellmann or any other virtuoso who may have subsequently given him "finishing lessons."

As to the Cours Préparatoire, I can only testify to its completeness and intelligibility. Not being a 'cellist, I must take Gerardy's playing as evidence of its soundness. It is published by Schott, has its instructions printed in French, German, and English, and is remarkably cheap, considering its bulk and quality, at ten shillings, or in two volumes at six shillings each.

I have received from Messrs Sampson Low & Co. a Life of Chopin, by Mr Charles Willeby, which strikes me as really supplying a want. For some years past the Liszt-George Sand stereo on the subject has been wearing out; and the arrival of an exceedingly cool young gentleman, adequately skilled in music, who gives his own account of the matter without the least regard for the expiring Chopin fashion, is highly refreshing. The older I grow, the more I appreciate the sang-froid of early manhood. Middle age makes me sentimental, hot-headed, and withal conscious of the folly of the multitude and the ease with which that folly can be exploited by anybody with a moderate power of self-expression in politics or in any of the popular arts. This I call becoming wise; but if I were anybody else, I should doubtless call it becoming stale.

Anyhow, it is a condition in which I could not write as freshly about Chopin as Mr Willeby; and I welcome his book accordingly; though I cannot refrain from giving utterance to the melancholy conviction that time will mellow his stern judgment of George Sand, and shake his incredulity as to her having boxed her son-in-law's ears and turned him out of the house for smiting one of her guests on the nose. "Were we dealing with children, and the nursery our scene," says Mr Willeby, "we might accept this story. But when we think that the parties concerned were men and women of the world, it is laughable, and to accept it seriously, impossible." Alas! alas! it is precisely the men and women of the world who do these things, whilst the novices are furtively studying manuals of etiquette to ascertain the proper use of the finger-bowl.

Mr Willeby, to tell the truth, rather breaks down over George Sand. He says:

"However lenient we may be towards the woman who so worthily added to the art of her country, one cannot deny the fact that she was of a nature the reverse of admirable—a woman who, while stopping at nothing in the gratification of her desires, yet was ever ready with an excuse for herself, and who *posed* before the world as an example of all that was good and upright in womanhood. Moreover, she seems to have been wanting alike in tact, reserve, and dignity of conduct; while by no means the least noticeable feature in her character was the manner in which she succeeded in deceiving even herself."

All of which, though irrefutable from its point of view, is entirely worthless as a description of George Sand, because it would be equally irrefutable of dozens of other eminent women who were not in the least like George Sand. One does not refute that sort of criticism; one repudiates it. Again:

"One of the vices of George Sand seems to have been not an extraordinary one in women generally, that of curiosity. This fatal feeling," etc.

Observe the implication that "this fatal feeling" is a stranger to the nobler male breast. Only once does Mr Willeby relent:

"Inasmuch as she kept his accounts, wrote many of his letters, and tended him with the greatest devotion in the many trying times when his disease laid him up, *she is worthy of some praise*."

I should rather think so. I do not hold a brief for George Sand; but Mr Willeby provokes me to ask what would have been said if the shoe had been on the other foot. Suppose Chopin had been George Sand's benefactor. Suppose he had found after a time that she was as exacting as an invalided child; that she spoiled the home life of his other children by quarrelling with them; and that he could not spare from his own work as a composer the energy wasted in combating these circumstances. Would any reasonable person have blamed him for refusing to share his home with her any longer? If not, how can any reasonable person blame George Sand, except on the gratuitous assumption that she and her children were Chopin's slaves, with no duty to anybody but to him? For the life of me, I cannot see how she behaved worse than Chopin.

The fact that he appears to have suffered more by the separation than she did is clearly a proof that he gained more than she by their association. Mr Willeby has certainly made out a case of ingratitude against Chopin, as well as one of levity against George Sand; but neither of them is more interesting or convincing than the cases against Salvini for vagabondism, against Mr Hamo Thornycroft for breach of the Second Commandment, against the Duke of Wellington for rapine and murder, or against any English Mahometan for not attending his parish church. Nothing is more idle and tedious than the sort of criticism which deals with a man who is acting up to his own convictions, right or wrong, as if he was simply violating his critic's convictions, or those of his critic's publisher.

On the whole, Mr Willeby's moral judgments must be taken as a trifle disabled by the very quality of youth which gives value to his book as a whole. To say, for instance, that Chopin was not a man to grasp opportunities merely because he did not jump at a chance of giving a paying concert, is to substitute the business standard of a smart agent for the artistic standard of the critic of a great composer. A man who died of consumption at thirty-nine, and yet produced what Chopin has left us, was clearly a man of immeasurably greater energy and practicality than the late Mr Jay Gould, who worked far longer than Chopin, and produced nothing.

On musical ground I agree better with Mr Willeby, though even here I am made somewhat restive by such passages as:

"In the Concerto, Chopin's subordination to, and inability to cope with, form was as conspicuous as was his superiority and independence of it in his smaller works."

This implies that form means sonata form and nothing else, an unwarrantable piece of pedantry, which one remembers as common enough in the most incompetent and old-fashioned criticisms of Chopin's ballades, Liszt's symphonic poems, and Wagner's works generally, but which is now totally out of countenance. Mr Willeby himself evidently would not stand by it for a moment. Yet on another page (229) he goes still further in the same direction by identifying music in sonata form with "absolute music," and describing all other music as "program music." Now a Chopin ballade is clearly no more program music than the slow movement of Mozart's symphony in E flat is.

I submit that a definition which makes program music of Chopin's tone poems, and abstract music of Raff's symphonies, clearly wants a little further consideration. However, I must not unduly depreciate Mr Willeby's book by dwelling too much on our differences. A few slips in the critical analyses may very well be condoned for the sake of a readable biography of Chopin which is not nine-tenths a work of pure imagination.

14 *December* 1892

I HAVE to complain strongly of the Royal College of Music for its neglect to exclude the parents and relatives of the students from its performance of Gluck's Orfeo on Saturday afternoon. The barbarous demonstrations of these Philistines, who treated the band just as they would have treated a quadrille player at one of their own dances, spoiled many a final strain in the score. Surely, if the students are to be nurtured as artists, the first and most obvious step is to cut off all communication between them and their families.

A member of an ordinary British household cannot become an artist: the thing is impossible. This was well understood in former ages with regard to the religious life, the devotees of which invariably began by cutting all their people dead, knowing full well that on no other terms was any unworldly life possible. Now the artistic life is the most unworldly of lives; and how can it be lived in any sort of association with people who, rather than wait for the band to finish Che faro senza Euridice? break into uncouth noise the moment the singer's mouth is closed?

Giulia Ravogli came to the performance, presumably to see what Gluck's Orfeo looked like. The unfamiliar spectacle must have made her envy those obscure students the artistic framework which she, one of the greatest Orfeos in the world, cannot get in the richest capital in Europe. The work was admirably put on the stage. One scene, in which a soul newly released from earth came groping into the Elysian fields, bewildered and lonely, and was discovered and welcomed by two child-shades, was a most pathetic piece of pantomime. That shade one believed to be the lost Euridice, until Euridice appeared later on in the person of quite another young lady—no great pantomimist. Very pretty, too, was the array of spirits stretching their hands after the departing Orpheus as he started on his return to earth.

The Elysian fields were situated on the uplands between Frensham and Selborne: I know the place, and thought it well chosen for the purpose. The furies and spectres were not quite up to the artistic level of the blesseder shades; and they gave no adequate sign of the shock given to them by the first note of Orpheus's lute in that dreadful region. I think, too, that the orchestral piece in D minor, since it was not danced to by the spectres, should have been played with the tableau curtain down, instead of as a storm symphony to a lightning and thunder cloth which became ridiculous after its levin bolts had remained for a couple of minutes without getting along. But the fact that these two matters exhaust my fault-finding speaks for the general excellence and artistic integrity of the staging.

The principal performer, Miss Clara Butt, a comparatively raw recruit from Bristol, far surpassed the utmost expectations that could have been reasonably entertained. She has a good voice, and went at her work without the least conceit, though with plenty of courage and originality, shewing an honesty of artistic character which is perhaps the most promising quality a novice can display. She has a rich measure of dramatic sympathy; and, considering that the management of the costume and deportment proper to the part would tax the powers of our most experienced actresses, her impersonation suffered surprisingly little from awkwardness. If Miss Butt has sufficient strength of mind to keep her eyes, ears, and mind open in the artistic atmosphere of the Royal College, without for a moment allowing herself to be taught (a process which instantly stops the alternative process of learning), she may make a considerable career for herself.

Euridice (Miss Maggie Purvis) sang like a pupil of the Royal Academy. She had apparently been taught to practise all over her voice on the vowel *a*, because that is the most beautiful vowel. The way in which a soprano produces the G or A flat above the stave had been taken as a model for the production of every sound within her compass. To make a crescendo she simply breathed harder; and she attacked her notes with the *coup de glotte*. I have heard basses—actually basses—who had been taught to do exactly the same thing; and the difference between their voices and that of Edouard de Reszke was very striking.

Imagine that genial giant with his voice trained like the top register of a soprano, bleating a few genteel notes between his upper B and D with the feather-edge of his vocal cords (the E natural and F not to be practised too much lest they should fatigue the larynx), and with all the middle of his voice worn to the sound of a cracked Pandean pipe. I do not know the names of the teaching staff at the Royal College, nor of Euridice's preceptor, whose instructions she may, of course, have been systematically violating, as the wont of pupils is when they get before the public.

But I am bound to say that though she sang prettily, and is not at all deficient in capacity, the sort of voice she produces would never stand the knocking about of real dramatic work, nor has it the least force or variety of color. It is impossible for me to go at length into the system of teaching singing which has prevailed for so long in our own Royal Academy and many of the foreign Conservatoires, and which has been maintained so ably by that clever and dramatically gifted family, the Garcias. Suffice it to say that I have heard a good many pupils of the Garcias in my time, and a good many pupils of other masters, too, from Santley to Melba and our modern American prima donnas; and I must frankly say that though I do not doubt that all the great Garcias were masterful people and powerful actors, I am a confirmed sceptic as to the practical value of their system of vocal instruction. And I was sorry to infer, from Euridice's singing, and from my recollection of the previous annual operatic performances, that the Garcia method is in the ascendant at Kensington as well as in Tenterden Street.

My observation has led me to believe that if you take an ordinary English girl and try to make her sing, your business is not to elicit from her sounds as fine as G above the stave on the vowel *a* (Italian) as Patti would sing it, but to work her voice on *aw* (without rolling her tongue up into a ball, *bien entendu*) below the stave, on *oo* and *ee* in the middle, and on *a* at the top only, shewing her how to manage her breathing and so forth meanwhile, and keeping her at that until she has learnt the physical act of singing, and is in possession of a fully developed voice well under her control, which she can use as vigorously as she wants to without any damage. Then, and not until then, is the time to awaken her artistic conscience, to purify her pronunciation, refine her tone, and, in short, turn your mere singer into an artist.

Try to make her into an artist before she can sing by worrying her at the very first lesson to produce the ideal tone aimed at by Garcia, and unless her physical endowment is so rich and her vocation so strong that she stumbles into the right path in spite of you, you will arrive at that melancholy result, the ordinary Academy pupil who, after a brief trial of her thin and colorless perfections on the public, takes to helping herself out by brute force, and presently grinds away her voice and takes to teaching the art in which she has failed. Of course she has been repeatedly warned that she must not force her voice; but when she finds that she can produce no effect in any other way, all these excellent negative precepts are thrown to the winds. No method that is merely negative is of any use to a dramatic singer, or indeed to any artist whatever.

Unless singers have a positive method, into which they can throw their utmost energy and temper at moments when they are about as much interested in the quality of the vowel *a* as a tiger is in the quality of his roar as he springs on a sheep, they *must* resort to brute force on the stage, or else fail through an obvious gingerly preoccupation with their negative instructions. The first demand of the dramatic instinct is for safe and powerful *fortissimo*. To tell students of dramatic singing that there is no need for vehemence in singing is only an evasion, like telling the student who wants to paint a white cat that "in the grand school, all cats are grey." Shouting is not necessary in political oratory; but I should like to see the political speaker who would put up with a teacher unable to put him in the way of thundering a little occasionally.

It so happened on Saturday that Miss Purvis did not particularly want to be vehement. But if she had been playing Elvira or Valentina or Fidelio, I wonder how much use her academic method in its negative purity would have been to her. Much less, I venture to affirm, than no method at all. She would simply have had to scream through all the formidable passages.

I turn with relief to the subject of the band. Here the performers, having all been taught their instruments by men who earn their living by playing them, knew their business, and were no worse than their instructors in respect of not always sustaining the tone for the full duration of the notes. The execution was smart, and the quality of sound remarkably bright and fine.

The conductor, Professor Stanford, guided, as I judged, by a genuine love of the work and an intimate knowledge of it, only went astray once—in the immensely grand chorus Che mai dell' Erebo, which he took, like a true Irishman, as he would have taken the first movement of the Eroica, and not in the *tempo* of God Save the Queen, which would have been much nearer the mark, reserving the quicker *tempo* for the later repetitions. For the performance as a whole there can be nothing but praise. It could only be possible in an institution where there was a well-spring of genuine enthusiasm for art. The credit of stimulating and centring that enthusiasm belongs, I imagine, to Sir George Grove, whose life-work has been of more value than that of all the Prime Ministers of the century.

Let me add, by the way, that the Royal College has selected its opera much better this year and last than it used to. Tales like those of The Barber of Bagdad, and classic legends like Orpheus, are understood by young students far better than silly intrigues like Cosi fan tutti, or—with all due respect to Shakespear—explosions of what I may call sex-Podsnappery like that atrocious play The Taming of the Shrew.

21 *December* 1892

THE Nursing Homes of St Mary's, Plaistow, succeeded in making up a program at St James's Hall on Thursday, which induced me to go, for once in a way, to a miscellaneous concert. I there heard Mrs Katharine Fisk, the American contralto, who seems to have made a considerable impression on her first appearance (at which I was unable to assist) some weeks ago. She selected a song called Calm as the Night, by Bohm, and, by dint of grinding and driving her voice hard down on every note, produced a certain effect which may have appealed to some of the audience as one of brooding intensity. To me it seemed a mechanical device which any contralto could acquire at the risk of being left presently with a hollow and unsympathetic voice, almost useless for what I, according to my particular prejudice on the subject, consider legitimate singing. However, Mrs Fisk obtained her share of applause; and, as it is her business to please the public and not to conform to my notions of voice production, I have nothing more to say.

Giulia Ravogli sang a scena from Vaccai's Giulietta e Romeo, chosen for the sake of one of those long recitatives beginning with In questo loco (In this neighborhood), and proceeding with the usual observations. I like to hear Signorina Giulia singing In questo loco, just as I should have liked to hear Mrs Siddons asking the linen-draper "Will it wash?" But let there be no mistake about the fact that In questo loco is as dead as My name is Norval. No doubt if Mr Irving suddenly took a fancy to Norval and began reciting about the Grampian Hills, and his father feeding his flock, a frugal swain, whose constant care was to increase his store, we should listen to him with high enjoyment, much as we listen to Miss Ellen Terry bringing Monk Lewis back to life with her pet recitation of Stay, gaoler, stay: I am not mad. But we should not regard the entertainment as up to date. And that is my objection to Vaccai. Like Monk Lewis and Home, he was a man for an age, but most emphatically not for all time.

Sofia Ravogli joined her sister in a duet from Le Roi de Lahore, which they sang with a distinction and quiet perfection of style which shewed that they have found out the good side of the London artistic atmosphere, and profited by it. Their former touch of provinciality, which one did not care to mention, so trivial a drawback was it to their genuine musical and dramatic force, has vanished without taking any of their intensity away with it; and we may now esteem ourselves rarely fortunate in having, apparently, attached them to England. No doubt we shall shew our sense of that by offering them the chance of some half-a-dozen appearances on the stage every year in the height of the season, with a turn at the Philharmonic and Crystal Palace, a liberal allowance of charity concerts, and plenty of private engagements. Nothing is sadder than the way in which London attracts dramatic genius to itself and then helplessly wastes it.

The concert, I should explain, was varied by the appearance from time to time of a cheerful clergyman, who made the most sinister announcements without blenching, and retired each time smiling blandly at the horror-stricken audience. Thus he would say, after waiting for dead silence with a reassuring beam in his eye, "Ladies and gentlemen: Miss Esther Palliser will not be able to sing for you this afternoon, as she is all but asphyxiated"; or, "Ladies and gentlemen: we must omit the next item, as one of the ladies in the quartet has suddenly lost her voice"; or, "Ladies and gentlemen: if Mr Wyndham and Miss Mary Moore give us their duologue, they will fall into the hands of the law, as this hall is not licensed by the County Council for dramatic entertainments; but they will do the best they can separately under the circumstances." He might have thrown in an apology for the excruciating discrepancy between the pitch of the pianoforte and that of Miss Eldina Bligh's fiddle.

I had rather have drunk a tumbler of vinegar than listen to those Brahms-Joachim Hungarian dances with the violin virtually in one key and the piano in another. It was a pity; for the young lady would have pleased the audience very well if there had been no accompaniment. When she reappeared later on with Miss Macintyre, to play the obbligato to the inevitable intermezzo from Cavalleria, the audience received her with the liveliest apprehensions. This time, however, the pitch was adjusted; and she played the obbligato much better, I must say, than Miss Macintyre sang the Ave Maria.

Miss Macintyre's style is not prayerful, nor her execution smooth; and when she finished her self-assertive orison with a vigorous *forte* on the last note, we thought of the saintlike Calvé and her touching *pianissimo*, and blessed the singer for resisting the encore which the intermezzo-manias promptly tried to force upon her. I rather admired her for singing the piece in her own way instead of imitating Calvé; but I cannot say that I thought her own way particularly appropriate; though far be it from me to make a serious matter of the treatment of what is, at best, an arrant piece of claptrap.

An interesting point in the program was Mr Henschel's singing of Schumann's setting of Heine's Two Grenadiers, followed by Mr Bispham with Wagner's setting of a French version—one of the *pièces de salon* which he produced in his early Parisian days. Mr Henschel sat down comfortably to the piano and murdered Schumann in cold blood. He played the mournful, weary-footed, quasi-military dead march accompaniment anyhow, flicking off the semiquaver turn in semidemisemiquavers, and beginning the Marseillaise at the top of his voice, which is the surest way I know to make the song fail. And it did fail, in spite of Mr Henschel's popularity, his staleness in it being obvious.

Mr Bispham, thoroughly on the alert, took his turn like the intelligent and cultivated artist he is; and though Wagner's setting taxed his voice fully twenty shillings in the pound, he came off solvent. I then fled from the miscellaneous scene, and so cannot say how the last quarter of the program was done, or whether it was done at all.

On the previous Tuesday I went to the Royal Academy of Music to hear Mr Ashton Ellis confront the Musical Association on the subject of Wagner's prose. There was a time when Mr Ellis would have taken his life in his hand on such an errand; but he now holds the field unopposed. I looked round for the old gang (if I may use that convenient political term without offence), and looked in vain.

When Mr Ellis sat down, after a sufficiently provocative exposure of the garblings of Opera and Drama which used to appear in the Musical World in the old days of anti-Wagnerism, I asked myself was there no man left to get up and complain of the "false relations" in Tristan, to plead for "a full close in the key" at frequent intervals during Der Ring, to explain that Wagner's music shattered the human voice and overpowered it with deafening instrumentation, to deplore the total absence of melody in Lohengrin, to praise the Tannhäuser march as the sole endurable work of Wagner (because plagiarized from the great scena in Der Freischütz) —in short, to put himself totally out of the question, for ever and a day, with every musician whose ideas of art were wider than those of a provincial organist?

But the enemy was chapfallen and speechless—that is, if the enemy was present; but I think he had stayed away. At any rate, Mr Ellis's party had the discussion all to themselves.

4 January 1893

THESE are not busy times for musical critics. In London everything serves as an excuse for having no music, from the death of a Royal personage to Christmas, just as in school everything serves as an excuse for a holiday. I have been in the country, in an old-English manor-house, where we all agreed to try and forget the festive season. We were not altogether successful. On the very first evening we were invaded by "the mummers," who were not in the least like the husbands of Mr George Moore's Mummer's Wife. They were laborers, overgrown with strips of colored paper as a rock is overgrown with seaweed; and they went through an operatic performance which I did not quite follow, as they were quite equal to professional opera-singers in point of unintelligibility, and, being simple country folk, were so unversed in the etiquette of first nights that they neglected to provide me with a libretto. I gathered that one of them was King Alfred, and another St George. A third, equipped with a stale tall hat, was announced as "the doctor." He drew a tooth from the prima donna, whom I did not succeed in identifying; revived the other characters when they were slain in single combat; and sang a ballad expressive of his aspiration to live and die "a varmer's b'woy." This he delivered with such a concentrated lack of conviction that I at once concluded that he actually was a farmer's boy; and my subsequent inquiries as to the rate of wages in the district confirmed my surmise. We of the audience had to assume the character of good old English gentlemen and ladies keeping up a seasonable custom; and it would be difficult to say whether we or the performers were the most put out of countenance. I have seldom been so disconcerted; and my host, though he kept it up amazingly, confessed to sharing my feelings; whilst the eagerness of the artists to escape from our presence when their performance was concluded and suitably acknowledged, testified to the total failure of our efforts to make them feel at home. We were perfectly friendly at heart, and would have been delighted to sit round the fire with them and talk; but the conventions of the season forbad it. Since we had to be mock-baronial, they had to be mock-servile; and so we made an uneasy company of Christmas humbugs, and had nothing to cheer us except the consciousness of heartily forgiving one another and being forgiven. On Christmas Eve there was more music, performed by the school-children, the carol-singers, and finally by an orchestra consisting of a violin, tambourine, a toy instrument with a compass of one wrong note, which it played steadily on the second and third beats in the bar, and anything else that would make a noise *ripieno*, *ad lib*. The singers sang traditional—*i.e.* inaccurate—versions of old airs and modern music-hall songs, the latter strangely modified by transmission from mouth to ear along the whole length of the Thames.

On my return to town I was casting about me in an unsettled state of mind for some pretext for keeping away for another evening from my work, when I found myself, as luck would have it, outside the Lyceum Theatre. Recollecting that I had not heard Mr Hamilton Clarke's incidental music to King Lear, I went inside, and found myself late for the overture, and only just in time for the march to which the Court enters. Mr Hamilton Clarke's music is graceful, and sensitive to the tenderer emotions of the drama. It is far too civilized for Lear; but it is, perhaps, unreasonable to expect a composer to aim at the powerful and barbaric when he well knows that the orchestral resources at his disposal will not be adequate to much more than sentimental *mélodrame*. I may add that I decidedly prefer Mr Ford Madox Brown as an illustrator of Shakespear to Mr Frank Dicksee; and as Mr Hamilton Clarke is in music exactly what Mr Frank Dicksee is in painting, his interludes do not altogether satisfy me. Which is nobody's fault, and my own misfortune.

Whilst I am on the subject of the Lyceum, I may as well extract the following from a letter in one of the musical papers: "Speaking of the letter O, Mr G. B. S. says that Mr Irving is the only living Englishman who makes it a pure vowel. What a marvellous being Mr G. B. S. must be! All the English, twenty-seven millions in number, have passed in review before him, and only one has succeeded in properly pronouncing the vowel O!" Now I did not say that Mr Irving pronounces O *properly*; I said that he makes a pure vowel of it. The effect was so strange at first that for years his pronunciation of "gold," "bowl," "pole to pole" (in Vanderdecken), etc., was unsparingly ridiculed and mimicked. I should like to have it settled whether Mr Irving is right or wrong.

There can be no doubt that the usage is to make O a diphthong: one hears "goh-oold," "gowld," "gah-oold," in all directions, but never pure "gold," except from Mr Irving or his imitators. On the other hand, the pure vowel is, to my artistic sense, much pleasanter. Which, then, should be recommended to the young actor? This question is much better suited for discussion in a musical paper than the misapprehensions arising from my unfortunate habit of saying things I do not mean, such as "the barbarous thoroughbass of Handel and Mozart." My critic has deserved well of his country for nipping that thoughtless slander in the bud.

I also hasten to explain that when I called Sterndale Bennett a convinced Dayite, I did not mean that he agreed with Day's derivations of chords. The first symptom of inveterate Dayism used generally to be a violent attack on one of Day's imaginary "roots." My impression is that Bennett believed in "roots," and that certain "intellectual harmonies" of his are logical applications of the root theory. Also, that the change from the rule-of-thumb thoroughbass taught by Mozart to Sussmayer, to the pseudo-scientific systems of Day and Macfarren, was forwarded instead of opposed by Sterndale Bennett. My critic contradicts me; but as his style does not inspire me with unreserved confidence, I remain, pending further information, in the same mind still.

11 January 1893

THE Incorporated Society of Musicians has been holding its annual conference. Being rather short of subjects to confer about, it has taken to listening to music—even on the organ—to wile away the time. It is a pity we have not an incorporated society of critics, so that the musicians and critics might confer together, with a strong police force present to maintain order. It would be more amusing, even to the provincials, than organs and schools for the musical training of the blind; and the eternal question of raising the status of the musician could perhaps be met by the previous question as to what is the matter with the musician's status that he should want it raised.

It seems to me that the social opportunities of the musician are greater, instead of less, than those of other craftsmen. The church organist may find, like the rest of us, that those who pay the piper insist on calling the tune; and if they happen to have no ear and no soul for music—nay, if, as may very easily be the case, they actually make a virtue of disparaging it—the unfortunate musician may be grievously oppressed; but he is not compelled to put up with oppression because he is a musician, but solely because he depends on his post for his bread-and-butter. He is at a disadvantage, not as artist, but as employee, just as he would be in any other trade or profession. He is certainly at no social disadvantage: on the contrary, it is always assumed that the professional player of a musical instrument is socially superior to the skilled mechanic or artisan, though there is no reason in the world why he should be.

An orchestral player may be a person of distinguished culture and address; but he may also be illiterate, coarse, drunken, not scrupulously honest, and, in short, a person whom sensitive composers and conductors would not employ if his mechanical dexterity could be dispensed with. An organist may be in every respect the superior of the rector; but he is just as likely to be the inferior of the keeper of the village shop, who does not complain particularly about his status. Some of the more innocent of my readers may be shocked at this, and may demand of me whether a man whose occupation is to interpret Handel, Mozart, Beethoven, or even Jackson in B flat, is not likely to have a more elevated soul than a buyer and seller of pots and pans. I reply, not in the least. You might as well ask whether a navvy, constantly employed on vast engineering schemes, is not likely to be more large-minded than a watchmaker.

Take a man with a quick ear and quick fingers; teach him how to play an instrument and to read staff notation; give him some band practice; and there you have your "professional," able to do what Wagner could not have done for the life of him, but no more necessarily a musician in the wider sense than a regimental marksman or broadsword instructor is necessarily a general or a master of foreign policy. He need make no more distinction between Beethoven and Brahms than a compositor does between Shakespear and Tennyson: even when he has an exceptionally fine sense of the difference between good and bad execution, he may not have the ghost of an idea of the difference between good and bad music.

Orchestral players, good enough to find constant employment in the best European orchestras, and yet with the manners, ideas, and conversation of ordinary private soldiers, are less common than formerly; but they are still contemporary facts, and not at all anomalous ones, except to muddle-headed people who imagine that every man who can play a string of notes written down by Mozart or Bach must have the heart and mind of Mozart and Bach. No doubt I shall presently be told that I have slandered an honorable profession by declaring that the members of our London orchestras are all illiterate, drunken, private-soldierly rapscallions. That is quite as near what I have just said as some of my musician-critics ever get to the meaning of my most careful and discriminate statements, let alone my more epigrammatic ones.

But the fact remains as I have stated it, that the professional musician, as such, can have no special social status whatever, because he may be anything, from an ex-drummer-boy to an artist and philosopher of world-wide reputation. It would be far more reasonable to demand a special status for the musical critic as such, since he is bound to be skilled in music, in literature, and in criticism, which no man can be without a far wider culture than an executive musician need possess. But I never have any trouble about my status, though I probably should have if I were asked to draw the line between myself and the country-town reporter who occasionally copies out a concert program and prefaces it with a few commonplaces. I am welcome among the people who like my ways and manners; and I believe musicians enjoy the same advantage.

When we are not welcome, probably the ways and manners are to blame, and not the profession.

With this soothing contribution to the ever-burning question of the conference, I pass on to the part of it which I personally attended: to wit, the lecture on the spinet, harpsichord, and clavichord by Mr Hipkins, and that on the lute and viols by Mr Arnold Dolmetsch. Mr Hipkins's proficiency as a player on the harpsichord and clavichord is an old story upon which I need not dwell. If any swaggering pianist is inclined to undervalue that proficiency, let him try his hand on a clavichord and see what he can make of an instrument which depends for its "action," not on the elaborate mechanism of Erard or any modification thereof, but on the dexterity of the player.

Not to mention, by the bye, that clavichord music is mostly of that sort in which every wrong note or rough touch betrays itself at once, unlike your modern thickly harmonized pieces, in which one fistful of notes is as good as another when a grandiose chord is wanted. The Rosencrantzes who know no touch of the old instruments, but who are not content to leave them alone, should go to Mr Hipkins, consider his ways, and be wise. For my own part, I hope Mr

Hipkins will find many imitators. There is no sort of doubt that the pianoforte must succumb sooner or later to the overwhelming objection that you can hear it next door. In an age of general insensibility to music this does not matter: the ordinary citizen today, who regards pianoforte playing as a mere noise, may drop an oath or two when the young lady at the other side of the party-wall begins practising; but he soon gets used to it as he gets used to passing trains, factory hooters, fog signals, and wheel traffic. Make a musician of him, however, and his tolerance will vanish. I live, when I am at home, in a London square which is in a state of transition from the Russell Square private house stage to the Soho of Golden Square stage of letting for all sorts of purposes. There are a couple of clubs, with "bars" and social musical evenings, not unrelieved by occasional clog dances audible a quarter of a mile off. There is a residence for the staff of a monster emporium which employs several talented tenors behind its counters. There is a volunteer headquarters in which the band practises on the first floors whilst the combatants train themselves for the thousand yards range by shooting through Morris tubes in the area. Yet I have sat at work on a summer evening, with every window in the square open and all these resources in full blast, and found myself less disturbed than I have been by a single private pianoforte, of the sort that the British householder thinks "brilliant," played by a female with no music in her whole composition, simply getting up an "accomplishment" either to satisfy her own vanity or to obey the orders of her misguided mother. Now if such females had spinets to play on instead of pianos, I should probably not hear them. Again, take the fiddle. It is a good sign, no doubt, that it is so much more generally practised than it used to be. But it is a terribly powerful instrument in neighborhoods where only millionaires can afford to live in detached houses.

How much pleasanter it would be to live next to Mr Arnold Dolmetsch, with his lutes, love viols, and leg viols, than to an ordinary string quartet! You can study the difference at Convent Garden on a Huguenots night, when the leader of the violas, after playing the prelude to Raoul's air in the first act on a ravishingly harmonious *viol d'amour*, reverts to his modern viola when he begins the obbligato to the air itself, and is promptly execrated for a harsh and tuneless scraper. A mouthful of margarine after a mouthful of honey would be far less disappointing. But if we went back to the old viols with sympathetic strings and the old harpsichords, I suppose we should have to begin to make them again; and I wonder what would be the result of that.

To me the difference between the beautiful spinet which Mr Hipkins played the other day and a modern cottage pianoforte of the sort that sells best in England is as the difference between the coloring of Bellini or Carpaccio and that of the late Frank Holl. But hereupon comes the horrible reflection that most of us prefer Frank Holl's pictures to Bellini's. Is there the smallest reason to suppose that if we took to making harpsichords we would make good ones? Alas! the question is already answered. Mr Hipkins not only played on the beautiful spinet already mentioned, and on a comparatively middling harpsichord, but also on a new harpsichord manufactured by a very eminent Parisian firm of pianoforte makers; and not only did it prove itself a snarling abomination, with vices of tone that even a harmonium would have been ashamed of, but it had evidently been deliberately made so in order to meet the ordinary customer's notion of a powerful and brilliant instrument.

Mr Dolmetsch did not exhibit any modern lutes, perhaps because none have been made; but if our fiddle-makers were to attempt to revive them they would probably aim at the sort of "power" of tone produced by those violins which ingenious street-players make out of empty Australian mutton tins and odd legs of stools.

I must not omit to say that Mr Dolmetsch's viol concerts, apart from their historical interest, are highly enjoyable from the purely musical point of view, his own playing and that of his daughter (on the viol da gamba) being excellent.

18 *January* 1893

LEST I should seem to slight that deservedly esteemed champion of good singing, Mr Charles Lunn, by taking no notice of his criticism of my utterances on his pet subject, I shall answer it, in spite of the difficulty created by the fact that whilst Mr Lunn firmly believes himself a disciple of Garcia and an advocate of the *coup de glotte*, he has, as a matter of fact, spent his life in fighting against the practical results of Garcia's method of instruction, and is no more a *coup de glottist* than I am. It will be remembered that I recently mentioned Santley and Melba as examples of the long line of good singers who have had nothing of the Academy method about them.

Mr Lunn, in reply, claims Santley and Melba as virtual pupils of Garcia. He says, "I have a letter before me in which I am informed 'Santley told me he had learned more in twelve lessons from my father than in all the years he had studied with others.' " To which I answer (1) that there is no evidence that when Santley made that polite but ingeniously ambiguous speech to Garcia's son he was alluding to the subject of voice production; (2) that in Santley's history of himself lately noticed in this column I read of his having grown up as a choirboy to the profession of singer, and of his obligations to his master Gaetano Nava of Milan, but not a solitary word of Garcia; and (3) that I have heard a Garcia sing, and that he did not sing like Santley. However, I must honestly add that the one lesson I ever had from a pupil of the Garcia school was prodigiously instructive, especially as to whether it was advisable to take another.

Mr Lunn proceeds: "Next, as to Melba. She was trained by Marchesi; and Marchesi was trained by Garcia and Viardot his sister." This proves exactly nothing. Marchesi may, for aught I know, have greatly modified, or even entirely abandoned, the method imparted to her by the Garcias.

And Melba's method is not the method of the Academy pupils, nor of the young ladies whom I have heard as they came fresh from the tuition of Madame Viardot. If I knew Madame Melba's personal history, I might possibly be able to shew that it was her success as a singer in Australia that induced her to seek from Marchesi and others that criticism and advice as to style, habits, phrasing, pronunciation, stage business and tradition, which make our eminent professors of singing so useful to pupils who, like Santley, already know how to sing.

Mr Lunn defends the vowel *Ah* on the extremely cheerful ground that "with death the jaw drops, and the last exhalation is *ah!*" Therefore *ah*, says Mr Lunn, is not metaphysical, like the other vowels, but physical. It is nature revealing itself. But I did not say it was not: all I contended for was that if, when the ordinary young Englishwoman is not dropping her jaw in death, but simply singing scales in life, she practises on *ah* instead of *oo* and *ee* in the middle, and *aw* in her lowest register, she will sing like an Academy pupil instead of developing the full vocal capacity, physical and metaphysical, needed by a public singer.

Sing on Garcia's method when you are dead by all means; but whilst you are alive you will find Edouard de Reszke's more useful: only dont abuse your power when you have gained it by wilful bawling for the mere fun of making a thundering noise, as he sometimes does. If you want to study nature freely expressing itself in vowels, and are averse to post-mortem examinations, you can pursue the following methods. To get the vowel O, with a marked *coup de glotte*, surprise a gentleman of full habit by a smart dig of your finger into his epigastrium at the moment when he has taken a full inspiration. For *oo*, with a B prefixed, simply write a play and appear before the curtain at the end. For *ah*, stick a pin into a lady. And so on.

The notion that *ah* is the best vowel and that no other should be used for practice is cognate to that of the gentlemen who tell you that D or F or B flat is the best note on their voice, though they do not go on to recommend you to practise exclusively on that note and to mistrust the others as "metaphysical." In Mr Lunn's own terminology, my contention is that the vowel which is physical at one pitch is metaphysical at another, and that nature does not freely express itself on a bass's low G in the same vowel as on the soprano's high A. Also that the dead-man, "no effort," unvolitional theory of singing, though it has arisen, naturally enough, in protest against the tight chin, rolled-up tongue, squeezed throat, and blowhard method, is just as impracticable, and consequently just as revolting to the student's common sense, as the celebrated instruction in the old volunteer drill-book, "Bring the rifle smartly to the shoulder without moving the hands."

Expert teachers and singers, knowing what the "no effort" precepts mean, approving of their drift, and careless of accuracy of statement, may declare their adhesion to it off-hand; but I, as an expert writer, have to say what I mean as exactly as possible. And I mean, among other things, that dramatic singing is one of the most arduously volitional acts that man can perform; and whoever compares it in that respect to moribund collapse, says (to quote a well-known controversialist) that which is not the truth, but so far from it, on the contrary, quite the reverse.

Whilst I am on the subject of my critics (whom I pass over in dignified silence only when they happen to have the best of the argument), I may as well astonish the gentleman who gives me such a tremendous taking-down over the competition of the School Board children. He is evidently a professional musician; for in no other class could such innocence be found as he displays in his interpretation of my recent remarks about the extent to which systems of sight-reading get credited with feats that are really due to the pupils having the power of remembering the absolute pitch of sounds.

Long ago I compared Hullah's "fixed Do" system with the Chevé and Tonic Sol-fa systems, and drew the inevitable conclusion that Hullah's was impracticable, whereas the other two were reasonable enough, though Rousseau's objection that no notation is so graphic as the staff, as far as pitch is concerned, rather inclined me to recommend some method of applying the movable Do system to the ordinary notation. But when I came from theory to practice, and found that the Hullah system seemed to produce much the same sort of result in classes as its more plausible rivals, I became sceptical.

My attention was presently drawn to a young lady who was exhibited as a marvellous example of the success of the Chevé system as a training for the staff notation. I was impressed at first; but eventually I discovered that she was an absolute pitcher, and could not only have read the staff notation just as well if she had never heard of Chevé or Galiné, but that she could get the hang of any sort of notation, numeral or syllabic, with amazing quickness, and translate it into absolute pitch. I was slow to find this out, because I cannot remember absolute pitch myself; and the faculty for doing so was at first as inexplicable to me as were the feats of the pupils of "Professors of Memory" until I read Mr Galton's work on Human Faculty, and learnt for the first time that there was such a faculty as "visualization."

Granted a faculty of "auralization," by which the auralizer can remember notes quite independently of one another, just as the visualizer remembers numbers; and the practicability of Hullah's system becomes quite intelligible. I soon came to the conclusions set forth in my previous article, which will probably be accepted by most disinterested musicians who have themselves the sense of absolute pitch, or have discovered its existence. For example, that excellent musician, Mr W. H. Cummings, whom I once heard inform an audience that when he was a boy his father struck a note on the piano and told him that it was A, and that he always remembered A from that, would be easily able to explain to my critic what has puzzled him so much.

However, I rather object to being contemptuously informed that the Chevé and Tonic Sol-fa systems are relative pitch systems. If I am ignorant of these systems I may deserve to be snubbed; but I ought to be told the truth. The Tonic Sol-fa is not a relative pitch system; and that is just where it is superior to the movable Do system applied to the staff notation—I think they call it the Lancashire Sol-fa. The genuine Tonic Sol-faist remembers his note by its dramatic effect in the key. He feels Soh (Tonic Sol-faese for Sol) as Wagner felt it when he wrote the Flying Dutchman motive, and not by calculating a fifth above Doh. Some day I must write a supplement to Schumann's Advice to Young Musicians. The title will be Advice to Old Musicians; and the first precept will run, "Don't be in a hurry to contradict G. B. S., as he never commits himself on a musical subject until he knows at least six times as much about it as you do." But then I hate saying conceited things, however true they may be, even to people who seem to regard me as a mere Aunt Sally instead of a fellow-creature.

A notable event of the week is the publication by Messrs Kegan Paul & Trübner of the first volume of Wagner's prose works, translated by Mr Ashton Ellis. It contains two works of the first importance, The Art-Work of the Future (once well known to those who had not read it as The Music of the Future), and the Communication to My Friends, a unique artistic document, and one, by the bye, which every woman who admires Lohengrin should read, as it contains that remarkable account of his conversion to the view that Elsa, whom he at first conceived as having "failed" Lohengrin, was quite right in insisting on knowing all about him. In the later dramas, you will remember, the woman's part is as heroic as the man's.

The rest of the volume is taken up with Art and Revolution, a classic example of brilliant pamphleteering; the Autobiographic Sketch, which will amuse those for whom the Communication is too deep; the essay on Art and Climate, and the tolerably full design for the unfinished poem of Wieland the Smith. This instalment will suffice to open the eyes of English readers to the absurdity of the notions concerning Wagner and his views which were current here until quite lately, and which only began to collapse when the public, instead of reading about his music, got opportunities of listening to it, and lost all patience with the old nonsense about its dullness, harshness, lack of melody, and so on.

Mr Edward Dannreuther's translation of On Conducting, too, revealed the supposed obscure and fantastic theorist as a very practical person, with simple and broad tastes in music, and with that saving salt of humor and common sense which are so vital to the sanity of an art enthusiast. And his attacks were so sympathetically aimed at the very incompetencies and impostures from which we ourselves are suffering that those who read the essay at once concluded that the disparagement and ridicule which had been heaped on Wagner the writer were just as stupid as those which had been heaped on Wagner the composer. Besides, Wagner never stopped short at the merely negative "Thats not the way to do it": he always said "This is the way to do it," and did it forthwith.

There is something pleasant, too, in the thorough popularity of his likes and dislikes in music. His love of Beethoven and Mozart, and of the Mendelssohn of the Scotch symphony and the Hebrides overture, and his sovereign contempt for the efforts of Schumann and Brahms to be "profound," taken with the positive productive power of the man to realize his own ideas with his own hand, make up a personality as convincing and as genial as that of William Morris, who has a prodigious appetite for Dickens and Dumas (need I say which Dumas?), and his masterpieces in poetry, in prose, in printing, in picture-glass, in tapestry and household wares of all kinds.

In proof of my own sympathy with the practical and popular side of Wagner, I hasten to add that the volume in question costs 12s. 6d. net, and is well worth the money. The translation is so good that it deserves the praise that Wagner gave to Liszt's interpretation of Beethoven's sonatas.

Grateful acknowledgments to the member of "the

Rag" who sets me right as to the key of "Jackson." I said "Jackson in B flat": I should have said in F. "Only fancy the additional horror of the thing a fifth higher," exclaims my correspondent. I shake that warrior's hand. He, too, has suffered as I have.

25 January 1893

TO Miss E. M. Smyth, the composer of the Mass performed for the first time at the Albert Hall last Wednesday, I owe at least one hearty acknowledgment. Her Mass was not a Requiem. True, it was carefully announced as "a Solemn Mass"; but when it came to the point it was not so very solemn: in fact, the Gloria, which was taken out of its proper place and sung at the end by way of a finish, began exactly like the opening choruses which are now *de rigueur* in comic operas. Indeed, the whole work, though externally highly decorous, has an underlying profanity that makes the audience's work easy.

If you take an average mundane young lady, and ask her what service to religion she most enjoys rendering, she will probably, if she is a reasonably truthful person, instance the decoration of a church at Christmas. And, beyond question, a girl of taste in that direction will often set forth in a very attractive and becoming way texts of the deepest and most moving significance, which, nevertheless, mean no more to her than the Chinese alphabet. Now I will not go so far as to say that Miss Smyth's musical decoration of the Mass is an exactly analogous case; for there are several passages in which her sense of what is pretty and becoming deepens into sentimental fervor, just as it also slips back occasionally into a very unmistakeable reminiscence of the enjoyment of the ballroom; but I must at least declare that the decorative instinct is decidedly in front of the religious instinct all through, and that the religion is not of the widest and most satisfying sort.

There are great passages in the Mass, such as "I look for the life of the world to come," which stir all men who have any faith or hope left in them, whether the life they look for is to be lived in London streets and squares, or in another world, and which stand out in adequate modern settings of religious services from among the outworn, dead matter with which creeds inevitably become clogged in the course of centuries. Every critic who goes to hear a setting of words written hundreds of years ago knows that some of them will have lost their sincerity, if not their very meaning, to the composer of today; and at such points he looks for a display of pure musicianship to fill the void; whilst he waits with intense interest and hope for the live bits.

Miss Smyth, however, makes no distinctions. She writes undiscriminatingly, with the faith of a child and the orthodoxy of a lady. She has not even those strong preferences which appear in the early religious works of Mozart and Raphael. Consequently, her Mass belongs to the light literature of Church music, though it is not frivolous and vulgar, as so much Church music unfortunately is. It repeatedly spurts ahead in the briskest fashion; so that one or two of the drum flourishes reminded me, not of anything so vulgar as the Salvation Army, but of a crack cavalry band.

There is, too, an oddly pagan but entirely pleasant association in Miss Smyth's mind of the heavenly with the pastoral: the curious trillings and pipings, with violin obbligato, which came into the Creed at the descent from heaven; the Et vitam venturi, on the model of the trio of the Ninth Symphony; and the multitudinous warblings, as of all the finches of the grove, at the end of the Gloria, conveyed to me just such an imagination of the plains of heaven as was painted by John Martin. Much of the orchestral decoration is very pretty, and shews a genuine feeling for the instruments. The passage in the Hosanna for the long trumpet which Mr Morrow mastered for the use of the Bach Choir, fairly brought down the house.

I have often tried to induce composers to avail themselves of this instrument; and now that Miss Smyth has set the example, with immediate results in the way of applause both for herself and the player, I do not see what there is to prevent a triumphant renovation of the treble section of the brass, especially now that Mr Wyatt's application of the double slide to the trumpet has at last made the slide-trumpet as practicable as the incurably vulgar but hitherto unavoidable cornet. Miss Smyth's powers of expression do not go beyond what the orchestra can do for her. None of the vocal solos in the Mass have that peculiar variety and eloquence which are distinctively human: the contralto solo, in which the voice is treated merely as a pretty organ-stop, and the setting of the Agnus Dei for the tenor, which is frank violin music, conclusively prove her limitations, which, let us hope, are only due to want of experience of what can be done with really expressive singers.

The work, as a whole, is fragmentary, with too many pretentious *fugato* beginnings which presently come to nothing, and with some appallingly commonplace preparatory passages before the sections of the continuous numbers; but it is very far from being utterly tedious and mechanical like Dvořák's Requiem, or heavy, sententious, and mock-profound like—well, no matter. Above all, it is interesting as the beginning of what I have so often prophesied—the conquest of popular music by woman. Whenever I hear the dictum, "Women cannot compose," uttered by some male musician whose whole endowment, intellectual and artistic, might be generously estimated as equivalent to that of the little finger of Miss Braddon or Miss Broughton, I always chuckle and say to myself, "Wait a bit, my lad, until they find out how much easier it is than literature, and how little the public shares your objection to hidden consecutives, descending leading notes, ascending sevenths, false relations, and all the other items in your *index expurgatorius*!"

What musician that has ever read a novel of Ouida's has not exclaimed sometimes, "If she would only lay on this sort of thing with an orchestra, how concerts would begin to pay!" Since women have succeeded conspicuously in

Victor Hugo's profession, I cannot see why they should not succeed equally in Liszt's if they turned their attention to it.

The night before the Mass I went to a comic opera at the Shaftesbury; and the night after it I went to another at the Lyric. Miss Smyth could have written up both of them with considerable advantage to the finales. They resemble one another in shewing the composer to much greater advantage than the librettist. The book of La Rosière is by Mr Monkhouse, who has never shewn himself such a thorough actor as in the invention of this opera-book. Such a hotch-potch of points, situations, *contretemps*, and Monkhousisms, unattached, unprovoked, uncaused, unrelated, and consequently unmeaning and unsuccessful, was never emptied out of any actor's budget. The utmost that can be said for it is that there are some passages which would be funny if the author himself were on the stage to take them in hand. Unfortunately, they do not suit the style of Messrs Robertson and Barrington Foote. The one advantage of Mr Monkhouse's dramatic method is that the opportunity for improvisation offered to the actors is only limited by the need for finishing in time for the last trains, since the characters and circumstances are nebulous enough to admit of any possible remark falling from the persons on the stage without incongruity. The who, the what, the when, the where, and the how of the play remain undecided to the last; and Mr Elton took full advantage of this on the night of my visit, when his colleagues were obviously wondering half the time what he was going to say next. He certainly did manage to dance and droll an impossible part into toleration, and even into popularity. But what saved the piece was the music, the Czardas in the second act (a hint taken, possibly, from the vogue of Liszt's Hungarian Rhapsodies in the concert-room), and, I hope, the scenery— I can only hope it, because it is not easy to guess how far audiences appreciate the fact that the finest art presented to them on the stage is often to be found, not in the music, or the singing, or the acting, but in the painting of the back-cloth. Such a scene as Mr Hann's Outside the Village is not only charming in itself, but critically interesting in a high degree to those who remember how Telbin would have handled the same subject; and yet it passes unnoticed, whilst yards of criticism are written every week about Bond Street exhibitions of water-color sketches which are the merest trumpery compared to it or to Mr Hemsley's scene in the first act. For my part, I am bound to say that these two scenes gave me greater pleasure than any other part of La Rosière; and since they have no chance of being "collected" and passed down to future generations, with an occasional airing at Christie's or the Winter Exhibition at the Academy, there is all the more reason why I should make my acknowledgments on the spot.

The music of La Rosière presents no new developments; but it is more generous and vigorous than the French work to which we are accustomed, the treatment of the orchestra in particular being as broad as the work will bear, and so escaping the reproach of timorous elegance and mean facetiousness which many recent comic-opera scores have incurred. The orchestra, conducted by Mr Barter Johns, is remarkably good. Miss Marie Halton acts somewhat in the manner of Mrs Bancroft, and sings somewhat in the manner of Miss St John, though, of course, chiefly in her own manner, which is vivacious and effective enough to keep her part from obeying the laws of Nature by falling flat. Miss Violet Cameron and Miss Lucille Saunders add to the interest of the cast, if not of the opera.

The Magic Opal, at the Lyric, is a copious example of that excessive fluency in composition of which Señor Albéniz has already given us sufficient proofs. His music is pretty, shapely, unstinted, lively, goodnatured, and far too romantic and refined for the stuff which Mr Arthur Law has given him to set. But Albéniz has the faults as well as the qualities of his happy and uncritical disposition; and the grace and spirit of his strains are of rather too obvious a kind to make a very deep impression. And he does not write well for the singers. It is not that the phrases are unvocal, or that the notes lie badly for the voice, but that he does not set the words from the comedian's point of view, his double disability as a pianist and a foreigner handicapping him in this department. The favorite performers of the company are not well fitted with parts. Poor Miss Aida Jenoure, whose forte is dancing, pantomime, and sprightly comedy with some brains in it, is a mere walking prima donna doomed to execute a florid vocal waltz. She could not sing it the least bit; but she dodged her way through it with a pluck and cleverness which earned her an encore. Mr Monkhouse, of whom it has been apparent any time these two years that he is potentially much more than a mere buffoon, has to buffoon away all the evening for want of anything better to do with his part. Mr Fred Kaye, too, is wasted. The only success of the first night was made by a Miss May Yohe, who, though she spoke the American language, actually had *not* ordered her florist to deliver half his stock to her across the footlights. She is personally attractive; her face, figure, and movements are lively and expressive; and her voice is extraordinarily telling: it sounds like a deep contralto; but the low notes beneath the stave, which are powerful in a normally trained contralto, are weak; and she has practically no high notes. But the middle of her voice, which she uses apparently by forcing her chest register, is penetrating and effective. In giving this account of her method I am describing what an ordinary singer would have to do to imitate her (with inevitably ruinous consequences), rather than what she does herself, as to which I am not quite assured. Probably she has one of those abnormal larynxes, examples of which may be found in Sir Morell Mackenzie's list of the singers whose registering he examined. Mr Wallace Brownlow was restless and off his balance, which is exactly what an artist ought not to be. Miss Susie Vaughan helped matters considerably as an amiable Azucena, her mock ballet with Mr Monkhouse being one of the funniest things in the piece. I must apologize to Mlle Candida for having missed her dance through running away for half an hour to the London Symphony Concert, where Mr Henschel, with an ingratitude that took me quite aback, celebrated my entrance by striking up Brahms in F.

8 *February* 1893

MR HENSCHEL is to be congratulated on his last Symphony Concert, not only for having brought a really practicable choir into the field, but for having shewn by an exceptionally good performance of the Pastoral Symphony that he had fully completed his first labor of forming a first-rate orchestra before attempting to add a choir to it. In the long intervals between the visits of Richter it is an unspeakable relief to hear a London band in St. James's Hall that has spirit and purpose in its execution, and in its tone a firmness, and at need a depth and richness, which it can sustain for as many bars as you please in the broadest movements without flinching or trailing off.

When we last heard the Pastoral Symphony from the Philharmonic (potentially and by common consent of the profession—on strictly reciprocal terms—the finest band in the world, and actually the most futile), the conductor had to apologize for the performance beforehand. On Thursday last Mr Henschel had to return to the platform twice *after* the performance to be tremendously applauded. This is the second time that he has deliberately picked a specially remarkable orchestral work out of the Philharmonic program in order to shew us the difference between the Philharmonic accomplishment of reading band parts at sight and the true art of orchestral execution. In Raff's Lenore he achieved a comparatively easy and certain success. In Beethoven he has gone deeper and been more conclusively successful. The first two movements were presented in a masterly way: I have not yet heard Mr Henschel accomplish so convincing a reading of a classic. In the third movement he was a little hampered by individual shortcomings in the band, the oboe being painfully out of tune;

and the climax to the storm was a trifle discounted by letting the band explode too freely before it was reached; but these blemishes were outweighed by the bringing out of many touches which usually go for nothing.

The only thing that was old-fashioned about the concert was the inevitable remark in the analytic program that Beethoven had "*descended* to positive imitation" (of the quail, cuckoo, and nightingale) in the andante. Now I appeal to Mr Bennett as a man and a brother whether we need keep waving this snippet of impertinent small-talk over the Pastoral Symphony for ever. There is no more beautiful bar in the work than that which consists of the "imitations" in question. It is exquisitely constructed and infinitely poetic; and we all like it and wait for it expectantly, and shiver with agony whenever some confounded flautist who never appreciated the nightingale—perhaps never even heard one—dots half the quavers and turns the other half into semiquavers. And then we go and gravely reproach Beethoven for having "descended" to the low and inartistic device of imitating a vulgar bird that never had a proper singing lesson in its life.

I can only say that after many years of attentive observation, devoted to determining which of the two parties—Beethoven or the critic—cut the more foolish figure after each repetition of the rebuke, I have reluctantly come to the conclusion that we had better drop it. Our profession affords us so many suitable and unobtrusive opportunities for making donkeys of ourselves when we are so disposed, that there is no excuse for our clinging to the most conspicuous and unpopular of them all.

The work selected for the début of the choir was Mendelssohn's Hear my Prayer. I desire to skate over this part of the concert as lightly as possible; but I must just ask Mrs Henschel to hear *my* prayer and never again meddle with Mendelssohn. Mind, I do not asperse Mrs Henschel's professional competence. I do not find fault with her technical execution: she sang the notes in time and tune; pronounced the words duly; and longed for the wings of a dove and worked up to the shouting of the enemy very intelligently. Nothing could have been more thoroughly businesslike from beginning to end.

But that is not enough for Hear my Prayer. Unless you can sing those opening lines with the rarest nobility of tone and the most touching depth of expression, your one duty to them is to let them alone. They are like the opening phrase of the quartet in Don Giovanni, "Non ti fidar, O misera": success in delivering them is only possible to singers who have the finest temperamental sympathy with their spirit; and anything short of success is utter failure. And that is what befell Mrs Henschel—failure, not apparent, as an ordinary breakdown would have been, to those who did not know the work—for they, indeed, applauded her plentifully—but deeply disappointing to us who have it in our hearts as a cherished early love. Perhaps it is strength of character rather than any artistic weakness that makes Mrs Henschel sing Die Lorelei charmingly, and Kennst du das Land or Hear my Prayer most disenchantingly; but in any case it is clear that it is the charm of romance and not the depths and heights of emotion and devotion that she was born to sing for us.

However, Hear my Prayer was soon over; and the Pastoral Symphony and the Meistersinger selection made amends for the disappointment. The choir is bright, vigorous, and spirited; and the volume of tone they produce is adequate to their numbers, instead of, as usual, every ten young women producing about as much voice as might be expected from a very little girl with a very bad cold. Their introduction was certainly most promising; and I begin to think that I shall hear some decent choral work at St James's Hall before I die, after all.

Curiosity to see the New English Opera House in its latest character of "Palace Theatre of Varieties" led me the other evening to make another trial of music-hall art. Previous attempts had taught me to be careful as to how far I should permit myself to criticize. I had learnt that writers of music-hall songs attribute to their verses a moral elevation which David would have modestly hesitated to claim for the Psalms, and that a remark which would be taken by Broadwood or Steinway as a handsome compliment is resented as an actionable insult by makers of music-hall instruments. Add to this that the Palace Theatre of Varieties is under highly sensitive management, and the perils of my position may be faintly realized. However, I ventured in, and found palatial provision for smoking, lounging, and drinking. This was thrown away on me, as I do not smoke, do not drink, and feel like a pickpocket whenever circumstances compel me to lounge. So I hastened to the auditorium to see the performance, and found palatial provision for this also in a comfortable chair, to the elegance and luxury of which I can pay but a feeble tribute by calling it, on the suggestion of the bill, a "fauteuil." Herein reclining, I contemplated the "new and novel act-drop by Mr J. Harker," representing a magnificent studio in which a model, undeniably a fine figure of a woman, stood posed before a number of infantine art-students, certain portions of whose persons were colored up to the point of presenting an inflamed appearance, as if they had been unmercifully corrected for faults in their drawing. For in this studio the model was draped and the artists were naked, the model being the person on whom the suspicions of the iconoclastic section of the County Council were most likely to fall. The performance, apart from the usual "turns," shewed a determination on the part of the management to popularize ballet by mixing it with comic opera. Even if this were the right way to popularize ballet—and I shall presently explain why I think it the wrong way—the first ballet we had, The Sleeper Awakened, seemed to me an example of how not to do it. A couple of scenes of the usual pantomime-opening kind were tacked on to an ordinary ballet finale, the dancers having nothing to do with the dramatic section, nor the actors with the dancing section. The result was, of course, that the beginning, played by ordinary burlesque actors with none of the grace, the agility, the distinction of the pantomimic dancer, was common to a degree; and the ending, owing to the sudden withdrawal of all pretence of meaning from a piece which had begun as a good story, was even more vapid than ballet finales usually are. Much more successful was From London to Paris, in which there is a genuine collaboration between the authors (Mr Cecil Raleigh and Sir Augustus Harris) and the composer (Mr J. M. Glover); whilst in the representation there is a genuine collaboration of the actors with the pantomimists. The result is a really amusing entertainment. Mr Glover has entered thoroughly into the spirit of the piece: his score grows naturally out of the action, and is consequently free from the stereo which makes most ballet music so worrying. The allusions to popular comic songs come in with a musical humor and a daintiness which makes them quite witty and pretty; and some of the points—for instance, the sea-sickly harmonies to Rule Britannia in the storm scene—are irresistibly funny. In short, Mr Glover's music has all the liveliness and adroitness of the ordinary imported French ballet music, without its staleness and without its foreignness. Mr Raleigh has made the Palace Theatre a present of a character from one of his comedies in the person of Velvet Sam, created, if I mistake not, by Mr Somerset some years ago at a *matinée*, and now brought back to life in a speechless condition by Mr Paul Martinetti, whose admirable and original pantomime strikes the highest note attained in the acting of the piece. The combination of spoken dialogue with pantomime leads to a scene between the low comedian and the high pantomimist in which the comedian, hopelessly misunderstanding all the exquisitely graphic gestures of the subtler artist, gives gratifying expression to the feelings which we have all shared when trying to follow the conventional Italian dumb-show. The panoramic scene of the voyage from Dover to Calais ought to be prohibited: it carries the joke too far. The moment those two sponsons and the bridge began to rock I began to feel ill; and the flying clouds and general moving and pitching and rolling that went on so intensified my symptoms that if the Calais light (exactly like the real thing, and not less welcome) had not appeared much sooner than it usually does, I should have had to leave the auditorium precipitately. This sort of stage realism is all very well for good sailors; but as these gifted persons form considerably less than one per cent of the population, I make bold to remind the managers that all the great composers have recognized that a Calm Sea is an indispensable condition of a Prosperous Voyage. The following scenes, like the preceding one at Charing Cross Station, are of the same topical sort; and the piece goes on vivaciously enough until it fades into pure *ballet divertissement*, relieved only by a funereal clog-dance and a *cancan* at the end. It left me more convinced than ever that what is wanted to make the ballet more popular is not its wholesale adulteration with comic opera, but its internal reform. It should be recognized that the stock of movements out of which the principal dancers make up their solos is so limited that the frequent playgoer soon learns them off by heart, and comes to regard the solo as a dreary platitude, only to be endured when the dancer has extraordinary charm of person and brilliancy of execution. In order to get even a very conventional round of applause, and that, too, from people who obviously have no more sense of dancing than the oratorio audiences who applaud interpolated high notes have of music, a principal dancer must spoil her solo by a silly, flustering, ugly, teetotum spin, which no really fine dancer should condescend to. Then there is the *corps de ballet*, consisting of rows of commonplace dancers, individually uninteresting (from the artistic point of view), but useful for the production of lines and masses of color in rhythmic motion—for realizing, in short, the artistic conception which was in Mr Swiveller's imagination when he described the dance as "the mazy." Now in planning the evolutions of the *corps de ballet*, nothing is easier than to ring the changes on mere drill, or harder than to devise really artistic combinations and developments. The natural result is a tendency to give us an intolerable deal of drill with each halfpennyworth of poetic color and motion. The last scene of a ballet is generally a bore, to which some sort of non-artistic interest is occasionally imparted by such desperate devices as making successive squads of girls represent different nations, or different uniforms in the services, or different periods of civilization, or what not, with the result, generally, of making the whole affair twice as stale and tedious. All such mechanical efforts to make lifeless entertainments attractive invariably lead to frightful expenditure, the last thousand pounds of which rarely produce sixpenn'orth of effect. Why not, then, call in the services of a dramatic story-teller, with the requisite sense of the poetry of motion and movement and spectacle, and make a clean sweep of all the merely habitual business that has no purpose and no meaning? The monotony and limitation of the dancer's art vanishes when it becomes dramatic. The detestable bravura solos which everybody hates, and which belong to the same obsolete phase of art as the eighteenth-century florid arias written for the singing virtuosi of the Italian stage by Hasse, Porpora, and Mozart in his boyhood, would soon fall into disuse and ridicule; and we could say to our prima ballerina assolutissima, when she attempted a "variation," "Spare us, dear lady. Dont do it. Our cherished Cavallazzi, a superb dancer, never does it. It was not that sort of thing that made the success of Yolande, of Asmodeus, of Excelsior, or of any of the ballets that are still borne in mind years after their withdrawal. Hundreds of forgotten assolutissimas have done it just as well as you are going to do it; and none of them are remembered save those who stamped themselves on our memories in their dramatic moments. Move us; act for us; make our favorite stories real to us; weave your grace and skill into the fabric of our life; but dont put us off for the thousandth time with those dreary pirouettes and entrechats and arabesques and whatd'yecallems." That is the cry of humanity to the danseuse, the ballet-master, and the manager; and it is in response to it that we are getting Round the Town and From London to Paris.

But in The Sleeper Awakened and From London to Paris there are signs of a movement to substitute, not dramatic pantomime for mere step exhibition, but comic opera of the lowest type for ballet; and this false start must not be followed up. It is one thing to give us what Martinetti does instead of what Albertieri does: it is quite another to give us what any vulgar low comedian can do. I am very fond of dramatic pantomime and of the dancing that grows out of it; and I think it important to the stage in general that we should have a school of the art among us. But I have had more than enough of the sort of gorgeously spectacular, farcical, rather rowdy comic opera that flourished at the old Alhambra in the days of Stoyle, Paulton, Kitty Munroe, and Rose Bell. People of taste went to the Alhambra in those days only to see Pertoldi and Gillert dance; and in the end it proved that even from a commercial point of view the ballet paid well enough to be worth retaining when the comic opera was dropped. I therefore suggest that the true policy is to follow the line so successfully pursued at the Empire, of reforming and developing the ballet as ballet, without allowing a single spoken word to open the way for a relapse into decadent comic opera. And the Palace management can do it at this advantage, that they have in Mr Cecil Raleigh and Mr Glover just the dramatist and musician for their purpose. As to the people who have no sense of the art of theatrical dancing at all, they will be satisfied if the music-hall turns are kept up to the mark, and if the ballet exhibits plenty of feminine beauty.

15 *February* 1893

I DO not know how far the matter is worth mentioning, but music is dying out in London. The Monday Popular and Ballad concerts go on from mere force of habit; the Crystal Palace concerts will begin again next Saturday, because they rashly promised to do so last year; oratorios are solemnized at the usual intervals in the Albert Hall; Sarasate goes and Joachim comes; and Mr Henschel's band is heard twice a month as usual. It is true that early February is not exactly the height of the musical season, and that this year the light-opera-houses produced their novelties much earlier in the year than is customary.

But when all allowances are made, it must be admitted that things for the moment are slack; and I have once or twice thought of raising an Unemployed Deadheads' agitation, and calling on the Government to at once set on foot a series of Relief Concerts, at which these unhappy people may pass their afternoons and evenings. The Abolition of Piece-work for critics would be a prominent plank in the program of such an agitation; for even a critic must live, and if the agents will not give concerts and recitals, the critics will be driven to invent them; that is the long and short of it.

A man cannot go on repeating what he has said a thousand times about the way the Monday Popular quartet played Haydn in G, No. 12 of Opus 756, or about Santley as Elijah. I turn in desperation to the musical journals, and my hopes rise as I see the words, "Ignorant Misstatement." But it is actually not G. B. S. this time; somebody else, I suppose, has made a remark sufficiently obvious to shake the foundation of make-believe on which "art" of the usual professional type is built. The tenants of that fashionable edifice are always protesting that I am an impudent pretender to musical authority, betraying my ignorance, in spite of my diabolical cunning, in every second sentence. And I do not mind confessing that I do not know half as much as you would suppose from my articles; but in the kingdom of the deaf the one-eared is king.

The other evening I was looking into a shop-window in Oxford Street, when a gentleman accosted me modestly, and, after flattering me with great taste and modesty into an entire willingness to make his acquaintance, began with evident misgiving and hesitation, but with no less evident curiosity, to approach the subject of these columns. At last he came to his point with a rush by desperately risking the question, "Excuse me, Mr G. B. S., but *do* you know anything about music? The fact is, I am not capable of forming an opinion myself; but Dr Blank says you dont, and—er—Dr Blank is such a great authority that one hardly knows what to think." Now this question put me into a difficulty, because I had already learnt by experience that the reason my writings on music and musicians are so highly appreciated is, that they are supposed by many of my greatest admirers to be a huge joke, the point of which lies in the fact that I am totally ignorant of music, and that my character of critic is an exquisitely ingenious piece of acting, undertaken to gratify my love of mystification and paradox.

From this point of view every one of my articles appears as a fine stroke of comedy, occasionally broadening into a harlequinade, in which I am the clown, and Dr Blank the policeman. At first I did not realize this, and could not understand the air of utter disillusion and loss of interest in me that would come over people in whose houses I incautiously betrayed some scrap of amateurish enlightenment. But the naïve exclamation, "Oh! you *do* know something about it, then," at last became familiar to me; and I now take particular care not to expose my knowledge. When people hand me a sheet of instrumental music, and ask my opinion of it, I carefully hold it upside down, and pretend to study it in that position with the eye of an expert. When they invite me to try their new grand piano, I attempt to open it at the wrong end; and when the young lady of the house informs me that she is practising the 'cello, I innocently ask her whether the mouthpiece did not cut her lips dreadfully at first. This line of conduct gives enormous satisfaction, in which I share to a rather greater extent than is generally supposed. But, after all, the people whom I take in thus are only amateurs.

To place my impostorship beyond question I require to be certified as such by authorities like our Bachelors and

Doctors of music—gentlemen who can write a Nunc Dimittis in five real parts, and know the difference between a tonal fugue and a real one, and can tell you how old Monteverde was on his thirtieth birthday, and have views as to the true root of the discord of the seventh on the supertonic, and devoutly believe that *si contra fa diabolus est*. But I have only to present myself to them in the character of a man who has been through these dreary games without ever discovering the remotest vital connection between them and the art of music—a state of mind so inconceivable by them—to make them exclaim:

> Preposterous ass! that never read so far
> To know the cause why music was ordained,

and give me the desired testimonials at once. And so I manage to scrape along without falling under suspicion of being an honest man.

However, since mystification is not likely to advance us in the long run, may I suggest that there must be something wrong in the professional tests which have been successively applied to Handel, to Mozart, to Beethoven, to Wagner, and last, though not least, to me, with the result in every case of our condemnation as ignoramuses and charlatans. Why is it that when Dr Blank writes about music nobody but a professional musician can understand him; whereas the man-in-the-street, if fond of art and capable of music, can understand the writings of Mendelssohn, Wagner, Liszt, Berlioz, or any of the composers?

Why, again, is it that my colleague, W. A., for instance, in criticizing Mr Henry Arthur Jones's play the other day, did not *parse* all the leading sentences in it? I will not be so merciless as to answer these questions now, though I know the solution, and am capable of giving it if provoked beyond endurance. Let it suffice for the moment that writing is a very difficult art, criticism a very difficult process, and music not easily to be distinguished, without special critical training, from the scientific, technical, and professional conditions of its performance, composition, and teaching. And if the critic is to please the congregation, who want to read only about the music, it is plain that he must appear quite beside the point to the organ-blower, who wants to read about his bellows, which he can prove to be the true source of all the harmony.

Some weeks ago, in speaking of the lecture and viol concert given by Mr Arnold Dolmetsch before the conference of the Incorporated Society of Musicians, I seized the opportunity to put in a protest on behalf of opera-goers against the horrible custom of playing the prelude to the tenor air in the first act of Les Huguenots on the viol d'amour, and then returning to the ordinary viola, with detestable effect, for the obbligato. Mr Dolmetsch, who is giving viol concerts on alternate Tuesdays at Barnard's Inn, Holborn, promises to bring a viol d'amour, tuned for playing this obbligato, to his next concert on the 14th, and to say something on the subject. I hope the upshot will be to get the obbligato played at the opera as Meyerbeer meant it to be played. The difference to the singer, who would be coaxed into the dulcet style, instead of having his teeth set on edge and his worst shouting propensities stirred up, would be considerable, and the difference to the audience incalculable.

I see that Mr Lunn is not quite convinced that he and I mean the same thing by the *coup de glotte*. But it is clear from his last utterance on the subject that we do. Marchesi's "sudden and energetic drawing together of the lips of the glottis an instant before expiration commences" is exactly what I mean, and what I object to. I never heard Titiens sing Hear ye, Israel; so I will take it on Mr Lunn's authority that she used to attack the allegro with a *coup de glotte* on the I, I am He that comforteth, although Titiens was certainly not a *coup de glottist* in her ordinary practice. I myself, in the very rare instances when I pronounce the word "I" in a self-assertive mood, may sometimes attack it with a *coup de glotte*; but I always regret it the moment the sound strikes my conscience, which, in my case, as in that of all musical critics, is situated in my ear.

But when Mr Lunn goes on to say that if Titiens had not used the *coupe de glotte* she must "inevitably" have pronounced the sentence as "Hi! Hi! am He that comforteth," I can only assure him that he is wrong on the point of fact. If Titiens had been an Academy pupil, with no power of distending and bracing her pharynx, and helplessly dependent on a carefully cultivated method of bleating with the vocal cords alone, then undoubtedly she could not have produced any vowel whatsoever without a *coupe de glotte*, except by fairly gasping it into existence by a strong aspirate.

Being what she was, a practical dramatic singer, she could have attacked any vowel with a perfectly open glottis and without an aspirate, exactly as an organ flue-pipe attacks its note, or as I can attack a note in whistling, without closing my lips, by simply putting them in the proper position first, and then directing a stream of air through them. Now a flue-pipe is just as "natural" an instrument as a reed-pipe; and I will by no means admit that a vocal method based on the analogy of the reed mechanism is any more "natural," or "normal," or "spontaneous" than a method based on the analogy of the flue construction. Infants may, as Mr Lunn says, yell with a *coup de glotte* (the method of the yelling infant being instinctively vicious); but children croon or "sing to themselves" on the other plan; so I claim the child's evidence as on my side, though I attach no importance to it.

Consequently we may get rid of all discussion as to whether the *coup de glotte* reed-pipe method or the open glottis flue-pipe method is Nature's method. The question is, which of the two sounds better and wears better. The first point is a matter of taste: the second, a matter of experience and observation; and I declare for the flue-pipe on both issues.

22 February 1893

MANY who hear Gounod's Redemption cannot but feel somewhat scandalized by the identity in treatment and spirit of the death on the Cross with the death of Valentine in Faust. He has to remind himself at such moments that it is in the opera and not in the oratorio that the music is out of place. Goethe's Valentine is a blunt and rather ruffianly medieval soldier, with all the indignant insistence on the need for virtue in other people which a man would naturally have after studying human nature in the course of helping to sack a town or two. His last words are a quaint combination of a regret that he cannot get at old Martha to blacken her eyes, with a reminder to the Almighty that a brave soldier is about to exercise his right of going to heaven.

Gounod, who has no turn for this sort of realism, made Valentine a saint and a martyr; and the ideal actor for a true Gounod performance of the part is a dreamy and pathetically beautiful youth with a pure young voice. Jean de Reszke, when he sang baritone parts, and was eighteen years younger and some thirty odd pounds lighter than today, was far more moving and memorable as Valentine than Maurel is now, though Maurel acts with great power, and reconstitutes the medieval soldier in spite of Gounod's teeth, or than Lassalle, who, conscious of his merits as a singer, avoids invidious comparisons by the quick-witted expedient of not acting at all. The chief disadvantage of turning the death of Valentine into a Calvary was that when Gounod wrote Passion music he was told that it sounded operatic. To which he can only reply that if operatic means like a Gounod opera, the term is not one of reproach. This is a good answer; but Gounod should not have pressed us too hard on the point. When we have been led to associate a particular eight bars of music with the words in which the dying Valentine warns Margaret that she, too, must face her day of reckoning, it is rather disconcerting, to say the least, to hear the central figure in the Redemption transposing those very eight bars from D into B, and using them to declaim, "If my deeds have been evil, bear witness against me," etc.

And those angelic progressions which lift the voice from semitone to semitone on ineffable resolutions of diminished sevenths on to six-four chords, though beyond question most heavenly, are so welded in our minds to Gretchen's awakening from her miserable prison dreams to the consciousness of Faust's presence in her cell, that it is not easy to keep in the proper oratorio frame of mind when they begin. In fact a knowledge of Gounod's operas is a disadvantage at the Albert Hall on Redemption nights, even to the ordinary occasional opera-goer. What must it be then to the professional critic, who has to spend about ten years out of every twelve of his life listening to Faust? If Gounod's music were less seraphically soothing, it would have long ago produced an inflammatory disease—Faustitis—in my profession. Even as it is, I am far from sure that my eyesight has not been damaged by protracted contemplation of the scarlet coat and red limelight of Mephistopheles.

That is why I was so grateful to Maurel for changing the customary hue to an unexciting mouse color. However, I am wandering away from the Redemption, as to which I have no more to say generally than that if you will only take the precaution to go in long enough after it commences and to come out long enough before it is over you will not find it wearisome. Indeed some people do not find it wearisome even at full length, just as, I suppose, they would not mind going through five miles of pictures by Fra Angelico; but I am unfortunately so constituted that if I were actually in Heaven itself I should have to earn my enjoyment of it by turning out and doing a stroke of work of some sort, at the rate of at least a fortnight's hard labor for one celestial evening hour. There is nothing so insufferable as happiness, except perhaps unhappiness; and this is at the bottom of the inferiority of Gounod and Mendelssohn to Handel as oratorio writers.

Whilst I am on this part of the subject, let me deplore the childish incapacity which the people who run after happiness always shew for being satisfied with it when they get it. For instance, when Miss Palliser sang They who seek things eternal, with a beautiful high C which should have made any reasonable person ashamed to ask for anything more for a whole month, the audience, with odious ingratitude, insisted on having it again, with the result that Miss Palliser, thrown into competition with herself, and hindered from letting well alone, could only give a comparative scrape to the C the second time. The greatest offenders in this encore were the choristers. Your chorister is generally a person who is always watching for high C's from sopranos and tenors, or G sharps from baritones, or low D's from basses, having, poor wretch! no other notion of what is excellent in music.

Even if this were not so, choristers ought not to be allowed to applaud at all, as under the existing toleration every choral concert and Handel Festival provides itself automatically with a huge army of *claqueurs*, full to their scalps with spurious connoisseurship. However, the Albert Hall connoisseurs did not sing badly, the performance on the whole being a very good one. Miss Marie Brema sang While my watch I am keeping with a gentler vocal touch and a nearer approach to purely lyric style than I had heard from her before; and it now seems not unlikely that Miss Palliser and Miss Brema may in the course of time succeed Albani and Madame Belle Cole on the oratorio platform. All the gentlemen, especially Mr Watkin Mills, were very efficient.

At Mr Dolmetsch's viol concert in Barnard's Inn yesterday week I enjoyed the unexpected sensation of having one of my criticisms read aloud to the audience. "This," added Mr Dolmetsch with an air of conviction, "is severe language; but it is true." Whereat the audience—well, I had better say they smiled, but sniggered is the expression I should use in unrestrained private conversation. The precedent appears to me an excellent one. I am confident that the Philharmonic concerts and those of the Bach Choir, nay, the very Opera itself, could be most agreeably enlivened by a judicious selection from my articles.

A legitimate development of the idea would be to engage me to mount the platform after each number in the program and deliver an impromptu five minutes' criticism. I shall be most happy to entertain any proposals of this nature; and I suggest that it might be possible to arrange for each of my appearances without adding to the expenses, as Mr Henschel would probably pay my Philharmonic fees, Signor Lago my Covent Garden fees, and againwards (which in modern English is *vice versa*).

I have a small criticism to offer on Mr Dolmetsch's method of explaining the construction of the old dances. Those who saw the Masque of Flowers in Gray's Inn Hall some years ago are probably the only amateurs in London who have any really artistic insight to the old dance forms. If you want to explain a dance form to me, there is only one way of doing it; and that is to shew me the dance for which the music was required. Until I see that, no information about sections and variations and ground basses can interest me in the least, because nothing that is arbitrary and unrelated to any artistic purpose can interest any human being unless he has taken a musical degree.

I know, of course, that Mr Dolmetsch cannot get up the dances for us, though that old hall of the Art Workers' Guild in Clifford's Inn would be the very place for a Masque if there were only a little more room in it; but I submit that if there is to be any oral description at all (and Mr Dolmetsch talks to his audience most discreetly and amusingly) the thing to describe is the suppressed part of the dance and not the performed part of it. If people hear a musical note or an harmonic progression, it does not add to their knowledge of it to tell them that its name is B flat or the plagal cadence. If it did we could teach music to the deaf. But if people hear B flat or the plagal cadence talked about, and they ask what these two terms mean, you can enlighten them completely by letting them hear the note and the progression.

Mr Dolmetsch's answer to the question "What is a pavan or a galliard?" should be to have it played and danced on the spot. This Mr Dolmetsch does, as regards the playing, to the entire satisfaction of his audience; and so he need say nothing about the music. What we are left in the dark about is the dance; and for the suggestion of this to the imagination, the chin music of the lecturer may legitimately be called in.

The Wagner program at the London Symphony Concert last Thursday drew a large audience. I never can quite reconcile myself to the entry of the gods into Valhalla across the rainbow bridge, as arranged for concert use without the voices and without the multitudinous harps of the original score; and matters were not improved on this occasion by the reeds giving us the lamentation of the Rhine daughters almost as flat as if they had been real German singers. But still, it is better to hear the Rhinegold music that way than not to hear it at all. The Meistersinger quintet soon degenerated into a mere bawling match, the tenor and soprano exciting general admiration by their stupendous and perfectly gratuitous exertions. I do not think their mistake arose from any lack of artistic feeling, but partly from the fact of the music not being sufficiently easily within their powers, and partly from exaggerating the difficulty of making themselves heard in St James's Hall against the orchestra. When I last heard the London Symphony band attempt the Siegfried Idyll, the result was a second-rate performance: this time it was first-rate, another proof of the artistic maturity of Mr Henschel's enterprise. The Liebestod transcription from Tristan was well played, but it was taken much too fast, in my judgment. The Eroica also suffered for a few moments in the middle of the last movement by expressive whipping up: otherwise it went admirably, especially the funeral march, but always excepting the first movement, which we shall hear in its glory, I suppose, when we get an orchestra of heroes to play it and a demigod to conduct it. Nothing will ever persuade me that Beethoven meant it to begin in a hurry, with the theme stumping along to catch the last train, and the syncopations for the violins in the fifth bar coming in like the gasps of a blown pedestrian. Imagine the effect of tackling Mozart's E flat symphony that way!

1 *March* 1893

I PRESUME I may congratulate Sir Charles Hallé this time on the result of his expedition to London. As I have lost no opportunity of opening the eyes of our London amateurs to the value of the Manchester orchestra as a real band with a mastered repertory and not a mere muster of good executants who can be depended on for sight-reading, Sir Charles Hallé's agents, fearing that they might seem to be corruptly returning a compliment, have carefully abstained from offering me any of the customary civilities by which a critic is kept informed of what is going on at St James's Hall. Consequently it was quite by accident that I learnt, last Wednesday evening, that the Manchester band was performing there. I hastened to the spot half an hour late and proffered a modest half-crown for admission, but was told that there was only standing-room, of which I decided not to deprive somebody else. I mention the incident partly to explain my having nothing to say about the performance, and partly to shew that the public has found out what a mistake it made last year in neglecting the Manchester band.

Let me, however, offer a criticism on the program. It was too long. Concert programs always are. The fact is, music is in much the same phase as that of the drama in "the palmy days." We have two farces, a Shakespearean tragedy, and a Christmas pantomime all in the same evening—a sort of thing only possible with audiences consisting of persons so callous that they are as triflingly affected by works of art as they are inconvenienced by bad ventilation. Now the completely sensitized listener is as intensely active in the theatre or concert-room as a photographic plate is during exposure; and when the light is of Wagnerian or Beethovenian power it cannot be endured for two hours without exhaustion. When Mr Henschel started the London Symphony concerts this season, he promised that they should be over always at a quarter past ten; but he is a deceiver: the last concert left that hour far behind, and sent me home a shattered man. At the Crystal Palace the same inhumanity passes without protest. Mr Manns appears to me to subordinate all other considerations, artistic and humanitarian, to keeping me late for the four-fifty-four train, which, if this country were properly governed, would be a five o'clock express. This may be all very well for the refreshment contractors, and for the victims of that most horrible form of dipsomania, the craving for afternoon tea; but to me it is only an aggravation of the trials of my profession. Besides, the tea-room is a mockery even to those who use it. Sometimes, when I have a dipsomaniac lady with me, she insists on being taken thither; and we enter at ten minutes past five, with twenty minutes to spare before the train starts. Five of these minutes are consumed in finding a place at the crowded tables, and five more in attracting the attention of the distracted waitress, a process which the crusty old gentlemen conduct by peremptory vociferation, the handsome young ones by what Darwin calls sexual selection, and mild and irresolute persons like myself by the silent pathos of infinite patience, which, however, is only practicable when the dipsomaniac is not of an impetuous disposition; for if she is, she nags, and declares aloud that the arrangements are scandalous. When the waitress is secured, she, if smart and willing, executes the order in five minutes more; and if you are wise you pay her on the nail lest you should have to find her all over again. Allowing two and a half minutes to catch the train, this leaves another two and a half to poison yourself in. And all this because there are seven—sometimes eight—numbers in a program which should contain five.

Let me come to the practical question, what would I cut out of the existing program scheme? Well, obviously not the symphony, nor the concerto, nor the overture. But what about the customary vocal pieces? Granted that a song forms a convenient interpolation between the concerto and symphony, is it worth while, when there is the cheap and simple alternative of a brief interval for reading Sir George Grove's inimitable programs, to secure the interpolation at the cost of having to give the vocalist another turn later on when nobody wants it? Besides, do the singers deserve any consideration? Have they done anything to make or maintain the reputation of the concerts? How many of them ever fill the gaps left for them in the programs with the faintest sense of appropriateness?

How often, on the contrary, do they not strut in between the Schumann concerto and a Beethoven symphony, and strike up some scena by Massenet, well enough in its place on the stage perhaps, but appearing only an ill-bred intruder in such noble company. And these singers are so insufferably unconscious of their ineptitude! You will see a woman who professes to be an artist expressing in every toss of her head her conviction that a pretty face, a smart bonnet, and a ripping B flat are of more importance than all the concertos and symphonies in the world. And nothing will ever convince her that she is mistaken until Mr Manns summarily removes her from the program scheme of his concerts. Why in the name of common sense should the singers have privileges which are denied to the instrumentalists?

Mr Manns would not for a moment dream of engaging a popular cornet-player to treat the Saturday audience to The Lost Chord or The Staccato Polka, or a popular drawing room pianist and miscellaneous concert "conductor" to rattle off a Grande Valse Brillante or Perles de l'Orient. Yet with the singers he is contemptuously indulgent. They may bring their ballads and bravuras straight from the miscellaneous and promenade concerts without any worse check than the discovery that the conductor does not take the smallest interest in them. Now I am for getting rid of these people, relics as they are of the savagery in which Sydenham was plunged when Mr Manns first arrived there —an heroic artist-missionary. Not that I would have vocal music altogether banned. On the contrary, I would elevate the singers to the level of the pianist and violinist by demanding an equally high class of work from them.

If anybody will sing for us some of those arrangements of Scotch songs by Beethoven, with string accompaniments —Treuer Johnnie, for instance—or the great concert arias of Mozart and Beethoven, let them by all means have the same importance and consideration in the making up of the program as Paderewski or Joachim. Provided we get rid of the promiscuous "vocal piece," the fragments of opera or oratorio, the sentimental trivialities in Norwegian and German which would not be tolerated if they were in familiar English; provided, above all, that I catch the four-fifty-four train, all will be well.

Before quitting this subject I may as well make my comment on the selection of choral works for the present season: that is, of Dvořák's new Mass in D on March 11th, and the Berlioz Faust on April 15th. I do not love these choral concerts: they bring down a horde of the oratorio public, which consists mostly of persons who mistake their curiosity to hear celebrated singers and celebrated compositions for a love of music. However, I admit—grudgingly—their right to live and enjoy themselves in their own miserable manner; and I recognize that they bring their money down and leave some of it behind for the better support of the concerts which please me; and so I put up with them for once in a way. But I do not see why they should not profit a little from the higher atmosphere of the Saturday concerts by being compelled to listen to their favorite singers in works that lie outside the ordinary Albert Hall repertory.

Of Dvořák's work I cannot of course speak, since the performance will be the first in England, though I should not greatly mind offering to eat the full score, covers and all, if it proves a serious contribution to Church music. Dvořák is a romantic composer; and the announcement of a Mass by him affects me much as if it were the announcement of a Divine Comedy in ever so many cantos by Mr R. L. Stevenson. His symphony in G, to which Mr Manns condescended last Saturday, is very nearly up to the level of a Rossini overture, and would make excellent promenade music at the summer fêtes out in the grounds. Berlioz' Faust seems to me to be altogether superfluous at the Crystal Palace, since it can now be heard often enough elsewhere.

Why not let us hear Schumann's Faust, with Mr Santley in the title part, or, if he does not care for it, Mr Bispham? Years ago I remember the Philharmonic producing the third section, and gravely informing the public that the first and second were not worth doing. As a matter of fact, the scene in which Faust is dazzled by the rising sun, with the trio of Want, Care, and Guilt, Faust's blindness, his orders to build the great dyke, the digging of the grave by the Lemures under the direction of Mephistopheles, Faust's quiet exultation at what he believes to be the progress of his great work, his declaration that life and freedom are for those alone who can fight every day for them, and his death in the moment of his fulfilled aspiration: all these are in the second part, which is the summit of Schumann's achievement in dramatic music, and is far superior to the rest of the work. I have often wondered that no baritone singer has succeeded in inducing one of our societies to undertake a performance; and it seems to me that at the Crystal Palace, where Schumann is especially beloved, and where the conductor is far more successful with him and more in sympathy with him than with Berlioz, Schumann's Faust would be heard to special advantage.

I may add that the Crystal Palace is rather on my mind for a reason altogether creditable to it. At the first concert of the spring season, on the 18th, the band, which is not usually at its best in the earlier concerts of the season, unexpectedly rose to the occasion with a performance of the C minor symphony so fine that it must have somewhat astonished Mr Manns himself. I hope Mr Henschel was present; for, in spite of his recent successes, he may take a lesson from Mr Manns as to the possibility of combining a vigorous and eloquent interpretation with refinement of execution and beauty of tone in the wind band. Young Hegner played Beethoven's fourth concerto, and, bar one or two little callousnesses proper to his juvenility, played it intelligently and appreciatively, shewing that he quite understood that he was there to give us the concerto and not to display his own powers. Later on he gave an excellent little performance of Schumann's Des Abends. The concert finished with some charming dance music by Nicodé, prettily spiced by certain fanciful polyphonic *hardiesses* in the style of Bruneau; Dvořák would have worked it up heavily into a symphony, and spoiled it. Last Saturday we had Dvořák in G, as aforesaid; and a Miss Mary Cardew, a remarkable violinist of the Joachim school, who ventured on Bach's Chaconne in D minor, and got through it and through Bruch's first concerto with adequate ambidexterity, but without quite settling the question as to the extent of her original artistic gifts. Santley sang L'orage s'est calmé, from Bizet's Pearl Fishers; and I wish the French baritone who introduced that air to us at Covent Garden had been present to hear what an unspoiled human voice, skilfully produced, and guided by a tender and upright artistic conscience, can do in French opera. Many of the audience had evidently expected him to howl in the customary manner, for they seemed a little surprised, and were probably disappointed, poor wretches. He also gave us his own Ave Maria; and I desire to be as gentle as possible in breaking to Mr Lunn and Signor Garcia the news of his having attacked the repeated Aves and Oras without the very least *coup de glotte*.

8 *March* 1893

A PERFORMANCE of the Ninth Symphony always brings a special audience to St James's Hall; for it is known to be the masterpiece of modern tone poetry, and the literary man comes to complete his culture by listening to it. I always pity him as he sits there, bothered and exhausted, wondering how soon the choir will begin to sing those verses which are the only part of the analytic program of which he can make head or tail, and hardly able to believe that the conductor can be serious in keeping the band moodling on for forty-five mortal minutes before the singers get to business. Time was when the conductor himself was often still more astray than the literary man as to the intention of Beethoven, and when those who knew the work by heart sat snorting in contemptuous rage, or enduring with the habitual resignation of tamed despair, whilst the dreary ceremony of reading through the band parts was proceeding.

When I say "time *was*," I do not for a moment question the ability of London to reproduce the same discouraging results still: no doubt anyone who may be curious to know exactly what I mean will find sufficient opportunity before we have lost all the traditions of the time when the Ninth Symphony was treated exactly as if it were a quintet for pianoforte, flute, etc., by Hummel, re-scored for full orchestra by Beethoven. But it has now become a matter of tolerably common knowledge that this sort of handling stamps a conductor, not as a leading authority on Beethoven, but as a nincompoop. How far the work has become really popular it would be hard to determine, because, as I have said, so many people come whenever it is in the bills, not to enjoy themselves, but to improve themselves. To them the culmination of its boredom in an Ode to Joy must seem a wanton mockery, since they always hear it for the first time; for a man does not sacrifice himself in that way twice, just as he does not read Daniel Deronda twice; and consequently, since it is pre-eminently true of the Ninth Symphony as of the hero of the music-hall song, that it is all right when you know it but youve got to know it first, he never becomes sufficiently familiar with the work to delight in it.

On the other hand, there must be a growing number of persons who, like myself, would rather have the Ninth Symphony, even from the purely musical point of view, than all the other eight put together, and to whom, besides, it is religious music, and its performance a celebration rather than an entertainment. I am highly susceptible to the force of all truly religious music, no matter to what Church it belongs; but the music of my own Church—for which I may be allowed, like other people, to have a partiality—is to be found in the Die Zauberflöte and the Ninth Symphony. I was born into evil days, when Les Huguenots was considered a sublime creation, and Die Zauberflöte "a damned pantomime" (as they say nowadays of its legitimate successor, Das Rheingold), and when the Ninth Symphony was regarded as a too long and perversely ugly and difficult concert-piece, much inferior to such august neo-classics as Spohr's Consecration of Sound and Mendelssohn's Italian Symphony; and if I had won all my knowledge of the great Singspiel and the great Symphony from their interpreters, instead of from Mozart and Beethoven themselves, small and darkened would that knowledge have been.

In bygone days I have often sat at performances, and said, under my breath, to the conductor or the artists, "Ah! if I were only a musical critic, how I would pay you out for this, you impostor, you pedant, you miserable artistic deaf-mute, you bawling upstart, you conceited minx," etc., etc., etc. That was in the day of my hot youth. Fortunately, I never became a professed critic—to my own great surprise—until age and experience had softened me to my present indulgent mellowness; but I am by nature vindictive, and find myself not always proof against the temptation to pay off old scores against hardened sinners; so that sometimes, when a fellow-creature is catching it in this column ostensibly for some shortcoming in the previous week, he (or she) is really expiating some murderous art-outrage perpetrated on a defenceless child a quarter of a century ago—perhaps even—and this, I admit, is the climax of injustice—by somebody else of whom the performance has too vividly reminded me.

Therefore I implore all young artists to do their best under all circumstances; for they can never know who is listening to them, or how soon some insignificant brat in the cheap seats in a provincial Town Hall or Athenæum may rise up, an avenging fury, armed with all the terrors of the London Press.

As to Mr Henschel and his performance of the Ninth Symphony last Thursday, when I say that he quite understood the nature of the work, and was not for a moment in danger of the old fundamental error of treating it as mere musical arabesque, I imply that the performance was a success; for, with a good band and a right understanding, the obscurities and difficulties of the Ninth Symphony vanish, and a child may lead it. The concert began with Schubert's unfinished symphony, which on this occasion ought to have been his uncommenced symphony. The Ninth Symphony is quite enough for one evening; and I purposely came late for the first movement of the Schubert part of the program, and did not listen to the second. When we got to Beethoven our minds were soon set at ease as to Mr Henschel's grasp of the situation by the vigor and decision with which we got the first subject, especially those two final bars with which Beethoven so powerfully clinches it. But though the main point was thus secured, the handling of the movement as it proceeded was not by any means above criticism.

Mr. Henschel, like Ibsen's Master Builder, and like all good conductors, has a troll in him; and this troll occasionally takes to rampaging and filibustering, at which seasons Mr Henschel will not only tolerate, and even relish, rough and blatant attacks on imposing passages, but will overdrive his band in a manner recalling some of the most remarkable achievements of Bevignani. Now, Beethoven must have known well that this was one of the common faults of the qualities he required in a conductor; and it seems clear to me that it was his dread lest any vulgar urgency or excitement should mar the grandeur of his symphonic masterpiece that led him to give the *tempo* of the first movement not merely as *allegro*, but as "*allegro*, but not too much so—rather majestically." Mr Henschel certainly missed the full significance of this "un poco maestoso." He made more than one undignified spurt; and at each of these incontinences the execution became blurred and confused, even to the point, if I mistake not, of notes being dropped and hasty recoveries made in the next bar by the wood-wind.

In the Scherzo, which lends itself to impetuous treatment, the *tempo* was perfect, varying between a normal hundred and seventeen bars per minute and an exceptional hundred and twenty. There were many admirable points in the execution of the slow movement, notably the cantabile of the second violins in the first of the andante sections; and the only matter on which I found myself at odds with the conductor was the concluding twelve-eight section, where the fact, hardly noticeable at first in the common time, that the pace was a shade too fast for a true Beethoven adagio, became quite obvious. Later on, Mr Henschel rather astonished some of us by the apparently very slow *tempo* he adopted for the *allegro assai*, in which the basses give out the theme of the Ode to Joy. We are so accustomed to hear this played exactly twice too fast, as if the minims and crochets were quavers and semiquavers, and treated as a Haydn allegro instead of as an expressive melody, that some of the older listeners felt a little indignant with Mr Henschel for not taking the usual wrong course.

I will even confess that I myself think that the thirty-three bars per minute, increasing to thirty-six at the *forte*, might have been changed to thirty-six and forty respectively without any worse effect than the correction of a slight failing that leaned to virtue's side. The choral portion was perhaps as well done as was possible under the circumstances at English concert pitch; but the strain was inhuman; and the florid variation beat both the choir and the principals, since it required smooth vocal execution as well as mere pluck, which quality the choir shewed abundantly as they held on desperately to high A after high A. On the whole, if we cannot get the pitch down, I am prepared to face the transposition of the choral section a semitone rather than have it marred by tearing and straining at impossibilities. The best points in the vocal work were the charming *piano* on the lines Who can not, oh let him, weeping, Steal away and live alone; the great chorus, Oh! embrace now all ye millions, and the martial tenor solo, which was sung with intelligence and spirit by Mr Henry McKinley.

May I suggest, on behalf of the choir, that if their voices are not to be relieved by the introduction of French pitch, at least their lungs might be refreshed by the introduction of a little fresh air? My enjoyment of the symphony was considerably interfered with by the background of young women, beauteous in their virgin robes, but visibly stifling, and agitating fans and sheets of music in all sorts of contradictory rhythms. At last, just as the exquisite coda of the adagio was stealing on me, I happened to catch sight of a face which had gone perfectly white; and then, of course, I gave up the adagio with a sigh, and resigned myself to watch the progress of the struggle not to faint and disturb the performance, the conviction that fresh air was the only salvation, the dreadful sense of the impossibility of climbing to the door over those giddy seats with the lights whirling round and the ground reeling, the alarm spreading to the neighbors, the proffering of fans and smelling-bottles, the commotion among gallant tenors and basses at the back, and the final desperate rally of the patient, and her triumphant postponement of her collapse to the top of the steep ladder at the other side of the door. During all which the band might have been playing Pop Goes the Weasel with no more fear of detection than if we had all been a St John's Ambulance class.

At the Crystal Palace on Saturday we had a Concert

Overture by Mr Marshall Hall. It began as if it really were going to be a concert overture, and a good one; but when it got to the double bar it rambled off into dreams and visions, dropped into Siegfried (the forest music) for a moment, much as Mr Silas Wegg used to drop into poetry, and finally lost all hold on my attention; so that I cannot say how it ended. Mr Marshall Hall will know that this is not a hostile verdict—I am of his faction, and not of the academic one; but I would sacrifice my own father if he wrote in sonata form and began to ramble in the fantasia section. Choose what form you please; but when you have chosen it, keep your grip of it like Beethoven, and dont wander and maunder like Schumann and Brahms. The aggravating part of the business in Mr Marshall Hall's case is that there is no lack of beauty and imaginative handling in his opening section; and he is hardly to be forgiven for not knowing the value and sufficiency of these for the work he had in hand.

Slivinski was the pianist at this concert, and he was mightily applauded. He played one of those concertos of Chopin's which should never have been written by a man of genius after Beethoven's fourth and fifth concertos had been given to the world. The edition used was Tausig's; and I am now more than ever convinced that Tausig's early death was, like that of Ananias, the result of supernatural interposition for the extermination of a sacrilegious meddler. The concert, I beg to add, was much too long.

15 *March* 1893

THE notices of the production of Cyrill Kistler's Kunihild at Würzburg remind me that I have often intended, and as often omitted, to call attention to the one composer who, as far as I know, has definitely set to work to continue Wagner's business on what I suppose I must now call the old lines, although it seems but yesterday that they were being denounced all over Europe as unbearably new lines. This, of course, is not altogether a fair description of Kistler; but I know so little about him that nobody can reasonably expect me to be accurate on the subject. I hear that he is very poor, and highly unpopular in academic circles; both of which facts, if they be facts, naturally predispose me to believe that he must be a man of some character and originality, and that he can easily get them recognized, even to the extent of a public statue, by simply begging or borrowing enough to keep him alive until he has produced a few great works, and then dying and waiting quietly in his coffin until his countrymen find him out. It is by offering the citizen every possible inducement not to be a man of genius that we keep him to safe everyday work; and this system is so completely successful that we may confidently boast that we never waste a man on high art unless he is so obsessed with it as to be fit for nothing else.

Kistler appears to be the victim of this sort of diabolic possession, brought on him, apparently, by exposure at a tender age to performances of Wagner's Ring trilogy; for he cannot get Valhalla and Odin and Loki and the Valkyries and dwarfs out of his head, and his solemn trombonings are beginning to be heard and talked of in the Fatherland. The Wagner Societies are charmed with him; but I do not regard their approval as conclusive; for I have had occasion to observe that it is possible to cultivate a taste for Wagner without cultivating a taste for music; and I suspect the Wagner Societies of including a considerable percentage of members who would rather have imitation Wagner than genuine Mozart, if, indeed, they do not positively dislike Mozart as their idol's rival before posterity. For in art, as in more personal matters, there is a love which means hating everybody else, and which ought to be capitally punished; as well as a love which spreads to everyone else, and which increases your regard for every man or woman, or piece of music, for the sake of one man or woman or piece of music.

Catholicity is the stamp of the higher love, as jealousy is of the lower; and I grievously mistrust the amateur who worships Wagner without sharing Wagner's delight in the works of other musicians, both great and small. Observe, catholicity is not Don Juanism. I much prefer Don Juan to the faithful French wife who throws vitriol in her rival's face, knowing that a French jury will let her off if she only dresses her part well enough; but still Don Juan did not love anybody: he was an Indifferentist. If I had been the petrified Commander, I should not have talked conventionally to him about repentance: I should have offered to let him off if he could rise for a moment to a preference for some woman above another, say for Elvira above her maid—though without in the least objecting to his appreciating the maid for what she was worth.

Nobody objects to Wagner's being delighted with La Sonnambula and Masaniello; but if they had served his turn as well as Die Zauberflöte and Fidelio, we should at once have seen that he had no more feeling for music than most bookbinders have for literature. Even the jealous lover is better worth consulting than the indifferent, who has no opinion at all, except that a book is a book, an opera an opera, and a petticoat a petticoat, and that books, operas, and petticoats are all enjoyable. But I prefer to consult the true catholic; and catholicism has not yet spoken on the merits of Kistler, except that he does not seem to be getting extinguished as the years go on—a fact which looks as if he were gaining ground with the final arbiter, Monsieur Tout-le-Monde. For my own part, I know nothing of his music, except what may be gathered from the vocal score of his Baldur's Tod, which does not contain his ripest work, and which, though it would certainly be a most remarkable and original music drama if there had never been such a person as Richard Wagner—just as Rienzi would have astonished the world greatly if Spontini and Meyerbeer had been out of the question—hardly proves more than a true discipleship (as distinct from a mere gleanership or imitatorship) on the part of its composer.

Of Kunihild I have very favorable accounts from trustworthy intelligencers; but for the moment I content myself with informing my readers that Cyrill Kistler should be noted as one of the coming men in Germany. It will take him longer to come all the way than it has taken Mascagni; but there will certainly be more to shew at the end of the journey: Baldur's Tod settles at least that much.

The first Philharmonic Concert took place last Thursday. It began at eight, and was actually not over at eleven. And as I am a living man, they played the overture to Marco Spada! Perhaps it is too much to ask the public to believe such a thing on my unsupported statement; but there are the papers, the printed program, the testimony of the audience to support me; and I repeat, they played Marco Spada—Auber's Marco Spada—at a Philharmonic Concert at the end of the nineteenth century, with the bust of Beethoven in its usual place before the orchestra! But that is just like the Philharmonic directors. They never could hear any qualitative difference between Rossini or Auber and Mozart or Beethoven. All four wrote overtures—William Tell, La Muette, Le Nozze di Figaro, Egmont; and an overture is an overture, as all the world knows—Don Juanism again, you see.

I may add that a band is a band, whether it is in St James's Hall or at a flower show: nevertheless, one does not draw up quite the same program for both places, except, apparently, at Philharmonic Concerts. I verily believe that if the composer of The Man that broke the Bank at Monte Carlo had only called his *chef-d' œuvre* an aria, and prefixed a recitative to it, we should have had Mr Coborn among the artists engaged during the Philharmonic season. One of the jokes of the present year is the reappearance in the programs of that history of the Society which figured in them all through last season. It will be remembered that this same last season ended somewhat scandalously for the Society through Mr Cowen, the conductor, publicly apologizing for the unrehearsed condition of the Pastoral Symphony, and being thereupon dislodged from his post by the indignant directors, who, having been exposed before all Europe and America by Wagner (whom they also dislodged after a year's trial in 1855) for offering monstrously long programs of scamped work to the public, were no doubt annoyed by being convicted by Mr Cowen of having persisted in their evil courses for nearly forty years.

However, before this happened they had, in the aforesaid historical sketch, made much of Mr Cowen in the following terms: "The Directors have ground for sincere congratulation for the choice [of a conductor] they have made for the present season." I quote the Philharmonic English verbatim, as the meaning may readily be guessed; and for the rest, why, as Rossini used to say when his serious style petered out too obviously into a galop, "*Excusez du peu.*" "It would scarcely be possible to find a more efficient or more popular conductor than Mr F. Cowen." The congratulations have been turned into condolements and gnashings of teeth, and the efficient and popular one has bitten the bosom that cherished him; yet the passage is still offered magnanimously to the public for a shilling, without even a note to indicate that the present conductor is Dr Mackenzie. He, in accepting the post, practically declared against Mr Cowen—a course which he has now to justify by producing better results than Mr Cowen, with no better preparation. When he appeared on the platform on Thursday there was an awful moment, caused by his coming somewhat pointedly to the front of the platform and facing the audience with a certain air of being about to make a speech; so that there began an awe-struck wondering whisper of "Is he also going to apologize?"

But he did not, happily; and next moment the band was shewing off in true Philharmonic style over the Euryanthe overture, as to which it is clear to me that either I know how Weber meant it to be played better than Dr Mackenzie does, or else Dr Mackenzie knows better than I do, which, as he is the Principal of the Royal Academy of Music, is no doubt the preferable view. Why, then, should I hesitate to express my opinion that the overture is thrown away on him—that he does not appreciate even the second subject, with that exquisite seventh bar which at its repetition in the last *fortissimo* becomes so gloriously transformed that no orchestra can ever saturate it with the flood of tone it requires? As it was, the band conveyed to me but one sentiment, which might have been expressed by the words "Ain't we just makin' it spin, eh?" And they certainly did make it spin: it sounded almost as smart as Marco Spada; and the *pianissimo* in the largo was undeniably *pianissimo*, if it was nothing else.

The Eroica Symphony was a great improvement on this: I judge that Dr Mackenzie knows and likes the work; and though the performance was not nearly so thoroughly studied as that recently given by Mr Henschel, and was consequently much less interesting, yet the score was very respectfully and delicately read through. The funeral march, of course, collapsed at the more powerful passages, as the wind would not hold their notes, perhaps because it is the custom for a Philharmonic conductor to throw up his hands in agony and cry "Sh—sh—sh!" at rehearsal whenever the brass ventures beyond a timid little bark. And the last episode, numbered 14 in the program, was made ridiculous in the traditional way by giving the quavers, obviously meant to be played very *legato*, as detached semiquavers, an absurdity which Mr Henschel also tolerated. But on the whole, the symphony did not need an apology. Marco Spada was of course brilliant—no one can pretend that the Philharmonic band cannot do justice to Auber, and Mancinelli's Suite, and Cowen's Language of Flowers, and all manner of pretty things. Decidedly Marco Spada was an excellent example of the best work the Philharmonic system can produce.

Slivinski played Schumann's concerto very brilliantly; but he made nothing of the slow movement, and did not throw any new light on the rest. He played Chopin's Nocturne in F sharp charmingly but inaccurately. *Tempo rubato* is all very well; but two semiquavers are two semiquavers all the world over, and not a dotted semiquaver and a demisemiquaver. Excuse these barbarous expressions.

Dvořák's rather amusing Mass in D and Goring Thomas's rather serious comic opera, The Golden Web, must stand over until next week.

22 *March* 1893

I WISH we had a Minister of the Fine Arts in this country, with a well-equipped statistical department behind him, and absolutely autocratic powers over everybody except myself. Were I such a Minister, I would allow the managers to do as they pleased in the way of producing plays; but I would compel them to submit their accounts to me, so that I might issue Blue-Books containing the exact truth as to the financial results of every play or opera produced in the kingdom. My object would be to shew that hundreds of thousands of pounds are wasted annually in producing obvious trash on the chance of its "catching on." Except actor-management and management to oblige a lady, management is mainly a department of sport into which artistic aims enter about as deeply as the improvement of national horse-breeding enters into the ambition of our gentlemen of the Turf. Consequently, we have an enormous proportion of failure to success; and we have the public going more and more to music-halls because a music-hall is the only place of entertainment where you can be quite sure of not having your evening and your money entirely wasted.

To avoid levelling these observations at any individual, I will now pass to the subject of Goring Thomas's Golden Web at the Lyric Theatre, since Goring Thomas attained a position as a dramatic composer which places the production of an opera of his beyond all suspicion as a legitimate artistic enterprise. Unfortunately, one of the effects of the experiment will be to confirm the association between the legitimate and the old-fashioned. In The Golden Web we have the composer utterly ignoring not only Wagner, but even Gilbert and Sullivan, by tacking so many numbers of what is practically "absolute music" to a book which, poor enough as a play, is quite wretched as a libretto, void as it is of a single passage which calls for musical expression: indeed, it is difficult to conceive how the work could have been made into an opera at all but for the stale interpolations of drinking-chorus, ballad, dance, and so forth, which have done duty in a hundred other operas before. Stuff of this kind apart, the music is essentially undramatic, and necessarily so, since the only truly dramatic music for such a play would be no music at all (I speak as an Irishman).

If Goring Thomas had been a dramatic composer instead of a mere musician ambitious to compose for the stage, he would have refused the book. There are degrees in the toleration of bad librettos: for instance, the late Franz Hueffer only pleaded for the reform of Now good red wine we will be drinking into Now let us drink some good red wine; whereas Sterndale Bennett insisted on total abstinence, and is said to have failed to leave us an opera only because he never could get a libretto in which some act did not begin with Soldiers discovered drinking. Bennett was quite right to object to the drinking-chorus altogether, not on account of its wording, but because no real dramatic poem could possibly contain such a thing. Goring Thomas, however, had no such scruples. He has provided music in The Golden Web for—

Let there be no more despair, boys;
Come along, tis share and share, boys,
Theres enough to drown all care, boys,
But remember, pray drink fair, boys.
A bottle—yes, a good old bottle,
Amazement and gratitude close up each throttle.
A glass of such medicine out of the bottle
Will stir up a blush our complexions to mottle.

It is quite unnecessary for me to state my opinion of these lines. I will do Mr Corder, one of the authors, the justice to assume that he entirely agrees with me; but Mr B. C.

Stephenson, his collaborator, must remain under suspicion of being rather proud of them until he writes to the papers repudiating any such notion. Mr Corder's excuse, no doubt, is that he has had to translate foreign opera texts into English versions capable of being sung to the original notes, a process in which all literary conscience and even common sanity vanishes, the job being in the nature of things an impossible one from the first. The public probably does not understand the difficulty; but it can easily do so by studying some of Schubert's settings of German translations of English poems by Sir Walter Scott. To the inconsiderate outsider, nothing would appear to have been simpler, when the time came to bring Schubert's settings to England, than to substitute the original text of Scott for the German translation. But the result would have been such an outrageous misfit, in consequence of the disparity in number of syllables and position of accent between many English words and their German equivalents, that it was necessary to contrive new English versions of the German translations, absurdly inferior to the original English.

Such English versions, which sometimes get re-translated into German and back again—for there is no logical end to the process—are makeshifts from beginning to end; and the difficulty of fitting them to the music is so great that the adapter soon grows desperate, and snatches at the most ludicrous and far-fetched solutions, not merely with resignation, but with positive complacency. Mr Corder achieved a surprising degree of success in making an English version of Wagner's Nibelungen tetralogy; but the success did not go to the length of enabling him to avoid making one of the giants remark, in dunning Wotan for the agreed wage of building Valhalla, Pay fails to appear—a flash of dialogue which, whilst fully up to the highest libretto standard, has not the atmosphere of "god-home" about it. But I not only should not think of finding fault with it, but do hereby absolve Mr Corder, as Nibelungen English versionist, from all literary responsibility for ever, in consideration of pre-eminent service and superhuman trials; and I shall not now say one unkind word about the following lyric, lest he, and not Mr Stephenson, should prove the author of it. Here it is:

> Oh dear! I am so frightened,
> My pulse is madly heightened,
> And every nerve is tightened—
>   Aunt Pamela is lost.
> I turned my head a moment,
> A lovely dress, for show meant,
> All lace and furbelowment,
> Had caught my eye a moment—
>   Aunt Pamela is lost.
> Geoffrey, say not our dream of love is o'er.
> Aunt Pamela in vain I search,
> In vain I call.

How Goring Thomas set this sort of poetry can be imagined by anyone who knows the facility with which he turned out opera scores musically as advanced as Gounod's, yet dramatically not an inch in front of Balfe's. In fact, Balfe was the more original of the two, since he came first, although of course Goring Thomas never bungled his music as Balfe would bungle a whole opera from the first page to the last, the ballads only excepted. In The Golden Web, the music, considered as absolute music, is graceful, workmanlike, and occasionally vigorous enough; but it does not even pretend anywhere to novelty—the very overture begins at once with a thoroughly well-worn Gounodism, and has for its second subject The heart bowed down from The Bohemian Girl, not more altered than it would have been by Balfe himself if he had used it in an overture and been able to handle it as cleverly as Goring Thomas. The non-musical part of the play is a rococo comedy, with a crusty father, a runaway pair of lovers, an elderly beau and belle, a gentleman's gentleman, a Fleet parson with a comic drunken servant, and so on. It is not actually stupid, but it is a poor affair, neither the authors nor the composer having taken their work seriously. If it succeeds, its success will be due largely to Miss Alice Esty, a born musician and singer, with an invaluable quickness and good sense, and a certain fresh charm of manner and appearance which at once broke down a virtuous resolution against encores promulgated by a man of few words in the gallery, who simply said, "No encores, boys," and carried his point thereafter against everybody except Miss Esty. It must be added that part of Miss Esty's freshness is due to the fact that neither her acting nor her speaking has any definitely artistic character. She turns her hand willingly and intelligently to the business of her part; but it is through the natural charm of her unspoiled voice, which tells through the heaviest ensembles by its quality alone (it is perfectly light and delicate), and through the pleasure taken by the public in her musical facility and confidence of execution, that she succeeds, and not in the least by the sort of artistic purpose and skill which have enabled less gifted persons to conquer a place on the stage in spite of refractory voices, slow ears, and unattractive faces and figures. Mr Wallace Brownlow acted humorously in an amateur way as the Fleet parson. The music suits his voice so well that he is on good terms with the audience all through; but I advise Mr Brownlow, now that he holds a leading position at a West End London theatre, not, even in a comic part, to allow his diction to sink to the point at which "gimme" passes for "give me," or "virchew" and "disconcerchew" for "virtue" and "disconcert you."

The Mass by Dvořák which was performed for the first time in England at the Crystal Palace last Saturday week, contains a good deal of *fugato*, which is all the funnier because the composer evidently meant it to be ecclesiastical and impressive. The Credo, in his romantic style, is not bad as an example of that style, though it is not good as a Credo. Some of the words of the Mass are omitted from the setting; but though the omissions seem to have been deliberate, I failed to infer from them the exact limits to Dvořák's orthodoxy.

At the Palace concert last Saturday, Joachim, whose finest qualities seem to improve as the years make him serener, gave us Mozart's concerto in A, the last movement in which is an experiment in combining the minuet and finale into a single movement in rondo form. Also a capriccio by Niels Gade—a novelty. Miss Mary Harris, who has been harmlessly—that is, excellently—trained, and whose purely musical qualifications are considerable, saw no difficulty whatever either in Mozart's Mi tradi from Don Giovanni or in Schubert's Ave Maria. In fact, finding both compositions rather uninteresting as they stood, she touched up the first with a B flat at the end, and even lent Schubert an A flat which was so unexpected that gentlemen were seen doubling up in all directions in the part of the room more especially affected by the connoisseurs.

I hope Miss Harris will understand that she must not do that again if she wishes to be respected as an artist as well as admired as a young lady with a pretty voice; and also, I must add, that she is not yet within ten years of attaining the expression and eloquence which can alone give her the right to touch in public a masterpiece like Mi tradi. For the rest, Miss Harris is to be congratulated on being a nice singer, since she is now in a position to begin to teach herself to be an artist.

29 *March* 1893

I SELDOM go to a Monday Popular Concert without wondering how many of the people who sit out the quartets and sonatas feel the heavy responsibility which they incur as the dispensers of applause and success to young artists. Last Monday week I heard them give a tremendous ovation to Joachim, who had played Bach's Chaconne in D minor, and played it, certainly, with a fineness of tone and a perfect dignity of style and fitness of phrasing that can fairly be described as magnificent. If the intonation had only had the exquisite natural justice of Sarasate's, instead of the austerity of that peculiar scale which may be called the Joachim mode, and which is tempered according to Joachim's temperament and not according to that of the sunny South, I should have confidently said to my neighbor that this particular performance could never be surpassed by mortal violinist.

But the thought that the miracle of miracles might arrive in the shape of a violinist with Sarasate's intonation and Joachim's style made me forbear. This peculiar intonation of Joachim's for a long time greatly hindered my appreciation of his art: the Celtic troll in me rebelled against intervals that were not the same as my intervals. For I may as well make known, as a remarkable discovery in psychical physics, that the modes in which we express ourselves musically, that is, the major and minor scales, though in theory series of sounds bearing a fixed pitch relation to one another, are in practice tempered by every musician just as the proportions of the human figure are tempered by a sculptor. Some physicist should make a tonometer giving a theoretically perfect major scale, in order that Joachim, Sarasate, Isaÿe, and Remenyi should have an opportunity of hearing how far the four different tone figures which they have made for themselves as major scales differ from the theoretic scale and from one another. Only the worst of it is that the tonometer would probably turn out to be inaccurate, as scientific instruments usually are.

Schumann's metronome led him a pretty dance; and Appun's tonometer bothered the late Alexander J. Ellis handsomely until it occurred to him that a box of reeds was much more likely to get out of condition than the organ of Corti inside the head of a musician. Still, the fact that a tonometer is quite as likely as a violinist to set up a scale peculiar to its individual self does not affect my contention that every artist modifies the scale to suit his own ear; that every nation does the same; and that the musical critic of the future, instead of crudely saying, as I do, that the Germans have every musical qualification except ear, will classify the national and individual modes, and dispassionately announce that the intonation of So-and-So, the new virtuoso, is German-lymphatic, or Spanish-bilious, or English-evangelical, or what not. And he will train himself to tolerate and appreciate all these different modes, just as I have come to such a perfect toleration of Joachim's that I no longer have the least feeling that he is playing out of tune except when he is false to his own scale.

I submit this enlightened attitude for the imitation of those rash persons who accuse Joachim of playing out of tune, and whose standard of intonation is often founded on the luscious strains of the accordion as made in Italy, or on keyed instruments like the common pianoforte, with its sharp thirds, flat fifths, and generally tinkered and compromised tuning. Even if Joachim played every note out of tune, the quality of his tone and the thoroughness of his interpretation would compel us to listen to him, though we groaned with anguish at every stroke of the bow.

However, I am wandering, as usual; for all I specially want to point out about this concert is that the same audience which apparently revelled in the masterly playing of Bach's Chaconne by Joachim, shewed equal delight at Miss Ilona Eibenschütz's attack on Beethoven's pianoforte sonata in F minor, popularly nicknamed "Appassionata." Now, at the risk of greatly astonishing Miss Eibenschütz, whose talent I quite appreciate and whose enthusiasm I should be sorry to damp, I must, on behalf of Beethoven, mention that the sonata could hardly have been worse played by an artist of Miss Eibenschütz's endowment. I am not now thinking of the last movement: a young player may be forgiven for trying to carry that by storm; and Miss Eibenschütz, who evidently enjoyed the excitement of the rush, at her age will be none the worse for it, though the music all but disappeared in the dust and hurry. But we have really had enough of hearing the first movement trifled with as if it were a mere bravura. No orator ever declaimed a sentence more gravely beautiful than that with which the sonata opens: words could add nothing to its feeling, though they could give it—quite superfluously—some specific relevancy. To seize such a poetic speech by main force and gallop it along as if it were a quickstep, and to follow it up in the same fashion, turning all its kindlings of heart into mere spurts of impetuosity, and retiring finally amid the sort of enthusiasm that follows a pluckily rowed boat-race, is to fail as a Beethoven interpreter in the most obvious way.

Every student knows that it is difficult to play the Appassionata or the Moonlight or the Waldstein sonata accurately, and exciting to play them fast. But that is not what they are for; and when a great artist wishes to give the public some fun of that kind, there are plenty of Hungarian rhapsodies and toccatas of all sorts ready to hand for the purpose. To put a tone-poem to such a use is like using an ivory sceptre as a singlestick; and if Miss Eibenschütz were ten years older there would be no pardon for her for having done this wrong to the F minor sonata, and that, too, with artists like Joachim and Piatti listening to her. Yet the audience, foolishly excited by the mere haste of the performance, encored her with enthusiasm, and thereby heavily discounted the value of the same compliment paid shortly afterwards to Joachim for the Chaconne. In the Eibenschütz furore, however, I think there was a passionate student element; for the young player, with her dark hair braided over her pale face and great eyes, her black dress emphasizing the slightness of her figure, and her quick, half-tamed movements, appealed with instinctive feminine art to the student imagination.

Fortunately, I have no imagination: I am proof against all illusions except illusions which flatter me; I am middle-aged in years and patriarchal in wisdom; and so before the end of the first bar I knew that the sonata was going to be a failure; and I hope Miss Eibenschütz will give due weight to that opinion from a critic whose first impression of her ability was highly favorable.

A very remarkable performance was that of Brahms'

violin concerto by Miss Wietrowetz at the Philharmonic last Thursday. It was not by any means musically satisfactory; for Miss Wietrowetz is powerful, impatient, and, like all modern women, somewhat contemptuous of manly gentleness. I confess I am afraid of Miss Wietrowetz: she is so strong and wilful that even her playing gives me a humiliating sense of being ordered about—positively of being henpecked. Joachim is called by courtesy her master; but I suspect that what really happened was that Miss Wietrowetz bought a fiddle; took it to his house; and said, "Here, shew me how to play this, if you please. Look sharp"; and that he meekly obeyed.

That is the way the younger generation comes knocking at the door nowadays. There is no longer any doubt about it: we of the nobler sex must give up the old assortment of "manly qualities"; for they are passing away from us to the young women, who beat all our records with triumphant ease. If the supremacy of man is to be maintained, we must develop a quite new set of qualities and hasten to the very heights; for I feel that nothing but a perfectly blinding moral splendor can protect me against the masterful will, the determined courage, the practicality, the executive skill of such a personality as Miss Wietrowetz's. Suppose she were to find out how easily I could be bullied into declaring her the greatest player that ever lived, where should I be?

But whilst I am still my own master I will maintain, even if I were to be taken by the collar and well shaken for it next day, that Joachim's patience, and his complete subjugation of his will to a purely artistic end, produce greater results in Brahms' concerto, or any other concerto, than the mettlesomeness of this formidable pupil of his, who, by the bye, has acquired his peculiar intonation as perfectly as Miss Nettie Carpenter has acquired Sarasate's. I repeat, they are wonderful, these young women: they do by sheer resolution what men are only able to do by extraordinary natural gifts.

Before I leave the subject of the Philharmonic concert, I must chronicle the performance of Mr Somervell's orchestral ballad Helen of Kirkconnel, a simple affair which disarmed criticism by its unpretentiousness. The band played the Brahms concerto in a rather ramshackle fashion (I think Miss Wietrowetz put them out of countenance); but in Sullivan's Macbeth overture they handled the wind parts with a firmness that quite took away my breath; and once or twice they positively approached a genuine fortissimo. My compliments, Dr Mackenzie! I begin to believe, for the first time in my life, that there is some use in criticism, and that the Philharmonic Society may earn its reputation yet, after all. I did not wait for Mr Cliffe's symphony, of which I have already expressed my opinion; but I have no doubt that, as the program promised, the first allegro gave "a general impression of the splendor of nature under the declining sun," and that the semiquaver figure duly "stood for the quivering beams of the great luminary."

The operetta called Mr Jericho, by "Harry Greenbank" (I take this to be an *alias*), which now precedes Haddon Hall at the Savoy, is funnily absurd and wittily funny, a fact which dawned on a rather stupid audience on the night of my visit after a page of really laughable dialogue had been listened to in dead silence. It has been passably upholstered with the requisite music by Mr Ernest Ford; and the acting and singing, though jolly enough to carry the piece through acceptably, are abysmally beneath notice from the point of view of the critic of skilled art.

The concerts of the Wind Instrument Chamber Music Society are now in progress at St James's Banqueting Hall. I can do no more than mention the fact, as the night fixed for the concerts (Friday) is one on which I am seldom able to attend.

12 *April* 1893

EASTER has afforded me an opportunity for a look through the vocal score of Verdi's Falstaff, now to be had at Ricordi's for sixteen shillings, a price which must obviously be reduced before the opera can get into the hands of the amateur at large. I did not go to Milan to hear the first performance for several reasons, the chief being that I am not enough of a first-nighter to face the huge tedium and probable sickness of the journey from Holborn to Basle (the rest I do not mind) in order merely to knock at the tradesman's door of Italy, so to speak, and turn back after hearing an opera half murdered by La Scala prima donnas with shattering tremolos, and witnessing a Grand Old Man demonstration conducted for the most part by people who know about as much of music as the average worshipper of Mr Gladstone does of statesmanship. In short, being lazy and heavily preoccupied, I cried sour grapes and stayed at home, knowing that the mountain would come to Mahomet soon enough.

Let it be understood, then, that since I have not been present at a complete performance of Falstaff I do not know the work: I only know some things about it. And of these I need not repeat what has already been sufficiently told: as, for instance, that Falstaff is a music drama, not an opera, and that consequently it is by Shakespear, Boito, and Verdi, and not by Verdi alone. The fact that it is a music drama explains the whole mystery of its composition by a man eighty years old. If there were another Il balen or La donna è mobile in it, I should have been greatly astonished; but there is nothing of the sort: the fire and heroism of his earlier works blazes up now only on strong provocation.

Falstaff is lighted and warmed only by the afterglow of the fierce noonday sun of Ernani; but the gain in beauty conceals the loss in heat—if, indeed, it be a loss to replace intensity of passion and spontaneity of song by fullness of insight and perfect mastery of workmanship. Verdi has exchanged the excess of his qualities for the wisdom to supply his deficiencies; his weaknesses have disappeared with his superfluous force; and he is now, in his dignified competence, the greatest of living dramatic composers. It is not often that a man's strength is so immense that he can remain an athlete after bartering half of it to old age for experience;

but the thing happens occasionally, and need not so greatly surprise us in Verdi's case, especially those of us who, long ago, when Von Bülow and others were contemptuously repudiating him, were able to discern in him a man possessing more power than he knew how to use, or indeed was permitted to use by the old operatic forms imposed on him by circumstances.

I have noticed one or two exclamations of surprise at the supposed revelation in Falstaff of a "hitherto unsuspected" humorous force in the veteran tragic composer. This must be the result of the enormous popularity which Il Trovatore first and Aïda afterwards attained in this country. I grant that these operas are quite guiltless of comic relief; but what about Un Ballo, with its exquisitely light-hearted E scherz' od è follia, and the finale to the third act, where Renato is sarcastically complimented on his domestic virtue by the conspirators who have just shewn him that the Duke's veiled mistress, whom he is defending from them after devotedly saving the Duke's life, is his own wife. Stupidly as that tragi-comic quartet and chorus has always been mishandled on our wretched operatic stage, I cannot understand anyone who knows it denying Verdi's gift of dramatic humor.

In the first act of Otello, the stretto made in the drinking song by Cassio when he gets drunk is very funny without being in the least unmusical. The grim humor of Sparafucile, the terrible ironic humor of Iago, the agonized humor of Rigoletto: these surely settled the question as to Verdi's capacity for Falstaff none the less because the works in which they occur are tragedies and not comedies. All that could be said on the other side was that Verdi was no Mozart, which was as idle as saying that Victor Hugo was no Molière. Verdi's vein of humor is all the more Shakespearean on that account.

Verdi's worst sins as a composer have been sins against the human voice. His habit of taking the upper fifth of the compass of an exceptionally high voice, and treating that fifth as the normal range, has a great deal to do with the fact that the Italian singer is now the worst singer in the world, just as Wagner's return to Handel's way of using the voice all over its compass and obtaining physical relief for the singer and artistic relief for the audience by the contrast of the upper and lower registers has made the Wagnerian singer now the best singer in the world. Verdi applied his system with special severity to baritones.

If you look at the score of Don Giovanni, you will find three different male voices written for on the bass clef, and so treated as to leave no doubt that Mozart, as he wrote the music, had a particular sort of voice for each part constantly in his head, and that one (Masetto's) was a rough peasant's bass, another (Leporello's) a ready, fluent, copious *basso cantante*; and the third a light fine baritone, the voice of a gentleman. I have heard public meetings addressed successively by an agricultural laborer's delegate, a representative of the skilled artisans, and a university man; and they have taught me what all the treatises on singing in the world could not about the Mozartian differentiation between Masetto, Leporello, and Don Giovanni.

But now please remark that there is no difference of range between the three parts. Any man who can sing the notes of one of them can sing the notes of the others. Let Masetto and the Don exchange characters, and though the Don will be utterly ineffective in the concerted music on Masetto's lower G's and B flats, whilst Masetto will rob the serenade of all its delicacy, yet neither singer will encounter any more impossibility, or even inconvenience, in singing the notes than Mr Toole would have in reading the part of Hamlet. The same thing is true of the parts of Bartolo, Figaro, and Almaviva in Le Nozze; of San Bris and Nevers in Les Huguenots; of Wotan and Alberich in The Niblung's Ring; and of Amfortas and Klingsor in Parsifal. The dramatic distinction between these parts is so strong that only an artist of remarkable versatility could play one as well as the other; but there is practically no distinction of vocal range any more than there is a distinction of physical stature or strength.

But if we turn to Il Trovatore, we find two vocal parts written in the bass clef, of which the lower, Ferrando, is not a *basso profondo* like Osmin or Marcel, but a *basso cantante* like San Bris or Leporello; yet the baritone part (Di Luna) is beyond the reach of any normal *basso cantante*, and treats a baritone voice as consisting of about one effective octave, from G on the fourth space of the bass stave to the G above. In Il balen there are from two hundred and ten to two hundred and twenty notes, including the cadenza, etc. Barring five notes in the cadenza, which is never sung as written, only three are below F on the fourth line, whilst nearly one hundred and forty lie above the stave between B flat and the high G. The singing is practically continuous from end to end; and the strain on a normal baritone voice is frightful, even when the song is transposed half a tone as it usually is to bring it within the bare limits of possibility. Di Luna is in this respect a typical Verdi baritone; and the result has been that only singers with abnormally high voices have been able to sing it without effort.

As to the normal baritones who have made a specialty of bawling fiercely up to G sharp, they have so lost the power of producing an endurable tone in their lower octave, or of pitching its notes with even approximate accuracy, that they have all but destroyed the popularity of Mozart's operas by their occasional appearances as Don Giovanni, Figaro, etc. I have often wished that the law would permit me to destroy these unhappy wretches, whose lives must be a burden to them. It is easy to go into raptures over the superiority of the Italian master in vocal writing because his phrases are melodious, easily learned, symmetrical, and often grandiose; but when you have to sing the melodious well-turned phrases, and find that they lie a tone higher than you can comfortably manage them, and a third higher than you can keep on managing them for five minutes at a stretch (for music that *lies* rather high is much more trying than music that *ventures* very high occasionally), you begin to appreciate the sort of knowledge of and consideration for the voice shewn by Purcell, Handel, and Wagner, and to very decidedly resent Verdi's mere partiality for the top end of it.

Now comes the question, what sort of voice is needed for the part of Falstaff? Well, Ferrando and the Count di Luna rolled into one—Amonasro, in short. A rich *basso cantante*, who can knock out a vigorous high G and play with F sharp as Melba plays with B flat. Polyphemus in Handel's Acis and Valentine in Gounod's Faust might do it justice between them. Barely reasonable this, even at French pitch, and monstrous at Philharmonic pitch. And yet it is the fashion to say that Verdi is a master of the art of writing singable music.

The score is necessarily occupied to a great extent by the discourses of Falstaff, which are set with the most expert ingenuity and subtlety, the advance in this respect from the declamation of Charles V in Ernani to that of Falstaff being as great as from Tannhäuser's to Parsifal's, or from Vanderdecken's to Hans Sachs's. One capital effect—the negative answers in the manner of Mr Chadband to the repeated questions as to what honor is—is, musically, a happy adaptation from Boito's Mefistofele, and is, as far as I have discovered, the only direct Boitoism in the work, though I imagine that Verdi has profited generally by having so fine an artist and critic as Boito at his elbow when composing Otello and Falstaff. There are some amusing passages of instrumental music: for instance, a highly expressive accompaniment to a colossal drink taken by Falstaff.

During the abundant action and stage bustle of the piece we get a symphonic treatment, which belongs exclusively to Verdi's latest manner. Some tripping figuration, which creates perpetual motion by its ceaseless repetition in all sorts of ingenious sequences, as in Mendelssohn's scherzos or the finales to his concertos, is taken as the musical groundwork upon which the vocal parts are put in, the whole fabric being wrought with the most skilful elegance. This is a matter for some of our musical pundits to consider rather anxiously. For, if I had said ten years ago that Ernani was a much greater musical composition than Mendelssohn's Scotch symphony or any of his concertos, words could not have conveyed the scorn with which so gross an opinion would have been received. But here, today, is the scorned one, whom even Browning thought it safe to represent as an empty blusterer shrinking amid a torrent of vulgar applause from the grave eye of—of—of—well, of ROSSINI! (poor Browning!) falling back in his old age on the Mendelssohnian method, and employing it with ease and brilliancy.

Perhaps, when Verdi turns a hundred and feels too old for opera composition, he will take to concerto writing, and cut out Mendelssohn and Schumann in the pretty pattern work which the pundits love them for. Which will shew how very easy it is for a good musician, when he happens to be a bad critic, to admire a great composer for the wrong thing.

19 *April* 1893

LAST week an unexpected event occurred—nothing less than a concert. I had been for a long time wishing to hear a little music; so I went off to Prince's Hall and found Miss Dora Bright wasting a very good program on a very bad audience, with the help of Messrs Willy Hess, Kreuz, and Whitehouse. They began with Mozart's pianoforte quartet in G minor, to my delight, as all my musical self-respect is based on my keen appreciation of Mozart's works. It is still as true as it was before the Eroica symphony existed, that there is nothing better in art than Mozart's best. We have had Beethoven, Schubert, Mendelssohn, Schumann, Götz, and Brahms since his time: we have even had Dr Parry, Professor Stanford, Mr Cowen, Dr Mackenzie, and Sir Arthur Sullivan; but the more they have left the Mozart quartet or quintet behind, the further it comes out ahead in its perfection of temper and refinement of consciousness.

In the ardent regions where all the rest are excited and vehement, Mozart alone is completely self-possessed: where they are clutching their bars with a grip of iron and forging them with Cyclopean blows, his gentleness of touch never deserts him: he is considerate, economical, practical under the same pressure of inspiration that throws your Titan into convulsions. This is the secret of his unpopularity with Titan fanciers. We all in our native barbarism have a relish for the strenuous: your tenor whose B flat is like the bursting of a boiler always brings down the house, even when the note brutally effaces the song; and the composer who can artistically express in music a transport of vigor and passion of the more muscular kind, such as the finale to the seventh symphony, the Walkürenritt, or the Hailstone chorus, not to mention the orgies of Raff, Liszt, and Berlioz, is always a hero with the intemperate in music, who are so numerous nowadays that we may confidently expect to see some day a British Minister of the Fine Arts introducing a local Option Bill applied to concert rooms.

With Mozart you are safe from inebriety. Hurry, excitement, eagerness, loss of consideration, are to him purely comic or vicious states of mind: he gives us Monostatos and the Queen of Night on the stage, but not in his chamber music. Now it happens that I have, deep in my nature, which is quite as deep as the average rainfall in England, a frightful contempt for your Queens of Night and Titans and their like. The true Parnassian air acts on these people like oxygen on a mouse: it first excites them, and then kills them. Give me the artist who breathes it like a native, and goes about his work in it as quietly as a common man goes about his ordinary business. Mozart did so; and that is why I like him. Even if I did not, I should pretend to; for a taste for his music is a mark of caste among musicians, and should be worn, like a tall hat, by the amateur who wishes to pass for a true Brahmin.

Miss Dora Bright's concert left me with a huge opinion of Mr Willy Hess, who gave a remarkable performance of

Brahms' violin sonata in G, in spite of the parching, freezing, north-east wind which was making even me conscious of having a liver. Mr Hess, always an exceptionally dexterous manipulator of the violin, used to lack artistic grip and earnestness; but he has matured, and is now a distinguished player, though an occasional careless phrase, or a final note petering out rather than being finished, still from time to time, reminds one of the old superficiality. His performance of the sonata, one of those compositions of Brahms which I can enjoy because, whilst they are rich in music, they are undisturbed by those intellectual pretensions which in Brahms (as in Tennyson) are so desperately commonplace, would, at a Monday Popular Concert, have roused a good deal of enthusiasm. Unluckily for him, Miss Dora Bright's enterprise being a new one, the genuine audience at this first concert was not very large, and was reinforced by a contingent of inferior miscellaneous concert deadheads; so that the success of the sonata remained a secret between Mr Hess and the critics, who had come chiefly to witness the first public appearance in England of Miss Atalja Van Niessen, who speedily made her mark as a sort of Scandinavian Giulia Ravogli. In personal appearance and artistic temperament she is as emphatically northern as Giulia is emphatically southern; but the corresponding difference in the quality of the two voices is not so great as might be expected: all the superficial differences which repudiate the comparison are overcome by the identity of the underlying dramatic force. Miss Van Niessen will make her way on to the stage without difficulty in any country where the opera is under intelligent artistic management. On the whole, Miss Bright is to be congratulated on her concert; and if the three which she is giving on successive Tuesdays do not succeed well enough to induce her to repeat and extend her enterprise next season, so much the worse for the public. Her own playing is satisfactory in Prince's Hall, where the absence of the athletic qualities which distinguish the pianist proper, as trained by Rubinstein or Leschetitzky, from the musician who plays the piano is not felt as a defect. Even if it were, the musicianly qualities of Miss Bright's playing would go far to make amends, her faults being those of an excess of musical facility. If her powers had cost her a harder wrestle she would probably have used them to enter more deeply into the poetic basis of modern music.

An attempt has been made to rescue Señor Albéniz's score of The Magic Opal from sinking under the weight of its libretto. It is now being played under the composer's bâton at the Prince of Wales Theatre as The Magic Ring, with considerable alterations and extensions. As far as these afford larger opportunities for the drollery of Mr Monkhouse and the appalling cleverness of Miss Susie Vaughan, they improve the chances of the opera. As far as they are meant to heighten the musical interest, they are failures, not in the least because Señor Albéniz has not risen to the occasion—on the contrary, the revised version of the opera leaves him easily ahead of the best of his rivals—but because they depend for their effect on having the tenor and soprano parts filled by singers of the same musical class as Mr Norman Salmond, who now takes Mr Wallace Brownlow's old part of Trabucos with excellent effect. Unfortunately the management has here put round pegs into square holes; and Señor Albéniz's labor has been consequently wasted. Mr Wareham is ineffective from beginning to end; and the part of Lolika is such a complete misfit for Miss Marie Halton that she appears to be playing as a superfluous second comedian to Miss Vaughan, and leaving the opera without a prima donna. I rather doubt whether The Magic Ring can survive on these terms, although, adequately cast on the musical side, the charm and vivacity of the score ought to secure it a handsome run.

Grieg has made a second orchestral suite out of his incidental music to Ibsen's Peer Gynt, concerning which I must really address a friendly remonstrance to Mr C. A. Barry, the author of the analytic program. On whose authority does he make Solveig "a gipsy woman" who had loved Peer "from a child," and in whose arms he dies as she sings a dream song over him? I admit the dream song; but the gipsy is really too much; and if Mr Barry thinks that Peer was the man to die in anybody's arms he little knows Mr Gynt's number, which was always number one. Nor do I recognize in Anitra "the very type of a hero-hunting woman," unless that means a woman who listens to an amorous hero without understanding a word he says, and then decamps with all his portable property. And why is Peer the bride-robber to be allowed the extenuating circumstance of "entertaining a secret passion for Ingrid," when it was plainly that lady's by no means secret passion for Peer that suggested his idea of shewing off before Solveig and the rest by abducting her.

I submit to Mr Barry that he has mixed up Anitra with Hedda Gabler, and Solveig with the gipsy mother in Brand; and as his program will be stereotyped for use in the Crystal Palace programs to all eternity if he does not alter it now, I implore him to read Peer Gynt two or three times (an inevitable result of reading it once) and then revise his narrative. It would be well, perhaps, to amplify the bald statement that Peer's friends "treacherously run off with his vessel and are blown up for their pains," which only suggests that he remonstrated vigorously with them, whereas they were actually and literally blown to smithereens. The suite will not be so popular as the first one, which naturally contained the pick of the music for suite purposes. It consists of the wedding prelude, the Arabian dance, the storm, and a transcription of Solveig's by this time rather hackneyed song from the fourth act. The first performance in England took place at the Crystal Palace on the 8th, when we also had a fine performance of Raff's Im Walde symphony (why dont they cut away all that repetition of the ghostly hunt stuff in the finale?), and a triumph for Miss Fanny Davies in Chopin's F minor concerto—the most successful feat of interpretation and execution I have ever heard her achieve.

26 *April* 1893

IN the eye of an inconsiderate public, concerts given by amateur orchestral societies hardly seem worth the serious attention of a critic who is busy watching the symptoms of the Philharmonic, the Crystal Palace, the London Symphony, the Richter, and the Hallé orchestras. Yet to me the amateur orchestra is all-important; for out of every ten people who support music in England, at least nine and three-quarters must have acquired their knowledge of it as amateurs and from amateurs. The musician of professional antecedents is an incorrigible deadhead: whether he performs or listens, music has to support him, instead of being supported by him.

It is clear that a man cannot cultivate a taste for orchestral music by listening once a week to a church service accompanied by the combination of pan-pipes and accordion which has replaced the old-fashioned village church band, or even by occasionally patronizing a travelling dramatic company in the town-hall, and studying the efforts of a pianist, backed by three fiddles and a cornet, to give a satisfactory account of the overture to William Tell, Mascagni's intermezzo, and a twenty-year-old waltz by Waldteufel. The moment you step outside the circle of London, Birmingham, Manchester, Bristol, Glasgow, and towns of their calibre, you have to choose between amateur music and no music at all; whilst even in these big towns music is really kept alive by professional musicians who as teachers discover amateur talent, and as conductors and concert-givers organize it for the performance of the masterpieces of modern music.

The professional orchestral conductor who is a conductor and nothing else, and who conducts professional singers and players exclusively, only exists in great capitals. It takes London and Vienna combined to keep Richter in this position, and Glasgow and the Crystal Palace combined to keep Manns in it; and both these eminent conductors have to depend on amateurs for the performance of choral works. Had Destiny buried them in a small provincial town, they would, whilst they remained there, have had to put up with an amateur band, and amateur principal singers into the bargain. And there are suburbs of London which are in darkness more deplorable than any country town.

Under these circumstances, it seems to me that the critic who considers an amateur orchestra beneath his notice stamps himself as a hopeless Cockney—that is, a man who does not know the country because he has never lived there, and does not know London because he has never lived anywhere else. Last week Mr James Brown, the conductor of the Richmond Orchestral Society, had the gumption to surmise that a stroll out to Richmond Hill to hear what his Society can do might seem to me at least as tempting a way of spending an evening as a visit to Steinway or Prince's Hall to hear the annual concert of Miss Smith or Miss Brown, aided by more or less distinguished artists singing exactly what they have sung on similar occasions for a whole generation of miscellaneous concerts. I accepted his invitation, and arrived at sundown on the terrace, where I mused over the site of that Wagner Theatre which yet remains unbuilt, until it was time to go into the "Star and Garter" and get to business.

The program was of the usual amateur kind: that is to say, it would have taxed the finest qualities of the best band in the world. Mozart's G Minor symphony, the Lohengrin prelude, Mendelssohn's Athalie overture and his violin concerto: only such works as these can inspire the mighty craving and dogged perseverance which carry a man through that forlorn hope, the making of an orchestra out of nothing. When you start you are received with enthusiasm by men who can play the posthorn, the banjo, the concertina, and every other instrument not used in the orchestra. You enlist trombone-players only to find that though they can "vamp" they cannot read, and propose to assist you by improvising a bass continuously to whatever may be going on. You can choose the two least execrable out of twenty cornet-players at the cost of making eighteen bitter enemies in the neighborhood; but you are lucky if you find one horn-player, although you require four. Flutes, too, are comparatively plentiful; whilst clarionets are scarce, oboes all but unknown, and bassoons quite out of the question (though there is a lady-bassoonist at Richmond).

In the string department the same difficulty arises. Young ladies who can play much better than the average professional "leader" of twenty years ago are discoverable with a little research in sufficient abundance nowadays (chiefly because Madame Neruda proved at that time that the violin shews off a good figure); and the violoncello, for some less obvious reason, fascinates tiny women sufficiently to keep itself fairly alive in amateur circles. But nobody will touch the double bass; and the viola comes to grief almost as signally as it used to do in the professional band in the old days, when only worn-out violinists scraped the tenor, and when such viola parts as those in Tristan or Harold, and such players as Hollander condescending to the instrument, were unknown.

When trying to get an orchestra together the conductor stops at nothing, except at houses whence come sounds of practising on an orchestral instrument. I have known a man, on catching this doleful noise at midnight on his way home from rehearsal, listen at the area-railings, take a note of the address, and call next day to kidnap the practiser by reckless flatteries. I have known valuable appointments, involving the transfer of learned professors from the Metropolis to provincial towns, decided by the frantic efforts of a local conductor to secure the election of a candidate who was said to be a proficient player on one of the scarcer instruments. But it is when the orchestra is actually formed and set to work that its creator tastes the full bitterness of his position.

The unredeemed villainy of the amateur nature is not easy to describe adequately. Its outrageous frivolity, to which no engagement is sacred, and its incredible vanity, to which art is nothing and the lower self everything, baffle my powers of description, and make me for once regret that I do not wield one of those bitter, biting pens which were made to lash offenders on whom mercy is thrown away—for instance, those two amateur extremes, the man who never attends a rehearsal but always turns up at the concert, and the man who attends all the rehearsals and blenches from the concert. Even your leader will miss a rehearsal to go to a dance, or will coolly tell you on the morning of the concert that he cannot play because his father is dead, or some such frivolous excuse. Then there is the incompetent wind-player who has a bit of solo which he cannot execute, and who, at the last moment, must have his part doubled by a professional to save public disgrace and breakdown.

On such occasions the professional, regarding all amateurs as blacklegs, is offensive; objects to having his part doubled; says, "Look here! Who's going to play this—me or you?" etc., etc. The amateur sulks, broods over his injuries, leaves the orchestra, and probably tries to establish a rival society for the performance of wind-instrument chamber-music. The difficulties are endless, and the artistic results agonizing, since the progress made by the people who stick to the rehearsals is always spoiled at the last moment by the backwardness of those who dont.

I will not pretend that the concert at Richmond did not bear the marks of these hard conditions. It began shorthanded, especially in the horn department. At the end of the overture a gentleman in irreproachable evening-dress, smiling, and carrying a black bag presenting the general outline of a French horn, appeared and climbed up on the platform with a sort of "Here I am, you see, safe and sound—never say die" air about him. As he mounted there was a crash of breaking wood, from which I gathered that he had succeeded in completing the sensation by shattering the platform. The conductor received him with grim patience, concealing all signs of the murderous thoughts that must have raged within him. Just imagine Mr Borsdorff, for instance, playing that trick on Richter! I wonder did it occur to the gentleman that money had been obtained from the public, with his consent, on the strength of his being in his place to play one of the horn parts in the overture. If it is too much to expect an ordinary English gentleman to be artistically conscientious, surely we may at least call on him to be commercially honest. However, justice forbids me to urge too harshly the offence of the man who came in after the overture, since I must perforce say nothing of the worse offenders who did not come at all. Almost immediately after the beginning of the Lohengrin prelude the band divided itself into two resolute factions, one maintaining that the bar in hand was the sixth bar, and the other equally convinced that it was the seventh. So they agreed to differ; and I listened with a drunken sensation of hearing the prelude double until the wind instruments rushed into the fray, and, mostly taking the side which the conductor had supported from the first, made the opposition waver and finally come over one by one, the fortissimo being played with almost entire unanimity. In the accompaniment to O star of eve! (Tannhäuser) the tremolando to the words Da scheinest du, etc., was ruined by the shirking of some lady-violinists, who, with faces expressive of the most shameful irresolution, and fear of being heard, rested their bows helplessly on the strings and sat quivering—an exceedingly amateur way of tremolandoing. But in spite of these and similar mishaps, I felt throughout that the thing was well worth doing. The conductor was always right in what he was driving at; and in some instances he had used that enormous advantage of the amateur—the unlimited rehearsal which is commercially impossible to the professional—to obtain graces of artistic treatment which were fresh and convincing: in fact, he snatched from that atmosphere of inevitable nervousness, blundering, and ineptitude (concerning much of which, however, *tout comprendre, c'est tout pardonner*) successful moments which I have too often missed from the performances of conductors with the best players in the world at their disposal. The leader, Mr J. S. Liddle, stood up to Mendelssohn's violin concerto, and dealt faithfully to the height of his powers. Mr Charles Phillips, a robust baritone, manfully shouted a most patriotically orchestrated ballad of Agincourt; but the first bar and a half led us to expect that what was coming was The Old Kent Road; and the disappointment was rather severe. Miss Florence Hudson got a tremendous encore for a harp solo; and Miss Emily Squire received a similar compliment for the Mignon gavotte, which she sang with a spirited facility which was none the less pleasant because of her thorough belief in the universality of the British vowel—"Say mwaw: Zjay too breezay, etc."

A comparatively unimportant matter was the Philharmonic concert of last Thursday, half an hour too long, and crowded to the doors. Sapellnikoff played Chopin's E minor concerto. He has turned his back on the thundering animal style, and has cultivated the purely musical and tactile quality of his playing to an extraordinary pitch, his left hand being now a marvel even among right hands for delicacy of touch and independence and swiftness of action. This time, it is to be hoped, he will not go away without giving recitals, or at least a technical demonstration at some of our musical schools. Miss Palliser was too ill to sing, and was replaced by Miss Marie Brema, who, happening to be tremendously in the dramatic vein, positively rampaged through a Schiller-Joachim scena and through Beethoven's Creation's Hymn, scandalizing the Philharmonic, but carrying away the multitude.

The band distinguished itself in Mendelssohn's Italian symphony, though I must again put it to Dr Mackenzie whether in his opinion a long note written for the brass, and marked fortissimo, should be played as a bark lasting one quaver, followed by a mezzo forte of depraved quality lasting a few more quavers, and tailing off finally into premature silence. I submit that Mendelssohn meant it to be sustained with full tone to the bitter end; and I take the liberty to add that a band that cannot hold up a powerful fortissimo in this way is only fit for quiet and select private parties and *tableaux vivants*, however genteelly it may pick its way through the Pilgrims' March. Imagine having a splendid band like that, and being afraid to let its full voice be heard. When a band is weak in the artillery department, its refinement becomes mere effeminacy and cowardice.

Two concerts at St James's Hall on Saturday afternoons (clashing, of course, with the Crystal Palace concerts) have been given—one by Sauret, and the other by Miss Agnes Janson. Sauret still remembers the days when he was famous for having mastered the difficulties of the concertos of Vieuxtemps; and now that his artistic interest in them is so utterly worn out that he rasps through them without one gentle touch or one moment of concern as to whether he is playing in tune or not, he still goes through the old display, and still finds a few old moustaches to cry Bravo because they know how horribly difficult the passages are. As for me, it tortures and exasperates me. Vieuxtemps's real name now is Vieuxjeu; and I appeal to Sauret to let him rest, with Alfred Mellon and other relics of the 'sixties. Otherwise the concert was enjoyable enough, Miss Muriel Elliot, Ernest Gillet, and Miss Dews reinforcing Sauret for the occasion. Miss Elliot, by the bye, requires a more thorough physical training to make her musical gifts fully effective in large rooms like St James's Hall. Miss Agnes Janson's concert, an excellent one of its kind, shewed, among other things, that Miss Janson knows how to make the most of her voice by a perfectly sound method, a good ear, and a nice sense of vocal touch. With this invaluable equipment, however, she takes things rather too easily, singing cheap operatic and quasi-operatic music frankly and genially, but without originality or conviction—in short, without having troubled herself seriously about its poetic or dramatic content. Mr Henschel's five vocal quartets *à la Russe* succeeded to admiration; and Sauret, again, won over the audience by a Beethoven sonata, only to disillusion them subsequently by a superannuated monstrosity of Ernst's—that wretched old fantasia on airs from Rossini's Otello. When Sauret's memory begins to fail he will become one of our most popular violinists.

3 May 1893

FOR some time past I have been carefully dodging Dr Hubert Parry's Job. I had presentiments about it from the first. I foresaw that all the other critics would cleverly imply that they thought it the greatest oratorio of ancient or modern times—that Handel is rebuked, Mendelssohn eclipsed, and the rest nowhere. And I was right: they did. The future historian of music, studying the English papers of 1892–3, will learn that these years produced two entire and perfect chrysolites, Job and Falstaff, especially Job. I was so afraid of being unable to concur unreservedly in the verdict that I lay low and stopped my ears. The first step was to avoid the Gloucester Festival. That gave me no trouble: nothing is easier than not to go to Gloucester.

I am, to tell the truth, not very fond of Festivals. It is not that the oratorios bore me, or even the new works "composed expressly," the word "expressly" here indicating the extra-special dullness supposed to be proper to such solemn occasions. These things are the inevitable hardships of my profession: I face them as the soldier faces fire, feeling that it is the heroic endurance of them that raises criticism from a mere trade to a profession or calling. But a man is expected to have the courage of his own profession only. The soldier must face cold steel; but he may without derogation be afraid of ghosts. The doctor who braves fever may blench from shipwreck; and the clergyman who wars daily against the Prince of Darkness is permitted to quit a field in which he unexpectedly meets a mad bull. The musical critic is ready at duty's call to stand up fearlessly to oratorios, miscellaneous concerts, requiems, and comic operas; but it is no part of his bargain to put up with the stewards at a provincial festival. It is not that these gentlemen intend to be uncivil, or are by nature more evilly dispositioned than their fellow-creatures; but they have no manners, no *savoir vivre:* they are unsocially afraid of the public, snobbishly afraid of being mistaken for professional attendants, unaccustomed to their work (which requires either experience or tact and self-possession), and inflated with a sense of their importance instead of sobered by a sense of their responsibility.

Consequently they are fussy, suspicious, rude or nervous, as the case may be, constantly referring helplessly to the one or two of their number who have their wits about them, and not unfrequently blundering unintentionally to within a perilous distance of the point at which the more choleric and muscular sort of visitor will threaten violence and execute profanity, and the more subtly malicious will patronizingly offer the blunderer a tip. By good luck, I have never myself been outraged by a festival steward; but the mere flavor of irresponsible and incompetent officialism poisons the artistic atmosphere for me.

It brings before me the appalling centralization of English intellectual and artistic life, and therefore of social grace, with the consequent boorification of the provinces. It will never be merrie England until every man who goes down from London to a festival or other provincial function will frankly say to his host, "My friend: your house is uncommonly comfortable, and your grub of the best. You are hospitable; and you gratify my vanity by treating me, who am a Nobody at home, as a Somebody from London. You are not bad company when you go out into the fields to kill something. But owing to the fact that you have been brought up in a town where the theatre, the picture-gallery, and the orchestra count for nothing, and the exchanges count for everything, you are, saving your presence, a hopelessly dull dog; and your son is growing up as dull a dog as you." Not a polite speech, maybe; but you cannot make revolutions with rosewater; and what is wanted in English provincial life is nothing short of a revolution.

Such being my sentiments, it will be understood that I forewent Gloucester and Job last autumn without regret. I have explained the matter at some length, not because I have not said all the above before, but solely to put off for awhile the moment when I must at last say what I think of Dr Parry's masterpiece. For I unluckily went last Wednesday to the concert of the Middlesex Choral Union, where the first thing that happened was the appearance of Dr Parry amid the burst of affectionate applause which always greets him. That made me uneasy; and I was not reassured when he mounted the conductor's rostrum, and led the band into a prelude which struck me as being a serious set of footnotes to the bridal march from Lohengrin. Presently up got Mr Bantock Pierpoint, and sang, without a word of warning, There was a man in the land of Uz whose name was Job. Then I knew I was in for it; and now I must do my duty.

I take Job to be, on the whole, the most utter failure ever achieved by a thoroughly respectworthy musician. There is not one bar in it that comes within fifty thousand miles of the tamest line in the poem. This is the naked, unexaggerated truth. Is anybody surprised at it? Here, on the one hand, is an ancient poem which has lived from civilization to civilization, and has been translated into an English version of haunting beauty and nobility of style, offering to the musician a subject which would have taxed to the utmost the highest powers of Bach, Handel, Mozart, Beethoven, or Wagner. Here on the other is, not Bach nor Handel nor Mozart nor Beethoven nor Wagner, not even Mendelssohn or Schumann, but Dr Parry, an enthusiastic and popular professor, forty-five years old, and therefore of ascertained powers.

Now, will any reasonable person pretend that it lies within the limits of those powers to let us hear the morning stars singing together and the sons of God shouting for joy? True, it is impossible to say what a man can do until he tries. I may before the end of this year write a tragedy on the subject of King Lear that will efface Shakespear's; but if I do it will be a surprise, not perhaps to myself, but to the public. It is certain that if I took the work in hand I should be able to turn out five acts about King Lear that would be, at least, grammatical, superficially coherent, and arranged in lines that would scan. And I doubt not at all that some friendly and ingenious critic would say of it, "Lear is, from beginning to end, a remarkable work, and one which nobody but an English author could have written. Every page bears the stamp of G. B. S.'s genius; and no higher praise can be awarded to it than to say that it is fully worthy of his reputation." What critic would need to be so unfriendly as to face the plain question, "Has the author been able for his subject?"

I might easily shirk that question in the case of Job: there are no end of nice little things I could point out about the workmanship shewn in the score, its fine feeling, its scrupulous moderation, its entire freedom from any base element of art or character, and so on through a whole epitaph of pleasant and perfectly true irrelevancies. I might even say that Dr Parry's setting of Job placed him infinitely above the gentleman who set to music The Man that broke the Bank. But would that alter the fact that Dr Parry has left his subject practically untouched, whilst his music-hall rival has most exhaustively succeeded in covering his? It is the great glory of Job that he shamed the devil. Let me imitate him by telling the truth about the work as it appeared to me. Of course I may be wrong: even I am not infallible, at least not always.

And it must be remembered that I am violently prejudiced against the professorial school of which Dr Parry is a distinguished member. I always said, and say still, that his much-admired oratorio Judith has absolutely no merit whatever. I allowed a certain vigor and geniality in his L'Allegro ed il Pensieroso, and a certain youthful inspiration in his Prometheus. But even these admissions I regarded as concessions to the academic faction which he leans to; and I was so afraid of being further disarmed that I lived in fear of meeting him and making his acquaintance; for I had noticed that the critics to whom this happens become hopelessly corrupt, and say anything to please him without the least regard to public duty. Let Job then have the benefit of whatever suspicion may be cast on my verdict by my prepossessions against the composer's school.

The first conspicuous failure in the work is Satan, who, after a feeble attempt to give himself an infernal air by getting the bassoon to announce him with a few frog-like croaks, gives up the pretence, and, though a tenor and a fiend, models himself on Mendelssohn's St Paul. He has no tact as an orator. For example, when he says "Put forth thine hand now and touch all that he hath, and he will curse thee to thy face," there is not a shade of scepticism or irony in him; and he ineptly tries to drive his point home by a melodramatic shriek on the word "curse." When one thinks—I will not say of Loki or Klingsor, but of Verdi's Iago and Boito's Mefistofele, and even of Gounod's stage devil, it is impossible to accept this pale shadow of an excitable curate as one of the poles of the great world magnet.

As to Job, there is no sort of grit in him: he is abject from first to last, and is only genuinely touching when he longs to lie still and be quiet where the wicked cease from troubling and the weary are at rest. That is the one tolerable moment in the work; and Job passes from it to relapse into dullness, not to rise into greater strength of spirit. He is much distracted by fragments of themes from the best composers coming into his head from time to time, and sometimes cutting off the thread of his discourse altogether. When he talks of mountains being removed, he flourishes on the flute in an absurdly inadequate manner; and his challenge to God, Shew me wherefore Thou contendest with me, is too poor to be described.

Not until he has given in completely, and is saying his last word, does it suddenly occur to him to make a hit; and then, in announcing that he repents in dust and ashes, he explodes in the most unlooked-for way on the final word "ashes," which produces the effect of a sneeze. The expostulation of God with Job is given to the chorus: the voice that sometimes speaks through the mouths of babes and sucklings here speaks through the mouths of Brixton and Bayswater, and the effect is precisely what might have been expected. It is hard to come down thus from the "heil'gen Hallen" of Sarastro to the suburbs.

There is one stroke of humor in the work. When Job says, The Lord gave, and the Lord taketh away: blessed be the name of the Lord, a long and rueful interval after the words "taketh away" elapses before poor Job can resign himself to utter the last clause. That is the sole trace of real dramatic treatment in this dreary ramble of Dr Parry's through the wastes of artistic error. It is the old academic story—an attempt to bedizen a dramatic poem with scraps of sonata music.

Dr Parry reads, The walls are broken down: destroyed are the pleasant places; and it sounds beautifully to him. So it associates itself with something else that sounds beautifully—Mendelssohn's violin concerto, as it happens in this case—and straightway he rambles off into a rhythm suggested by the first movement of the concerto, and produces a tedious combination which has none of the charm or propriety of either poem or concerto. For the sake of relief he drags in by the ears a piece of martial tumult—See! upon the distant plain, a white cloud of dust, the ravagers come—compounded from the same academic prescription as the business of the dragon's teeth coming up armed men in Mackenzie's Jason; and the two pieces of music are consequently indistinguishable in my memory—in fact, I do not remember a note of either of them.

I have no wish to linger over a barbarous task. In time I may forgive Dr Parry, especially if he will write a few more essays on the great composers, and confine himself to the composition of "absolute music," with not more than three pedal points to the page. But at this moment I feel sore. He might have let Job alone, and let me alone; for, patient as we both are, there are limits to human endurance. I hope he will burn the score, and throw Judith in when the blaze begins to flag.

As to the performance, it did not greatly matter. On the whole, it was somewhat tame, even relatively to the music. Mr Piercy's treatment of the high notes in his part offended all my notions of artistic singing. Mr Newman did what he could with the part of Job; and his performance was entirely creditable to him. Mr Bantock Pierpoint, as the Narrator, gave more pleasure than any of his colleagues. Miss Palliser was the shepherd-boy. The chorus was not very vigorous or majestic; but it made the most of itself.

10 *May* 1893

THE success of Professor Stanford's Irish Symphony last Thursday was, from the Philharmonic point of view, somewhat scandalous. The spectacle of a university professor "going Fantee" is indecorous, though to me personally it is delightful. When Professor Stanford is genteel, cultured, classic, pious, and experimentally mixolydian, he is dull beyond belief. His dullness is all the harder to bear because it is the restless, ingenious, trifling, flippant dullness of the Irishman, instead of the stupid, bovine, sleepable-through dullness of the Englishman, or even the aggressive, ambitious, sentimental dullness of the Scot. But Mr Villiers Stanford cannot be dismissed as merely the Irish variety of the professorial species.

Take any of the British oratorios and cantatas which have been produced recently for the Festivals, and your single comment on any of them will be—if you know anything about music—"Oh! anybody with a bachelor's degree could have written that." But you cannot say this of Stanford's Eden. It is as insufferable a composition as any Festival committee could desire; but it is ingenious and peculiar; and although in it you see the Irish professor trifling in a world of ideas, in marked contrast to the English professor conscientiously wrestling in a vacuum, yet over and above this national difference, which would assert itself equally in the case of any other Irishman, you find certain traces of a talent for composition, which is precisely what the ordinary professor, with all his grammatical and historical accomplishments, utterly lacks. But the conditions of making this talent serviceable are not supplied by Festival commissions. Far from being a respectable oratorio-manufacturing talent, it is, when it gets loose, eccentric, violent, romantic, patriotic, and held in check only by a mortal fear of being found deficient in what are called "the manners and tone of good society." This fear, too, is Irish: it is, possibly, the racial consciousness of having missed that four hundred years of Roman civilization which gave England a sort of university education when Ireland was in the hedge school.

In those periods when nobody questions the superiority of the university to the hedge school, the Irishman, lamed by a sense of inferiority, blusters most intolerably, and not unfrequently goes the length of alleging that Balfe was a great composer. Then the fashion changes; Ruskin leads young Oxford out into the hedge school to dig roads; there is general disparagement in advanced circles of civilization, the university, respectability, law and order; and a heroic renunciation of worldly and artificial things is insisted upon by those who, having had their fling, are tired of them, a demand powerfully reinforced by the multitude, who want to have their fling but cannot get it under existing circumstances, and are driven to console themselves by crying sour grapes.

This reaction is the opportunity of the Irishman in England to rehabilitate his self-respect, since it gives him a standpoint from which he can value himself as a hedge-school man, patronize the university product, and escape from the dreary and abortive task of branding himself all over as an Irish snob under the impression that he is hall-marking himself as an English gentleman. If he seizes the opportunity, he may end in founding a race of cultivated Irishmen whose mission in England will be to teach Englishmen to play with their brains as well as with their bodies; for it is all work and no play in the brain department that makes John Bull such an uncommonly dull boy.

The beginning of this "return to nature" in music has been effected, not by a sudden repudiation of the whole academic system, but by the smuggling into academic music of ancient folk-music under various pretences as to is archæological importance; its real recommendation, of course, being that the musicians like the tunes, and the critics and programists find it much easier to write about "national characteristics" and "the interval of the augmented second" than to write to the point. First we had Mendelssohn's "Scotch" Symphony, and then came a deluge of pseudo-Hungarian, gipsy, and other folk-music—Liszt, Bruch, Dvořák, and Brahms all trying their hands—with, in due course, "pibrochs" by Dr Mackenzie, Land of the Mountain and the Flood overture from Mr Hamish MacCunn, and Villiers Stanford's Irish Symphony. No general criticism of the works produced in this movement is possible.

The poorer composers, unable to invent interesting themes for their works in sonata form, gladly availed themselves of the licence to steal popular airs, with results that left them as far as ever behind the genuises who assimilated what served their turn in folk-music as in every other store of music. But, at all events, the new fashion produced music quite different in kind from the Turkish music devised by the German Mozart for Il Seraglio, the Arabian music copied by his countryman Weber for Oberon, or the African and Scotch music invented by Mendelssohn and Meyerbeer (both Jews) for L'Africaine and the Scotch Symphony. This sort of "national" music takes the artificial operatic or sonata forms quite easily, submitting to be soaped and washed and toiletted for its visit to Covent Garden or St James's Hall without the least awkwardness.

But in the recent cases where the so-called folk-music is written by a composer born of the folk himself, and especially of the Celtic folk, with its intense national sentiment, there is the most violent repugnance between the popular music and the sonata form. The Irish Symphony, composed by an Irishman, is a record of fearful conflict between the aboriginal Celt and the Professor. The scherzo is not a scherzo at all, but a shindy, expending its force in riotous dancing. However hopelessly an English orchestra may fail to catch the wild nuances of the Irish fiddler, it cannot altogether drown the "hurroosh" with which Stanford the Celt drags Stanford the Professor into the orgy. Again, in the slow movement the emotional development is such as would not be possible in an English or German symphony. At first it is slow, plaintive, passionately sad about nothing.

According to all classic precedent, it should end in hopeless gloom, in healing resignation, or in pathetic sentiment. What it does end in is blue murder, the Professor this time aiding and abetting the transition with all his contrapuntal might. In the last movement the rival Stanfords agree to a compromise which does not work. The essence of the sonata form is the development of themes; and even in a rondo a theme that will not develop will not fit the form. Now the greatest folk-songs are final developments themselves: they cannot be carried any further. You cannot develop God Save the Queen, though you may, like Beethoven, write some interesting but retrograde variations on it. Neither can you develop Let Erin remember. You might, of course, develop it inversely, debasing it touch by touch until you had The Marseillaise in all its vulgarity; and the doing of this might be instructive, though it would not be symphony writing. But no forward development is possible.

Yet in the last movement of the Irish Symphony, Stanford the Celt, wishing to rejoice in Molly Macalpine (Remember the glories) and The Red Fox (Let Erin remember), insisted that if Stanford the Professor wanted to develop themes, he should develop these two. The Professor succumbed to the shillelagh of his double, but, finding development impossible, got out of the difficulty by breaking Molly up into fragments, exhibiting these fantastically, and then putting them together again. This process is not in the least like the true sonata development. It would not work at all with The Red Fox, which comes in as a flagrant patch upon the rondo—for the perfect tune that is one moment a war song, and the next, without the alteration of a single note, the saddest of patriotic reveries "on Lough Neagh's bank where the fisherman strays in the clear cold eve's declining," flatly refuses to merge itself into any sonata movement, and loftily asserts itself in right of ancient descent as entitled to walk before any symphony that ever professor penned.

It is only in the second subject of this movement, an original theme of the composer's own minting, that the form and the material really combine chemically into sonata. And this satisfactory result is presently upset by the digression to the utterly incompatible aim of the composer to display the charms of his native folk-music. In the first movement the sonata writer keeps to his point better: there are no national airs lifted bodily into it. Nevertheless the first movement does not convince me that Professor Stanford's talent is a symphonic talent any more than Meyerbeer's was. In mentioning Meyerbeer I know I run the risk of having the implied comparison interpreted in the light of the Wagnerian criticism—that is, as a deliberate disparagement. I do not mean it so. The Wagnerian criticism of Meyerbeer is valid only as a page in the history of the development of opera into Wagnerian music drama. Taken out of this connection it will not stand verification for a moment.

If you try to form a critical scheme of the development of English poetry from Pope to Walt Whitman, you cannot by any stretch of ingenuity make a place in it for Thomas Moore, who is accordingly either ignored in such schemes or else contemptuously dismissed as a flowery trifler. In the same way you cannot get Meyerbeer into the Wagnerian scheme except as the Autolycus of the piece. But this proves nothing except that criticism cannot give an absolutely true and just account of any artist: it can at best explain its point of view and then describe the artist from that point of view. You have only to shift yourself an inch to the right or left of my own point of view to find this column full of grotesque exaggerations and distortions; and if you read the musical papers you will sometimes find some *naïf* doing this, and verdantly assuming that *his* point of view commands the absolute truth and that I am the father of lies.

Let me therefore make it clear that I am not likening Stanford to Meyerbeer from the Wagnerian point of view. I am thinking of Meyerbeer's individual characteristics as a composer: for instance, the singularity which is not always originality, the inventiveness which is not always fecundity, the love of the curious and piquant, the fastidious industry and cleverness, the intense and jealous individualism with its resultant treatment of the executants as mere instruments and not as artistic comrades and co-operators, the retreating from any effect that cannot be exactly and mechanically planned by himself as from an impossibility, the love of the fantastic, legendary, non-human element in folk-music (compare Stanford's settings of Irish songs with Dinorah), and the almost selfishly concentrated feeling, the fire, the distinction, the passion that flash out occasionally through much artifice and much trifling.

The parallel is of course not exact; and the temperament indicated by it does not disqualify Stanford from writing symphonies any more than it disqualified Raff; but it suggests my view of the composer of the Irish Symphony as compendiously as is possible within present limits. With the right sort of book, and the right sort of opportunity in other respects, Stanford might produce a powerful and brilliant opera without creating any of the amazement which would certainly be caused by any such feat on the part of his academic rivals.

The performance of the Irish Symphony was decisively successful. Except to briefly and gratefully note a marked improvement on the part of the Philharmonic band, I can say nothing more at present. Dozens of pianists and other concert-givers are hereby begged to excuse me until next week.

17 *May* 1893

I HAVE never heard an orchestra more completely thrown away than the one conducted by Sir Arthur Sullivan at the opening of the Imperial Institute. When I was outside, making my way to the hall, I heard it pretty well: when I got inside I heard it only now and then. In the march from Le Prophète, played as the Court withdrew, not a note of the section where the theme is taken up by the trumpet and bass clarinet reached me at the daïs end of the hall. The overture to Euryanthe was fitfully audible, the *pianissimo* for muted strings coming off rather better than the more powerful passages. Under these circumstances, the effect produced by the conductor's new Imperial March was very like a stage wait in the proceedings. I reserve my opinion until I get an opportunity of really hearing it, only certifying for the present that it contains a long flowing theme which shews off the strings very cleverly. In the evening, at the Albert Hall, we had Stanford's setting of Swinburne's Exhibition ode entitled East to West—Putney to Chicago. As a rule, Exhibition art is not high art. Doubtless it would be an exaggeration to say that the average exhibition gallery picture, or choral ode, or grand march, is something that no self-respecting hangman would condescend to burn; but there is no harm in recalling the fact that even Wagner, when he replenished his exchequer by the Centennial March, came rather nearer disgracing himself than Beethoven did in The Battle of Vittoria; and that is saying a good deal. The amateur who knows good art from bad may pick up treasures in Exhibitions just as he may pick them up in pawnshops and boxes of secondhand books: for example, it was at the Italian Exhibition at Earl's Court that the painter Segantini was introduced to English connoisseurs. But the treasures are never among the works commissioned and advertised by the promoters of the show.

Consequently Professor Stanford, if he had composed a particularly bad ode, might have pleaded that this is just what a great composer invariably does on such occasions. However, as it happens, the apology is not needed. The two qualities needed for a good Chicago ode are tunefulness and bounce; and there is an allowance of both in East to West, though it is certainly stinted by the professorism which is Stanford's bane. I cry "Professor!" whenever I hear the natural flow of music checked by some crude and wooden progression, inscrutable in its motive—perhaps an idle experiment in the introduction and resolution of a discord, perhaps an austere compliance with some imaginary obligation of the sham grammar which is called scientific harmony, perhaps—and of this I often very grievously suspect Stanford—a forced avoidance of the vernacular in music under the impression that it is vulgar.

The result of this last notion as a principle of composition may be illustrated by imagining an author not only searching the dictionary for out-of-the-way words so as to avoid using any that might drop from the man in the street, but distorting the more obvious ideas as well with the same motive. Professors of literature have tried to do this before now, and produced the tedious pedant's jargon that we all know and dread in books. Your men who really can write, your Dickenses, Ruskins, Carlyles, and their like, are vernacular above all things: they cling to the locutions which everyday use has made a part of our common life. The professors may ask me whether I seriously invite them to make their music out of the commonplaces of the comic song writer? I reply, unabashed, that I do.

That arrant commonplace, the opening strain of Dove sono, made out of the most hackneyed cadence in modern music, pleases me better than all their Tenterden Street specialities. When I wrote last week of Stanford's talent for composition, I was not thinking of the Mixolydian nonsense in his Eden—the angels' choruses written in no mode at all, because, as I take it, he conceives angels as too "genteel" to sing in anything so vulgar as the major and minor modes used at the music-halls. I was thinking, on the contrary, of his straightforward rum-tum setting of Browning's Cavalier Romances, as fiery and original as they are vernacular from beginning to end, and of that charming Bower of Roses song with its simple tonic and subdominant Irish harmonies, which is the only number I know from his opera The Veiled Prophet.

Well, East to West is not as good as either of these compositions, because it is too frequently turned aside from its natural course for the purpose, apparently, of taking it out of the common run, at which moments I find it dry, perverse, and unaffected. But the native audacity of the composer asserts itself more freely than in any of his recent compositions; and the entire welcomeness of the change was proved by a tremendous ovation at the conclusion of the performance, very different in spirit from that which greeted the Mixolydian angels at Birmingham.

Pianism has prevailed very fearfully for the last few weeks. Essipoff has given three recitals. No technical difficulties give her trouble enough to rouse her: sometimes she is interested and interesting, sometimes cold and absent, always amazing. The cobbler's wife may be the worst shod woman in the parish; but Leschetitzky's wife is undeniably one of the greatest exponents of his technique in Europe. If it were possible to believe that she cares two straws about what she plays, she would be also one of the greatest executive musicians in Europe. But she has discovered that all this also is vanity; and so, with her indifference cloaked by a superb habit of style, and by the activity of her unerring mechanism, she gets through a recital as a queen might through a drawing room, and sets one thinking about Arabella Goddard, who was a player of the same sort, and then wandering off into all manner of idle afternoon reveries. In addition to the usual classics she introduces Leschetitzky, Moszkowski, and Schytte, apparently finding them a relief. Mr Lennart Lundberg would have been more fortunate in his first recital if it had not happened on an Essipoff afternoon. He is a Dane, trained in Paris, which is the very last place in the world to train a Dane in, or indeed anybody else as far as music is concerned. A Beethoven sonata being *de rigueur* in London, he rattled off the Waldstein sonata, throwing in a French grace here and there to keep up our spirits. I have no patience with Paris: provincialism I do not mind, but a metropolitanism that is fifty years behind the time is insufferable. Why could not Mr Lundberg, with his northern temperament, have gone to Vienna, Brussels, Moscow—anywhither except to the city where, musically speaking, you still find 1850 fighting in its last ditch? Fortunately, the neatness and brilliancy which seem so artificial, and after a time become so wearisome, in players who are Frenchified without being genuinely French, are charming in their best native form as combined with the freshness and simplicity of the "adorable" variety of Parisienne. We had this type exemplified by Mlle Simmonet, who sang in Bruneau's La Rêve and in Gounod's Philémon at Covent Garden; and we have it also in Clotilde Kleeberg, who revived a barren but clever and elegant pianoforte concerto of Ferdinand Hiller's at the last Philharmonic concert with great success, and who was even petted at the Crystal Palace, where she ran her hands daintily up and down Beethoven's fourth concerto without once awakening it. For there are limits to the realm of adorability; and Beethovenland is some distance outside that frontier. Talking of Parisian freshness and adorability reminds me of German freshness and adorability, personified in a Mädchen named Margarethe Eussert, who made her first appearance at Prince's Hall on the 5th. She dressed the part, smiled it, curtsied it, and coifed it so consummately that her artistic instincts were proved before she struck a note. Her playing is still girlish; but it is vigorous and promising; and her master and discoverer, Klindworth, has laid the foundations of her technique with tolerable solidity. Another young lady, also in the stage in which the human female is called in America "a bud," and also most effectively got up for the part, is Miss Nellie Kauffmann. She is good-looking, confident, and not without some natural talent and dexterity; so she will be able without much trouble to persuade some first-rate teacher to take her in hand and shew her how to begin her apprenticeship. She seems to have had but little artistic guidance hitherto: otherwise she could hardly believe that gabbling thoughtlessly over the notes of a Bach fugue and a Beethoven allegro at breakneck speed is pianoforte playing in the St James's Hall sense. Besides, she does not even gabble accurately. Young as she is, we have players who are hardly more than children—Ethel Barnes and Elsie Hall, for instance—who are enormously superior to her as artists; and nothing could be more cruel than to applaud her mere musical handiness and engaging appearance at the risk of persuading her that she has finished the training that she has hardly yet begun, and that would possibly make her a very worthy artist. Herr Isidor Cohn has also given a recital in St James's Hall. To him it is not necessary to offer paternal advice, as he is an artist who has unquestionably made the most of his natural talent. He is not by temperament a Beethoven player; but in pieces by Hiller, Moszkowski, Dvořák, and Liszt he reaps the full reward of his skill and industry. Madame Grimaldi, another pianist, who has given an evening recital at Prince's Hall, is not very easy to criticize. As a rule I do not hazard guesses about artists until I have privately ascertained that my guesses are correct, which in this case I have had no opportunity of doing. Nevertheless I will venture to make public my surmise that Madame Grimaldi has played a great deal before fashionable audiences in drawing rooms, depending a good deal on her memory, and that she has not submitted her readings of Chopin to any very severe criticism for some years past. I find her exclusive, private, tastefully superficial, altogether wanting in that deep need for the sympathy, or at least the attention, of the farthest away and humblest person in the shilling gallery, which marks the great public artist. Further, I find the pieces she plays most extraordinarily mannered and transmogrified, apparently by a long course of repetition without occasional careful verification by the score. As Madame Grimaldi's powers are of no mean order, I think she might produce interesting results by becoming as a little child again for a few months and spending them under the tuition of, say, Leschetitzky.

Of violin playing I have heard comparatively little; but violin recitals are never so plentiful as pianoforte recitals, for the prosaic reason that they do not advertise the instruments of any living maker, and are therefore not given unless they pay directly, which many of the pianoforte recitals of course do not. In the fiddle department, then, I have only to record that Mr Willy Hess played Beethoven's concerto at the Philharmonic. What with his habit, gained as leader of the Manchester band, of driving fast movements along without much reference to their poetic content, and his weakness for exhibitions of his skill in trick fiddling, which led him to substitute a very flagrant display of it for a cadenza, he rather threw away his chance in the first movement, the only part of the work that really tries a player. Mr Arnold Dolmetsch, whose unique viol concerts in the hall of Clifford's Inn, Holborn, are gems of musical entertainment in their way, gave an Italian concert last Tuesday week, to be followed by a French concert on June 6th, and a Bach concert on July 4th. I heard the last half of the Italian one, and was delighted by a sonata for the viol da gamba by Marcello, with a peculiar effect made by an interrupted cadence which sounds as fresh now as it did when first written. It was beautifully played by Miss Hélène Dolmetsch. Mr Fuller Maitland, who was to have played the harpsichord, was unwell; and his place was taken at short notice by Mr C. H. Kempling, organist of St John's, Kennington, who rose to the occasion with an aptitude which was very remarkable considering that he had no great experience of the instrument. The two big "concertos" by Vivaldi and Corelli were interesting; but as they required eight or nine players they would have been the better for a conductor, failing more exhaustive rehearsal than they are worth nowadays. Among the miscellaneous concerts of which I have had somewhat precarious glimpses, I may mention those of Miss Elsie Mackenzie, who is sure to be at least a favorite ballad singer by the time she is personally as mature as her talent already seems to be; of Miss Kathleen Walton, a contralto whose powers I could not fully judge in the only song I was fortunate enough to hear during my brief visit to her concert; and of Mr Charles Phillips, who, with the co-operation of Mrs Trust, Miss Damian, and Mr Braxton Smith, introduced a set of five "Spanish" songs for four voices with pianoforte duet accompaniment, by Mr William Wallace. They were very pretty and fluent, and did not sound hackneyed, though I cannot say that they contained anything unfamiliar.

24 *May* 1893

THE new Savoy opera would not occupy me very long here if the comic-opera stage were in a reasonably presentable condition. If I ask Messrs Barrie and Conan Doyle whether I am to regard their reputations as founded on Jane Annie, or Jane Annie on their reputations, I have no doubt they will hastily declare for the second alternative. And, indeed, it would ill become me, as a brother of the literary craft, to pretend to congratulate them seriously upon the most unblushing outburst of tomfoolery that two responsible citizens could conceivably indulge in publicly. Still less can I, as a musical critic, encourage them in their want of respect for opera as an artistic entertainment. I do not mean that a comic-opera writer would be tolerable if he bore himself reverently; but there is a conscientious irreverence which aims at comic perfection, and a reckless irreverence which ridicules its own work and throws away the efforts of the composer and the artists; and I must say that there is a good deal of this sort of irreverence in Jane Annie.

After all, nothing requires so much gravity as joking; and when the authors of Jane Annie begin by admitting that they are not in earnest, they literally give the show away. They no doubt secure from the public a certain indulgence by openly confessing that their work will not bear being taken soberly; but this confession is a throwing up of the sponge: after it, it is idle to talk of success. A retreat may be executed with great tact and humor, but cannot thereby be turned into a victory. The question then arises, Is victory possible on purely humorous lines? Well, who is the great fountain-head of the modern humorous school, from Artemus Ward down to Messrs Barrie and Doyle themselves? Clearly Dickens, who has saturated the whole English-speaking world with his humor. We have whole squadrons of humorous writers who, if they had never read him, would have produced nothing but sectarian tracts, or, worse still, magazine articles. His ascendancy is greater now than ever, because, like Beethoven, he had "a third manner," in which he produced works which influenced his contemporaries as little as the Ninth Symphony influenced Spohr or Weber, but which are influencing the present generation of writers as much as the Ninth Symphony influenced Schumann and Wagner. When I first read Great Expectations I was not much older than Pip was when the convict turned him upside down in the churchyard: in fact, I was so young that I was astonished beyond measure when it came out that the convict was the author of Pip's mysterious fortune, although Dickens took care to make that fact obvious all along to every reader of adult capacity. My first acquaintance with the French Revolution was acquired at the same age, from A Tale of Two Cities; and I also struggled with Little Dorrit at this time. I say struggled; for the books oppressed my imagination most fearfully, so real were they to me. It was not until I became a cynical *blasé* person of twelve or thirteen that I read Pickwick, Bleak House, and the intervening works. Now it is pretty clear that Dickens, having caught me young when he was working with his deepest intensity of conviction, must have left his mark on me far more deeply than on his own contemporaries, who read

Pickwick when they were twenty, and Our Mutual Friend when they were fifty, if indeed they kept up with him at all. Every successive generation of his readers had a greater advantage. The generation twenty years younger than his was the first that knew his value; and it is probable that the generation which will be born as the copyrights of his latest works expire, and leave the market open to sixpenny editions of them, will be the most extensively Dickensized of any.

Now I do not see why the disciples should not be expected to keep up to the master's standard of hard work, as far as that can be done by elbow grease, which is a more important factor in good art work than lazy artists like to admit. The fun of Dickens without his knowledge and capacity for taking pains can only end in what I have called Jane Annie —mere tomfoolery. The pains without the humor, or, indeed, any other artistic quality, as we get it occasionally from an industrious "naturalist" when he is not also an artist, is far more respectable. There are a fair number of humorists who can throw off conceits as laughable as Mr Silas Wegg's comments on the decline and fall of the Roman Empire, or his version of Oh, weep for the hour! But Wegg himself is not to be had so cheaply: all the "photographic realism" in the world is distanced by the power and labor which gave us this study of a rascal, so complete inside and out, body and soul, that the most fantastic playing with it cannot destroy the illusion it creates.

You have only to compare Dickens's pictures of people as they really are with the best contemporary pictures of people as they imagine each other to be (Trollope's, for instance) to understand how Dickens, taking life with intense interest, and observing, analysing, remembering with amazing scientific power, got more hard work crammed into a thumbnail sketch than ordinary men do into colossal statues. The high privilege of joking in public should never be granted except to people who know thoroughly what they are joking about—that is, to exceptionally serious and laborious people. Now, in Jane Annie the authors do not impress me as having taken their work seriously or labored honestly over it. I make no allowances for their performances in ordinary fiction: anybody can write a novel. A play—especially a music-play—is a different matter—different, too, in the sense of being weightier, not lighter.

Messrs Doyle and Barrie have not thought so: they have, with a Philistinism as to music of which only literary men are capable, regarded their commission as an opportunity for a lark, and nothing more. Fortunately, they have larked better than they knew. Flimsy as their work is compared to the fiction of the founder of their school, they have made something like a revolution in comic opera by bringing that school on to the comic-opera stage. For years past managers have allowed themselves to be persuaded that in comic-opera books they must choose between Mr Gilbert's librettos and a style of writing which would have disgraced the Cities of the Plain.

In all populous places there is a currency of slang phrases, catch words, scraps from comic songs, and petty verbal indecencies which get into circulation among bar loafers, and after being accepted by them as facetious, get a certain vogue in that fringe of the sporting and dramatic worlds which cannot be accurately described without an appearance of Puritanism which I wish to avoid. An operatic style based on this currency, and requiring for its complete enjoyment nothing else except an exhaustive knowledge of the names and prices of drinks of all kinds, and an almost inconceivable callousness to, and impatience of, every other subject on the face of the earth, does not seem possible; but it certainly exists, and has, in fact, prevailed to the extent of keeping the comic-opera stage in a distinctly blackguardly condition for some time past.

Now the fun in Jane Annie, senseless as some of it is, is not in the least of this order. If anyone had offered at the end of the performance to introduce me to the authors, I should not have hastily declined; and this is saying a good deal. Further, the characters, always excepting the page-boy, whose point lies in his impossibility, and who is a most degenerate descendant of Bailey junior, are so sketched as to make it not only possible but necessary for the performers to act, thereby departing from the tradition of the "good acting play," the goodness of which consists in the skill with which it is constructed so as to require no acting for its successful performance.

Miss Dorothy Vane acted, and acted cleverly, as Jane Annie. I never knew before that she could act, though I had seen her in other comic operas. Mr Kenningham, whose want of skill as a comedian has not hitherto been any great disadvantage to him, was very decidedly hampered by it this time. The thinness of Miss Decima Moore's dramatic accomplishments were also more apparent than usual; and her efforts to make her part go by mere restlessness did not altogether help her out. The honors of prima donna fell virtually to Miss Rosina Brandram, who, like Mr Rutland Barrington and Messrs Gridley and Passmore, profited by the change in style.

A remarkable success was scored by a surpassingly beautiful young gentleman named Scott Fishe, with plenty of musical aptitude and a penetrating but agreeable bass voice, who looked the part of the handsome Lancer to perfection, and was received with shouts of laughter and an encore on the extravagantly silly occasion of his first entry. Mr Scott Fishe must, however, excuse me if, whilst admitting that he is a pleasant and amusing person, I dare not add anything as to his general ability on the strength of his success in the character of a consummate ass.

As to the music, a few numbers, notably the prelude, which sounds suspiciously like some old attempt at a concerto utilized for the occasion, and the love duet in the first act, have the effect of patches on the score; but the rest is often as adroit, lively, and humorous as Sir Arthur Sullivan's work. There is one plagiarism, curious because it is obvious enough to convince everyone of its unconsciousness. It is the "I dont know why" refrain to the proctor's song, treated exactly like the "I cant think why" in the king's song in Princess Ida. I may add generally that the effect of Jane Annie was so novel that I have no idea whether it was a success or not; but it certainly amused me more than most comic operas do.

I have to record the production by the Philharmonic Society of a Scotch ballad for soprano solo, chorus, and orchestra, entitled Annie of Lochroyan, by Erskine Allon. When Mr Hamish MacCunn hit on this form of composition with his spirited Lord Ullin's Daughter, I solemnly warned all whom it might concern that the feat, once invented, was an extremely easy one, and was likely to be extensively imitated if it were made too much of. And now in due course comes Mr Allon, tackling another ballad as solemnly as if it were the Mass, and spinning it out with wearisome interludes and repetitions beyond all patience. If Mr Allon will revise his score, and make a point of going straight through as quickly, concisely, and imaginatively as Mr MacCunn went through the better half of Lord Ullin's Daughter, I am prepared to deliver judgment on it; but as it stands I should only waste my time in attempting to pick the raisins out of the suet. Why Miss Liza Lehmann, with her very German intonation, should have been chosen to sing a Celtic ballad remains to be explained. With the utmost stretch of the high consideration which all musicians owe her, I cannot pretend that the effect was agreeable. At the same concert young Otto Hegner played a sort of glockenspiel obbligato to a bustling orchestral piece by Huber, the last movement of which was a rather barefaced attempt to make a finale by spinning a few barren figures out into sequences and rosalias. The work was announced as a pianoforte concerto. I did not hear the rest of the concert, a retouch of influenza having crippled my powers of endurance last week. It prevented me from hearing more than a portion of the last item in the concert of the Laistner Choir, the said last item being Schumann's Pilgrimage of the Rose, a work full of that original and expressive harmony which is so charming in Schumann when he is using it poetically instead of pedantically. What I heard of the performance gave me a highly favorable opinion of Herr Laistner's capacity as a choirmaster and conductor.

The most notable recent pianoforte recital has been that of Louis Diémer, a remarkably clever, self-reliant, and brilliant pianist, artistically rather stale, and quite breath-bereavingly unscrupulous in using the works of the great composers as stalking-horses for his own powers. The mere recollection of his version of the Zauberflöte overture causes the pen to drop from my hand.

31 *May* 1893

WHITSUNTIDE brought me a week's ticket-of-leave from St James's Hall. By way of setting me a holiday task, Messrs Chapman & Hall sent me Mr H. Heathcote Statham's Form and Design in Music to study. I always enjoy Mr Statham's essays on music, because, as he is a thorough architect, and writes about music like one, I get the benefit of a side-light on the art. This particular essay is only a chapter from his Thoughts on Music and Musicians. It contains his five famous examples of melody, taken from Bach, Mozart, and Beethoven, followed by a sixth example of which he says: "As an instructive contrast the reader may take this cacophonous string of notes, which is put forth as a melody, but has no analogy in structure with those quoted above except in the mere fact that it consists of a succession of notes; these, however, have neither a common law of rhythm nor of tonal relation, nor any definite form or balance as a whole; the passage has, so to speak, neither beginning, middle, nor ending, in any organic sense, and there seems no reason why it should not wriggle on in the same fashion indefinitely: it is a formless thing."

After this, what do you suppose the "cacophonous string of notes" is? Obviously (to those who know Mr Statham) something out of Wagner. And in fact it is the mother motive from Parsifal, that haunting theme that gives you "Herzeleide" merely to think of it. Mr Statham, having thus squarely confronted you with the dilemma that either Wagner was a cacophonous humbug or he himself hopelessly out of the question as an authority on form or design or any other artistic element in music, takes it for granted that you will throw over Wagner at once, and proceeds to kill time by making an "analysis" of Mozart's G minor symphony, which he parses in the most edifying academic manner.

Here is the sort of thing: "The principal subject, hitherto only heard in the treble, is transferred to the bass (Ex. 28), the violins playing a new counterpoint to it instead of the original mere accompaniment figure of the first part. Then the parts are reversed, the violins taking the subject and the basses the counterpoint figure, and so on till we come to a close on the dominant of D minor, a nearly related key (commencement of Ex. 29), and then comes the passage by which we return to the first subject in its original form and key."

How succulent this is; and how full of Mesopotamian words like "the dominant of D minor"! I will now, ladies and gentlemen, give you my celebrated "analysis" of Hamlet's soliloquy on suicide, in the same scientific style. "Shakespeare, dispensing with the customary exordium, announces his subject at once in the infinitive, in which mood it is presently repeated after a short connecting passage in which, brief as it is, we recognize the alternative and negative forms on which so much of the significance of repetition depends. Here we reach a colon; and a pointed pository phrase, in which the accent falls decisively on the relative pronoun, brings us to the first full stop."

I break off here, because, to confess the truth, my grammar is giving out. But I want to know whether it is just that a literary critic should be forbidden to make his living in this way on pain of being interviewed by two doctors and a magistrate, and haled off to Bedlam forthwith; whilst the more a musical critic does it, the deeper the veneration he inspires. By systematically neglecting it I have lost caste as a critic even in the eyes of those who hail my abstinence with the greatest relief; and I should be tempted to eke out these columns in the Mesopotamian manner if I were not the slave of a commercial necessity and a vulgar ambition to have my articles read, this being indeed the main reason why I write them, and the secret of the constant "straining after effect" observable in my style.

I remember once in bygone years accepting a commission as musical critic from a distinguished editor who has been described by Atlas as a Chinese gentleman, he being a native of that part of Cathay which lies on the west coast of Ireland. He placed himself in my hands with one reservation only. "Say what you like," he said; "but for—[here I omit a pathetic Oriental adjuration]—dont tell us anything about Bach in B minor." It was a bold speech, considering the superstitious terror in which the man who has the abracadabra of musical technology at his fingers' ends holds the uninitiated editor; but it conveyed a golden rule. The truth is that "Bach in B minor" is not criticism, not good sense, not interesting to the general reader, not useful to the student—very much the reverse, in fact, and consequently exceedingly out of place in "a brief outline of the æsthetic conditions of the art," as Mr Statham calls his essay, which would be quite unreadable by ordinary mortals if it were not for the fact that the author is a clever man, who knows and likes a great deal of good music (notably organ music, on which I always read him with pleasure), and therefore cannot help occasionally writing about it in an interesting way.

If Mr Statham will study the work of a modern experienced practical critic, and compare it with the work of an amateur like, let us say, the late Edmund Gurney, he will be struck by the fact that the expert carefully avoids "Bach in B minor," whilst the amateur is full of it; and that the amateur, when he dislikes a piece of music, invariably enters into an elaborate demonstration that the composer's proceedings are "wrong," his melody not being "true melody," nor his harmony "scientific harmony," whereas the expert gives you his personal opinion for what it is worth. Mr

Statham evidently thinks that it would not be criticism to say that he finds Wagner an offensive charlatan and his themes cacophonous strings of notes. He feels bound to *prove* him so by laying down the first principles of character and composition, and shewing that Wagner's conduct and his works are incompatible with these principles.

I wonder what Mr Statham would think of me if I objected to Brahms' Requiem, not on the ground that it bores me to distraction, but as a violation of the laws of nature.

Miss Martha Möller, who gave a concert at Prince's Hall last week, was clever enough to appear in a national costume, the most notable feature of which was a white tablecloth spread above her head by some ingenious contrivance. One gets so desperately tired of fashionable modes and materials that a stroke of this kind tells effectively at the height of the season. It gives Miss Möller a Swedish Nightingale air, raising expectations which are heightened by her intelligent face and interesting demeanor. But when the singing begins it becomes apparent that though Miss Möller has the strong natural feeling and quietly fervid expression which belong to the national costume and the silver ornaments, and can give an exceptionally able reading of anything from a folk-song to an aria by Meyerbeer, she has not been altogether successful in teaching herself to sing. Her voice is naturally a clear free soprano of normal quality; but she has been fascinated by the richer, stronger, more sympathetic tone natural to some contraltos, and has imitated it, much as if Madame Melba had taught herself to sing by imitating Miss Alice Gomez. The imitation has unfortunately involved a constrained action of the lower jaw and retraction of the tongue which are fatal to good singing. Her tone is dry and artificial, and her execution forced and uneasy; so the verdict for the present must be that though Miss Möller imitates good singing with remarkable talent she does not sing well. She was assisted by Miss Yrrac, who plays the violin with a trenchant, well-rosined bow, and knocks a good deal of exhilarating noise out of it; also by a young pianist who gave a presentable performance of Chopin's Berceuse, but made only a poor business of Rubinstein's Valse Caprice, which requires a degree of power admitting of immense abandonment on the part of the player.

We have had a casual orchestral concert at St James's Hall from Hans Wessely, one of the professors of the R.A.M. There was certainly no lack of masterpieces for our souls to adventure among. The overture (Le Nozze) was followed by Brahms' and Mendelssohn's violin concertos, with Beethoven's pianoforte concerto in E flat between them. Wessely was not altogether successful with Mendelssohn. There is a certain quality in the style of that fastidious and carefully reared composer which can only be described as his gentility; and Wessely, who is a sincere, unreserved, original player, made rather short work of some of Mendelssohn's more decorous measures. Even with Brahms he once or twice sounded a little brusque; but the fault is a refreshing one at St James's Hall, and it weighed very lightly against the qualities he revealed, chief among them being a considerable degree of that prime requisite of the concerto-player, a sympathetic comprehension of the whole score, instead of a mere readiness to give a verbatim report, so to speak, of the solo part. This stood him in good stead in the first movement of the Brahms concerto. Thanks to it and to his smart execution, his excellent intonation, and a cantabile which proclaimed the natural musician, he won ovations which were by no means confined to the Academy students in the gallery. The pianist, Mr Isidor Cohn, did not venture to approach the first movement of the great Beethoven concerto in the spirit of a masterplayer—indeed, he made less than nothing of the exordium; and he missed (in my judgment) the indicated treatment of the accompaniment in the second half of the slow movement. Still, his performance was conscientiously thought out and not uninteresting, which is more than could be said for some older and more eminent pianists than Mr Cohn. The band, a Philharmonic contingent under Dr Mackenzie, who is beginning to take advantage of his great opportunities as an orchestral conductor, played the Figaro overture in a little under four and a half minutes, a great improvement on the silly tradition of scampering through it in three and a half. I should add, by the way, that some songs were sung with exceptional skill and delicacy by Miss Schidrowitz, who, though her light agile soprano voice was the worse for a cold, shewed herself an accomplished vocalist and a clever interpreter. She has only one habit which I dislike; and that is the preparation of a minor trill by a slow alteration of the notes of the major trill. The effect of the change is not pleasant to my ear.

END OF VOL. II